Between the Ambo and the Altar

Biblical Preaching and The Roman Missal,
Year A

Guerric DeBona, OSB

LITURGICAL PRESS
Collegeville, Minnesota

www.litpress.org

1   2   3   4   5   6   7   8   9

Library of Congress Cataloging-in-Publication Data

DeBona, Guerric, 1955–
    Between the Ambo and the altar : biblical preaching and the Roman missal, year a / Guerric DeBona.
        pages   cm.
    ISBN 978-0-8146-3459-2 (alk. paper) — ISBN 978-0-8146-3484-4 (e-book)
    1. Church year sermons.   2. Lectionary preaching—Catholic Church.
3. Catholic Church—Sermons.   4. Catholic Church. Lectionary for Mass
(U.S.). Year A.   5. Catholic Church. Missale Romanum (1970)   I. Title.

BX1756.A1D43 2013
251'.6—dc23   2013008345

For the monks, co-workers,
students, alumni,
and benefactors of
Saint Meinrad Archabbey,
Seminary, and School of Theology

"that in all things God may be glorified."

Contents

Introduction: Biblical Preaching and the New *Roman Missal*   1

Advent

First Sunday of Advent   12
Second Sunday of Advent   17
Third Sunday of Advent   21
Fourth Sunday of Advent   25

Christmas Time

The Nativity of the Lord (The Mass during the Night)   30
Holy Family of Jesus, Mary and Joseph   35
Solemnity of Mary, the Holy Mother of God   40
Second Sunday after the Nativity   44
The Epiphany of the Lord   48
The Baptism of the Lord   52

Lent

First Sunday of Lent   58
Second Sunday of Lent   63
Third Sunday of Lent   68
Fourth Sunday of Lent   73
Fifth Sunday of Lent   78

Holy Week

Palm Sunday of the Passion of the Lord   84

Thursday of the Lord's Supper   89

Friday of the Passion of the Lord   94

Easter Sunday of the Resurrection of the Lord
    (The Easter Vigil in the Holy Night)   99

Easter Sunday of the Resurrection of the Lord
    (At the Mass during the Day)   108

Easter Time

Second Sunday of Easter   114

Third Sunday of Easter   119

Fourth Sunday of Easter   124

Fifth Sunday of Easter   129

Sixth Sunday of Easter   134

The Ascension of the Lord   138

Seventh Sunday of Easter   142

Pentecost Sunday   147

Ordinary Time

Second Sunday in Ordinary Time   154

Third Sunday in Ordinary Time   158

Fourth Sunday in Ordinary Time   162

Fifth Sunday in Ordinary Time   166

Sixth Sunday in Ordinary Time   169

Seventh Sunday in Ordinary Time   173

Eighth Sunday in Ordinary Time   177

Ninth Sunday in Ordinary Time   181

Tenth Sunday in Ordinary Time   185

Eleventh Sunday in Ordinary Time   188

Twelfth Sunday in Ordinary Time   193

Thirteenth Sunday in Ordinary Time   197

Fourteenth Sunday in Ordinary Time   202

Fifteenth Sunday in Ordinary Time   206

Sixteenth Sunday in Ordinary Time   210

Seventeenth Sunday in Ordinary Time   214

Eighteenth Sunday in Ordinary Time   219

Nineteenth Sunday in Ordinary Time   224

Twentieth Sunday in Ordinary Time   229

Twenty-First Sunday in Ordinary Time   234

Twenty-Second Sunday in Ordinary Time   238

Twenty-Third Sunday in Ordinary Time   242

Twenty-Fourth Sunday in Ordinary Time   246

Twenty-Fifth Sunday in Ordinary Time   250

Twenty-Sixth Sunday in Ordinary Time   254

Twenty-Seventh Sunday in Ordinary Time   259

Twenty-Eighth Sunday in Ordinary Time   263

Twenty-Ninth Sunday in Ordinary Time   267

Thirtieth Sunday in Ordinary Time   271

Thirty-First Sunday in Ordinary Time   275

Thirty-Second Sunday in Ordinary Time   279

Thirty-Third Sunday in Ordinary Time   283

Solemnities of the Lord during Ordinary Time

The Most Holy Trinity   288

The Most Holy Body and Blood of Christ   293

The Most Sacred Heart of Jesus   297

Our Lord Jesus Christ, King of the Universe   302

Introduction: Biblical Preaching and the New *Roman Missal*

The Geography of the Homily

It is no exaggeration to say that we live in a world choked with words. From texting with smartphones to blogging on the Internet, we face a glut of language day after day. Paradoxically, we strain to establish relationships with one another that really connect. Indeed, this age of global messaging has been far from communicative. Instead, we are a culture of individual selves, more often isolated than not by the very words we form, longing for true community and reconciliation. In the end, no multiplication of words or virtual encounters via the latest technology will satisfy the human yearning for connecting to the deepest center of our being and the lives of others. Only the Word made visible will satiate that terrible hunger.

That is the mission of Christian preaching when the community of faith gathers as the eucharistic assembly: to unearth a liberating Word to the weary, the downtrodden, and the alienated. As Christ tells those gathered to hear the words of Scripture broken open to them in the synagogue at Nazareth at the beginning of his ministry in Galilee, God has sent him "to proclaim liberty to captives / and recovery of sight to the blind, / to let the oppressed go free, / and to proclaim a year acceptable to the Lord" (Luke 4:18-19, NAB). The liturgical homily exists, then, for the purpose of deepening the faith of the baptized. In the often quoted words from *Sacrosanctum Concilium* of the Second Vatican Council, "By means of the homily, the mysteries of the faith and the guiding principles of the christian life are expounded from the sacred text during the course of the liturgical year" (52). Preaching is meant to guide the Christian community into a deeper celebration of the Eucharist and engage the faith community in the "richer fare"

1

of the Scriptures as they unfold in the Sunday Lectionary and in the experience of the faith community.

This banquet of God's saving word served at the eucharistic celebration emerges from the Scriptures and the church's liturgy itself. As the *General Instruction of the Roman Missal* says, the homily "is necessary for the nurturing of the Christian life. It should be an explanation of some aspect of the readings from Sacred Scripture or of another text from the Ordinary or the Proper of the Mass of the day and should take into account both the mystery being celebrated and the particular needs of the listeners" (65). The preacher, then, engages the assembly in its particular historical horizon with the language of faith and tradition in order to draw the congregation into the paschal mystery of Christ's sanctification for his church. Preaching is a grace-filled convergence among preacher, text, and God's people. As a constitutive component of the liturgy, the homily "points to the presence of God in people's lives and then leads a congregation into the Eucharist, providing, as it were, the motive for celebrating the Eucharist in this time and place."[1] As the USCCB document *Preaching the Mystery of Faith: The Sunday Homily* enjoins us, "Every homily, because it is an intrinsic part of the Sunday Eucharist, must therefore be about the dying and rising of Jesus Christ and his sacrificial passage through suffering to new and eternal life for us."[2] The preacher facilitates the congregation's discovery of the Word unfolding in the very midst of sacred space and, in so doing, discloses the mystery of God's faithful love, together with the thanks and praise that is at the heart of the Eucharist, the height and summit of our worship as the people of God. As Pope Benedict XVI writes in *Verbum Domini*, quoting *Sacrosanctum Concilium*,

> Here one sees the sage pedagogy of the Church, which proclaims and listens to sacred Scripture following the rhythm of the liturgical year. This expansion of God's word in time takes place above all in the Eucharistic celebration and in the Liturgy of the Hours. At the center of everything the paschal mystery shines forth, and around it radiate all the mysteries of Christ and the history of salvation, which become sacramentally present: "By recalling in this way the mysteries of redemption, the Church opens up to the faithful the riches of the saving actions and the merits of her Lord, and makes them present to all times, allowing the faithful to enter into contact with them and to be filled with the grace of salvation." For this reason I encourage the Church's Pastors and all engaged in pastoral

work to see that all the faithful learn to savor the deep meaning of the word of God which unfolds each year in the liturgy, revealing the fundamental mysteries of our faith. This is in turn the basis for a correct approach to sacred Scripture.[3]

I have titled this preaching commentary *Between the Ambo and the Altar* in order to locate the liturgical geography of the homily and call attention to the place of preaching as the site for the faithful "to savor the deep meaning of the word of God which unfolds each year in the liturgy, revealing the fundamental mysteries of our faith." As is well known, for many years the sermon functioned as a kind of misplaced little island at the Roman liturgy; it became a harbor for boatloads of parish announcements or themes that were loosely drifting out to sea. Most of these were well-intentioned sermons but something like castaways unmoored, poorly integrated into the liturgy itself. When the restoration of the ancient *homilia* was promulgated with the Second Vatican Council, the character of preaching the Word shifted from a lone island adrift in a vast ocean to a strategic bridge connecting two vast continents. The purpose of the homily in the age of the new evangelization is to preach the Good News of Christ's saving work as it is disclosed in the entire Bible, God's living Word among us, and this disclosure is to lead the baptized assembly to praise, thanksgiving, and mission. "The homily is a means of bringing the scriptural message to life in a way that helps the faithful to realize that God's word is present and at work in their everyday lives. It should lead to an understanding of the mystery being celebrated, serve as a summons to mission, and prepare the assembly for the profession of faith, the universal prayer and the Eucharistic liturgy. Consequently, those who have been charged with preaching by virtue of a specific ministry ought to take this task to heart" (*Verbum Domini* 59). By accounting for God's activity in Christ throughout salvation history, the homily deepens the faith of the Christian assembly, instilling in the faithful a heartfelt desire to gather at the eucharistic sacrifice. So by definition, the homily exists for the sake of the hearer of the Good News, to transition this congregation from Word to sacrament, from the ambo to the altar. And from the altar to mission.

The present series, which begins with this volume, is meant to be an application of preaching in the context of the church's Lectionary inside the language of the Sunday liturgy. From the perspective of the Sunday homily and the interests of those who preach week after week, I think that there remains a marvelous opportunity to discover a dialogue that exists between the liturgical texts—the presidential prayers and eucharistic prayers, the prefaces for Ordinary Time as well as feasts and solemnities—and the Scriptures themselves. I think we should view our dialogue with the Sunday liturgy as both culturally local and broadly universal. Just as the Scriptures have been passed down to us and are made applicable for our day by exegetical methods such as historical criticism and other ways of study, so too are we able to draw in the church's liturgical tradition for the homily as a constitutive dialogue partner. As of this writing, there have already been some fine introductions to the translation and implementation of the new *Roman Missal* (2011), such as Paul Turner's *Pastoral Companion to the Roman Missal* (WLP, 2010). Indeed, the probing of the vast resources of the liturgy and the Scriptures from which this celebration has emerged allows for what Louis-Marie Chauvet calls *"la Bible liturgique."*[4] Drawing from Chauvet and echoing the *GIRM*, Edward Foley and Jon Michael Joncas remind us that the preacher may explore further resources for the homily, among them the "liturgical bible," which "may refer to all liturgical texts apart from the lectionary." These include the major and minor euchologies such as the eucharistic prayers, prefaces, collects, the invariable (e.g., the "Holy, Holy"), and optional texts for the day (e.g., prayers for the blessing of an Advent wreath or newly restored Blessing over the People during Lent), "as well as the words of the hymns, songs and acclamations that are sung during worship."[5] I hasten to add that this liturgical language is not simply a resource for the preacher, but the living text of the faith community that has unfolded over the centuries. Yes, we are a historical, culturally specific faith community but always in dialogue with sacred history and how God has shaped us through the mediation of the church. The liturgy and the Scriptures that are the spine of the Body of Christ, as it were, form a marvelous dialectic for the preacher to witness the proclamation of the Good News of Jesus Christ.

The Homiletic Arc

In addition to providing a resource for the preacher by way of commentary, my hope is that the present text will contribute to an understanding of homiletic process as well. After teaching preaching to seminarians for over a dozen years and giving workshops to priests, deacons, and other ministers, I can say that one of the most difficult concepts to grasp—but one of the most essential to learn—is the essential organic unity of the homily. The late Ken Untener and others have stressed the frustration present in hearers in the congregation who complain about the homily having too many ideas and failing to challenge the call to mission in the world on a practical level.[6] Every preacher should certainly have some kind of method that serves as a kind of armature for the text, moving the homily along and structured around the listener. We cannot rely on our subjective, privatized voice to preach to a community of believers. All of us have been trained as solitary writers from an early age, but those who preach write for a congregation of ears, not a single pair of eyes. In this regard, homiletic strategy is very much in order so that the baptized assembly might listen to the word of God with faith and understanding, unencumbered by the personal eccentricities of the preacher. For those who are interested in developing a method of homiletics more fully, I would recommend the works of David Buttrick, Eugene Lowry, and Paul Scott Wilson, all of whom have written extensively on crafting the homily.[7]

With *Between the Ambo and the Altar*, I have in mind something less like a method and more like process, moving from Scripture to liturgical text to homily. Therefore, I have structured the book around three coordinates that seem to me to be the most productive way of engaging a preaching dialogue between the Sunday Lectionary readings and the liturgical texts that surround them. The first section is meant to be a prayerful reflection on the Lectionary for the day. I have avoided commentaries but used only some (minor) native ability in biblical languages, together with a good study Bible. Over the years, I have found that scholarly biblical commentaries are quite useful but usually only *after* a kind of naïve reading of the text, a precritical reflection, which Paul Ricoeur has called "the first naiveté" or "the spontaneous immediacy of reader to subject matter."[8] Such reading of the sacred text allows me to sink deeply into the word of God without a gloss. At the same time, a study Bible with adequate footnotes affords the opportunity to make very general historical and textual connections that aid in the life of prayer and contemplation. I am suggesting, then, that this first section of exploring the biblical text become the initial starting point for the homily, best accessed about a week before the homily is to be delivered and, ideally, integrated into Morning or Evening Prayer.

The second section is devoted precisely to establishing a substantial connection with the liturgical texts and making some links with the Scripture. "Connecting the Bible and the Liturgy" is rather subjective and personal, and it is my hope that the preacher will bring a wealth of associations to such a process of connections between Scripture and the liturgy, or between the ambo and the altar. These musings on the prayers in the liturgy are meant to be pastoral suggestions for homiletic building blocks rather than formal theoretical arguments. To this end, I have taken each of the Lectionary cycles (A, B, C) and evinced some connection with the liturgical texts for that particular Sunday. My goal here is certainly not exhaustive; in fact, it is far from that. As every seasoned preacher knows, homiletics relies on making associations and connections for an increasingly diverse congregation of listeners. My aim is that preachers, new and experienced alike, will begin to mine the wealth of material already present in the liturgy and the Scriptures for a multicultural and multigenerational assembly. Although there are numerous elements in the "liturgical Bible" to consider, as well as many possible partners for establishing the homiletic text, I have confined myself mostly to the newly revised translation of the presidential prayers and prefaces of *The Roman Missal* in an effort to glean material for preaching. There is a wealth of potential present in these texts for reflection. I have avoided historical explanations of the prayers, but simply recommend what might be considered a point of departure for constructing the liturgical homily. In some rare instances, I have alluded to the previous (revised) *Sacramentary*'s (1985) translation or, again, sometimes averted to the original Latin itself as a way of mining the depth of the church's liturgy. So saying, the wise homilist's attention to these prayers demonstrates an attention to what *Fulfilled in Your Hearing* (1982) refers to as the preacher's unique role as "mediator of meaning." The preacher stands in the midst of the Christian assembly as an interpreter of the Word within a particular culture articulating a powerful witness, nurtured by the faith of the church. As Daniel McCarthy has demonstrated with his commentaries on selected Collects originally published in *The Tablet*, the liturgy itself is a catalyst to such preaching.[9] Careful meditation on the liturgical prayers in the manner of *lectio divina*, while reflecting on a given Sunday, solemnity, or feast that celebrates these days, will undoubtedly assist the preacher not only in the homily itself but also with the entire Eucharistic Liturgy for the various needs of these particular hearers of the gospel.

Finally, I have included a third section on "Strategy for Preaching" as a kind of point of homiletic integration for each Sunday. As with the previous two sections, I hardly expect that each reader will come to the same homiletic text as I did in the course of this process, but I simply recommend one that strikes me as a plausible outcome of my own engagement with the texts. The paradigm remains the same, though, for each of the Sundays, feasts, and solemnities presented in the liturgical year. If we follow the process for preaching in this book, we move from a meditation on Scripture as it is given in the Lectionary then on to a connection of these texts with the liturgical prayers for the given Sunday (or perhaps some other relevant liturgical text) to the emergence of the homily itself. In terms of a watershed moment in preaching preparation, I regard the primary task of this third stage of the homiletic process a narrowing down to a single declarative sentence, which I have called here the homiletic core idea, but which has also been termed by others a "focus sentence."[10] Discovering a homiletic core idea, a foundation for an uncluttered, pristine armature from which to hang eight to ten minutes of words each week, is not easy, but absolutely necessary. It is the sentence that should be in the mind of every congregant after the homily is over in answer to the question, "What did you hear?"

Having come to a core homiletic sentence, the preacher will then need to develop practical tactics as to how this idea will become a reality for the congregation. For most Sundays, feasts, and solemnities, the best guide to understanding tactics is posing the question: What are some concrete images, relevant stories, or illustrations that will make the core homiletic idea a reality in the heart of the hearer? Tactics are culturally specific and will have strong pastoral application. The preacher ought to instinctively know that the day-to-day activity of the parish and the world at large will, by and large, inform tactics. If one is preaching to a youth group, there is no sense using stories, vocabulary, or illustrations that are more appropriate to the retired members of the parish. Then again, parishioners will be directly affected by the economic and political happenings around them, which will inflect the meaning of the homiletic core. If there has been a tragic death in the parish family, the homiletic event for the next Sunday (let's say, it is the Fifth Sunday of Lent, Year A, the gospel for which is the raising of Lazarus) will carry a different freight than if such sadness were not part of the community. Again, these homiletic strategies are only meant to be suggestive and not prescriptive.

As every seasoned preacher knows very well, abstractions are the kiss of death when it comes to homilies, and so the tactics for achieving a core homiletic idea should be as concrete as possible and structured in a way that the congregation may follow it with ease, with a logic that is slow and available. Remember—tactics are practical actions with measured goals; in this case there is a single target: the core homiletic idea. What must be done to achieve that goal? As I have suggested earlier, homiletic methods are designed to organize a structure around the listener. We cannot presume that simply because I am speaking the fruits of my meditation and study that the congregation is unpacking the homily and getting to the depth of the core homiletic idea. The homiletic idea gives something precious to the baptized, enfleshing the word of God; it is a deepening of the reality of faith, a pondering of the mysteries of Christ, an exploration into God's creation. So in order to get to a theological understanding of the word of God, we ought to taste the aroma of fresh bread in that language.

In a word: the people of God don't want our stale crumbs in our preaching. "Homilies are inspirational when they touch the deepest levels of the human heart and address the real questions of human experience."[10] The worst possible response anyone can evince after preaching the word of God is for a faithful member of the congregation to respond, "So what?" Good tactics in homilies, like creative strategic planning, ensure that there is a measurable outcome. "So what?" Homilists should take care that this primary question is the subtext of every preaching event because no congregation should walk away from the Eucharist with that question lingering in their hearts. If we don't have a method or a structure of some kind to achieve the incarnation of our words, then we may have a great private meditation, but not much by way of evangelization. Jesus did not preach in parables for nothing: they are stories designed around the hearer to challenge, affirm, and unfold the kingdom of God.

It is a great privilege to stand in the midst of the baptized assembly and mediate meaning for those who have faithfully gathered at the Eucharist. Our preaching begins long before we come to the ambo and remains in the hearts of the congregation well after we leave the altar. Pray God that our own words become sown in the field of the Lord and reap a bountiful harvest.

Feast of St. Gregory the Great
Saint Meinrad School of Theology and Seminary, 2012

Notes

1. USCCB, *Fulfilled in Your Hearing: The Homily in the Sunday Assembly* (Washington, DC: USCCB, 1982), 23.

2. United States Conference of Catholic Bishops, *Preaching the Mystery of Faith: The Sunday Homily* (Washington, DC: USCCB Publishing, 2012), 15.

3. Benedict XVI, Post-Synodal Apostolic Exhortation, *The Word of the Lord (Verbum Domini)* (Boston: Pauline Books, 2010), 52.

4. Louis-Marie Chauvet, *"La Dimensions bibliques des texts liturgiques,"* *La Maison-Dieu* 189 (1992): 131–47. Chauvet demonstrates the foundational influence of the biblical text on the Christian liturgy, citing just some of the more obvious examples.

5. Edward Foley, Capuchin, "The Homily beyond Scripture: *Fulfilled in Your Hearing* Revisited," *Worship* 73, no. 4 (1999): 355.

6. Cf. Kenneth Untener, *Preaching Better* (Mahwah, NJ: Paulist Press, 1999).

7. Cf. David Buttrick, *Homiletic* (Philadelphia: Fortress Press, 1987); Eugene Lowry, *The Homiletic Plot* (Louisville: Westminster John Knox, 2001); Paul Scott Wilson, *The Four Pages of the Sermon* (Nashville: Abingdon, 1999 [1980]).

8. Cf. Paul Ricoeur, *The Symbolism of Evil*, trans. Emerson Buchanan (Boston: Beacon Press, 1967), 347–53.

9. Daniel McCarthy, *Listen to the Word: Commentaries on Selected Opening Prayers of Sundays and Feasts with Sample Homilies* (London: Tablet Publishing, 2009).

10. Cf. Thomas Long, *The Witness of Preaching*, 2nd ed. (Louisville: Westminster John Knox, 2005 [1990]), 99–116.

11. United States Conference of Catholic Bishops, *Preaching the Mystery of Faith*, 15.

ADVENT

First Sunday of Advent

Isa 2:1-5; Ps 122:1-9; Rom 13:11-14; Matt 24:37-44

The three readings for this First Sunday of Advent disclose a common thread: time. There is a sense of urgency communicated in First Isaiah (his ministry can be dated in the last three decades of the eighth century BC) and his call to Judah to return to God. Since it is the commencement of the church year, Isaiah's oracle forecasting "the days to come" is especially evocative. We might recall that Isaiah of Jerusalem was both informed and commissioned to service by a transcendent vision of God and his eternal dwelling place (cf. Isa 6:1-13), and so what is at stake in the return to the Lord is nothing less than an ascent up the mountain where the Most High will deliver righteous instruction. The prophet envisions an endless procession of God's people streaming into the Lord's house. There we will find peace at last because "the nations will be no more training for war." Isaiah's utopia trumpets a call to Zion in what we might imagine as "the future perfect." God will gather all into the holy mountain where only justice and peace will be spoken.

Jesus alerts his disciples of that future time as well, albeit with more ominous realities than Isaiah. We know that this particular passage in Matthew forms a section of the fifth (and last), eschatological discourse; it seeks to initiate the hearer into a future reality: it is a warning that the Son of Man will come at a time when we least expect him. Indeed, Jesus uses concrete and vivid language to jar the complacent disciples into God's end time, the *parousia*, comparing the in-breaking of God's future to the days of Noah. As illustrations, he points to one man being taken in the field, while another is not; two women are grinding at the millstone, and only one remains.

Such an ending will be like a thief who comes upon a householder unawares. So the conclusion could not be more obvious—stay alert, be faithful, and keep vigil.

Paul is of the same mind as Jesus and turns the preparation for the days to come into practical, moral advice for the Romans. At the same time, Paul uses *kairos* to define the approaching moment as eschatological, a moment of crisis before the end time when God will collapse all things into the day at hand. The imagery Paul uses underlines his point. As we wait for the day, we must "throw off the works of darkness / and put on the armor of light." We are to clothe ourselves in right conduct, putting on the Lord Jesus Christ.

Connecting the Bible and the Liturgy

The First Reading positions the listening assembly in precisely the same frame as the opening prayer: both imagine a peaceable kingdom as part of God's future. As Isaiah recalls God's promise to gather all nations into a peaceable kingdom, the **Collect** petitions for unity in Christ. Indeed, the voices of these nations that Isaiah imagines ("Come, let us climb the Lord's mountain . . . that he may instruct us in his ways, and we may walk in his paths.") give voice to the congregation's own desire to be gathered at God's coming into an eschatological moment. The opening prayer is quite visual, even as it encourages the faithful to run forth to Christ at the last, who becomes not the place but the *person* for which the just long. The longing for Zion and the kingdom of justice and peace has been extended to the church that eagerly runs to meet the Just One.

The use of future time as a lens of the present recalls the church's liturgical posture itself on this Sunday. Our present hope is guaranteed by a faith in God's future coming. But with the **Collect**'s petition to gather the righteous at Christ's right hand, there is also something of a cataclysmic warning meant to drive home the importance of keeping vigil, beginning with this first day of the church year. It is worth recalling that on the last day of the church year in Cycle A, we will once again take up the metaphor of those who will be at the right hand of the Son of Man when he comes with his angels in glory and separates the sheep from the goats. This First Sunday of Advent is preparing the congregation for God's coming not only at the end of Advent, not only at the end of the church year, but at the *parousia*, at the end of time when the flock gathers to its Shepherd—or rather, is gathered by the Son of Man. Interestingly, the English translation of the third edition of the *Missale Romanum* (2011; hereafter *The Roman Missal*) strengthens the force of the gathering of the faithful considerably to "gathered to his right hand" (*eius dexterae sociati*) from what the second edition of the *Sacramentary* (1985) translated as "his side." With a vision of the last days, the church, like Paul, clearly implores the faithful to remain vigilant as in the day "with righteous deeds at his coming, so that, gathered at his right hand, they may be worthy to possess the heavenly Kingdom." The **Prayer after Communion** underlines the transitory nature of time and our need to look to the coming of the Lord when that oration reminds the congregation that "we walk amid passing things." Even these temporal things can become instruments for conversion if we allow the Lord to "teach us by them to love the things of heaven and hold fast to what endures."

If all the biblical readings remind us of the *kairos* moment at hand, then the **Preface I of Advent** makes it clear that it is God who has both initiated time and will bring it to completion. God is the "almighty and eternal God" whose Christ has "fulfilled the design you formed long ago and opened for us the way to eternal salvation." All of those gathered at the Eucharistic Liturgy await this same Lord to draw back the curtain of human history, "when he comes again in glory and majesty and all is at last made manifest." Like Isaiah, the **Preface** imagines a collective gathering of all peoples into the peace of God's kingdom in and through Christ. Far from an individualized waiting for the coming of Christ, the church's prayer is centered on the vision of unity, joined in fellowship not only with one another but with angels and archangels. The Eucharist becomes the place of vigil, the watchtower upon which God's people stretch forth their hands in prayer for which "we now dare hope."

Strategy for Preaching

The Advent Season then invites the church into silent vigil, urgent longing, and hopeful expectation for the coming of the Redeemer. Unlike preaching during Lent, which has a penitential character in its own right and is imbued with preparation for the baptized for the dawning of Easter, Advent homilies focus on the church that has assembled in eager anticipation for God's coming. The language of the liturgy for the First Sunday of Advent is particularly useful for preaching, and its exploration begins to surface homiletic strategies. Consider the three images in the **Collect**, for instance, which might be used to underline a homiletic core idea. The first of these implores almighty God to grant the faithful "the resolve to run forth to meet your Christ with righteous deeds at his coming." The second imagines that the place such a meeting would occur is "gathered at his right hand." The third projects these faithful as potential members or possessors of "the heavenly kingdom." The liturgy and the Scriptures remind us of God's promise for a future when Christ will gather those who wander into the kingdom of justice and peace.

Useful images for constructing the homily are vividly disclosed in the Scriptures and in *The Roman Missal*: running to meet Christ, a holy mountain, leaving a home unguarded. Clearly a dominant preaching thread present this Sunday is, perhaps obviously enough, the advent of God breaking into our historical time and how we prepare ourselves to run and meet him at the last. With that homiletic core idea in mind, the pastorally conscious preacher should, as always, exegete the assembly together with these biblical and liturgical texts. This combination is always nonnegotiable for liturgical preaching but all the more important at the beginning of the church year as we link our preaching to mission. Where do I want my congregation at the end of Advent? What about in a year on the Feast of Christ the King? Will the people of God be in a better place because of my preaching? It seems clear that this First Sunday of Advent is asking the church to lean into the *kairos* moment, the *parousia* held out to us as we await the coming of the Lord, and that raises the question of how we own the present moment. At the beginning of the church year, am I challenged to be present to something other than a secular calendar? Does God's claim on time and the gathering of all peoples on a holy mountain reorient all of us to consider the implications of peace and justice now? How does the vision of Zion inform our present circumstances?

Finally, the preacher's theology of Advent will determine the homiletic text. What is that theology, and how are these ideas shaped by the preacher's identity? In order to ponder this question of identity further, the preacher might examine narratives about exile in the literary canon. Foremost among exiles and return journeys is Homer's

Odyssey in which Odysseus must make his way back to his family
and homeland after a period following the Trojan War. The longing
for home and return seems to be a dominant theme in a great deal
of literature and an appropriate one to investigate when discovering a
preaching theology for Advent. The whole book of the prophet Isaiah
might prove another text worthy of careful meditation, alongside a
good commentary. If Isaiah sets the tone for this Sunday in Year A,
he is taking the role of the herald of things to come. I would suggest
that this heraldic character marks preaching identity for the Advent
season, perhaps most obviously on the first Sunday.

Second Sunday of Advent

Readings from the Ambo

Isa 11:1-10; Ps 72:1-2, 7-8, 12-13, 17; Rom 15:4-9; Matt 3:1-12

In contrast to the First Sunday of Advent, this week's readings focus our attention more on the person of the messianic king, rather than the place where he dwells. Where the very beginning of Advent exhorted the community to the ecstatically renewed city of Zion on God's holy mountain to await the end time, this Second Sunday celebrates the leader who will make such a world possible. Isaiah's passage here is exuberant with its hope for the one who will inhabit the Spirit of the Lord and all the divine gifts: wisdom, understanding, counsel, strength, knowledge, and fear of the Lord. Most of all, this messianic king will maintain justice, especially for the poor and the afflicted. It is interesting to contrast Isaiah 9:2-7 to the present passage, since it also famously reminds the community of the "Prince of Peace" who will establish and uphold justice and righteousness. The coming of the Just One means the establishment of a society rooted in rectitude and harmony.

On that promised day, everything will be transformed, including nature itself. Therefore Isaiah delivers a litany of what can only be described as impossible relationships; these would only be possible at the time of messianic deliverance present on God's mountain, where "the wolf shall be the guest of the lamb . . . the calf and the young lion shall browse together." Finally, this "stump of Jesse" will be a legacy not only for Israel but "a signal for the nations, / the Gentiles shall seek out, / for his dwelling shall be glorious." Paul underlines the universality of Christ's salvation when he tells the Romans that God's promise ratified the patriarchs of Israel but also extends to other nations as well so that they "might glorify God for his mercy." God's holy mountain is a place for all peoples, a place where there is no division, either by force of national boundaries or even by the barriers of nature itself.

John the Baptist sees his own mission in the desert of Judea as something of a level playing field as well. The message of salvation is meant not only for Israel but for those who repent, who have a change of heart. In fact, John singles out the religious "elite" of his day, the Pharisees and Sadducees, and condemns them for their self-justification. Just because they have Abraham as their father means nothing unless they have a change of heart. It is conversion that makes all of us equals, not our religious sects. John suggests that the coming of the one after him will bring a new order, gathering the wheat and burning the chaff.

Connecting the Bible and the Liturgy

Both Isaiah and Matthew's gospel promise one who will incarnate the very virtues for which the Christian assembly has been longing. "May no earthly undertaking hinder those who set out in haste to meet your son," the **Collect** prays. Indeed, the liturgy's focus on cultivating virtues finds its foil in the biblical articulation of the gifts of the messianic king, a kind of roll call of all the great moral virtues that lead to peace and justice. The embodiment of the Just One who will bring peace and concord to the nations is emblematic of the virtuous messianic king. God's power will undermine earthly corruption and realign an unjust and violent world with the manifestation of the coming of the kingdom through the Righteous One; this is, he whom John announces is near at hand, ready with an ax to cut down and throw all trees that do not bear fruit into the fire. The proximity of his coming and righteous judgment necessitates a conversion and repentance for all those who long for his appearance, the "root of Jesse" who will initiate God's reign. John's message is for the congregation attentive to God's teaching on this Second Sunday in Advent; it is a call to heed the instruction of the master so that we might be prepared.

The call to conversion is nothing less than a vision of reconciliation and peace, which Isaiah himself has proclaimed and echoed in the liturgy. Paul counts on a similar harmonic attitude in Romans ("with one accord you may with one voice / glorify the God and father of our Lord Jesus Christ"), reminding the community that the Scriptures provide "instruction" for carrying out this radical hospitality: "Welcome one another, then, as Christ welcomed you, / for the glory of God." This hospitality also extends to the congregation offering its "humble prayers and offerings . . . with no merits to plead our cause" (**Prayer over the Offerings**). Therefore the congregation begs the Lord for mercy and waits to be "replenished," as the **Prayer after Communion** puts it, by "the food of spiritual nourishment." Note that the special emphasis on the congregation being "replenished" is a striking change from the previous (1985) translation, which simply said, "you give us food from heaven." The translation in the new *Roman Missal* suggests that during the Second Sunday of Advent, those on the journey need to be refreshed and fed, even as they are waiting for the Word. The Eucharist, as always, is the invitation to conversion, the food that teaches us "to judge wisely the things of earth" (**Prayer after Communion**) and reminds us of the Baptist's invitation to "produce good fruit" as evidence of our repentance. The Eucharist becomes the wellspring for bringing forth an abundant crop as the congregation is sent forward into mission.

Strategy for Preaching

With the initial burst of the First Sunday of Advent over, the Second Sunday concentrates on the hard work of Christian conversion, which could form a homiletic core idea. The word that Matthew uses is the imperative form of the verb *metanoeo* ("I repent"), which literally means beyond (*meta*) one's mind (*nous*). The preacher, then, becomes an instrument like Isaiah and John the Baptist, centering his message on the necessity moving beyond one's present mind into a newer reality. The homily might consider as a homiletic core idea how to motivate the assembly out of a shared complacency or status quo mentality into *corporate* conversion.

Initiating the call to conversion for the congregation is not an easy rhetorical strategy, to be sure. Most failed attempts to move folks to repentance begin with injunctions like "you ought" or "you should." These statements usually wind up as moralistic platitudes that never really engage anyone from moving beyond the present circumstances of their lives, and may even be a cause of resentment. An occasional "ought" statement here and there might be okay, but if the homily's spine is held together by "should," then the preacher reduces his congregation to a kind of Sunday school of dos and don'ts and he becomes the bearer of something like bitter tea, rather than the cup of salvation.

The careful reader of Scripture and the liturgical texts will recognize clues that help to discover how to motivate the congregation on the Second Sunday of Advent. Recall that John the Baptist does not only say, "Repent," but that there is a second, vital rejoinder: "the kingdom of heaven is at hand!" I take it that the **Collect** focuses our attention quite deliberately on the immediacy of that kingdom when it asks that "our learning of heavenly wisdom gain us admittance to his company." The homily, then, becomes the process of disclosing signs of the *nearness* of God's kingdom, which will motivate the congregation to repentance. Therefore the eucharistic assembly structures its desire to change around a yearning for the kingdom, now so near at hand. How urgent and how near becomes the rhetorical strategy of the homily.

In uncovering images or symbols or examples of the kingdom, there are an infinite variety of examples from which to choose. I am thinking here of one of the most obvious examples that Jesus himself will point to as a window into the kingdom: children. They are the most visible, energetic, and obvious signs in the Advent season. They are the natural symbols present at almost every Eucharistic Liturgy and disclose the wonder and mystery of the season. Children disclose the kingdom of God during Advent because they have not lost the sense of expectation of the coming Christmas season that often accompanies adulthood. Children are signs that the kingdom is near at hand because they always live in the present, rather than a dark past or a vague future. A homily that focuses on a kingdom that comes to us like a child will transform the ubiquitous commercialized season (with its mutated, commercialized children as consumers) into a community seeking to transform its mind and heart. Like expectant children of God, all in the eucharistic assembly can await "the food of spiritual nourishment" in true humility and eager longing.

Third Sunday of Advent

Readings from the Ambo

Isa 35:1-6a; Ps 146:6-10; James 5:7-10; Matt 11:2-11

On this *Gaudete* Sunday, Isaiah's proclamation in the first reading imagines the impossible: the desert exulting, the steppe in bloom, the eyes of the blind opened, the ears of the deaf cleared. The passage is part of the oracle (the bulk of which we find in chaps. 40–55) of what has become known as "Second Isaiah," whose mission in the sixth century BC was to preach to the Israelites languishing in Babylonian exile that their affliction was at an end and their relationship with the Lord was renewed. A highly visual text, Isaiah's prophecy in chapter 35 is nothing less than a dream of God's splendor at its most spectacular. There is reason to rejoice, a reason to sing. Isaiah's text is the answer to the question, "Celebrate what?" It is humanity's very ransom from captivity into freedom, so that Zion will enter with hymns of praise from the foundations of creation itself. "[T]hey will meet with joy and gladness, / sorrow and morning will flee." The biblical text is the portrait of a people in ecstatic joy who have been released from bondage at long last; it is a preview of the Christian community in the middle of the Advent season when we have glimpsed the Promised One, like the sight of a loved one across an enormous, crowded room. We know that it is love that will set us free. It is as if the biblical text here before us is just a peek at what the liturgy asks the congregation to expect, long for, and, finally, celebrate in word and, of course, song.

At the same time, the Letter of James uses very earthy and practical language to express patience on this Third Sunday of Advent. Steadfastness or making "hearts firm" is the way to prepare for the coming of the Lord. Similarly, the prophets "who spoke in the name of the Lord" are not so much ecstatic visionaries as examples of those who remained faithful, despite hardship. In this regard, Matthew's portrait of John the Baptist is the tragic prophet in chains, a mighty voice that now becomes an open ear, a listening heart that now desires the Eternal Word. This section of Matthew's gospel initiates a third section or discourse in which Jesus will continue to disclose himself in mysterious ways to the disciples. In a certain sense, John is among the first to ask a question concerning Jesus' identity, "are you the one who is to come, / or should we look for another?" The Baptist is literally reduced to a voice, a disembodied self, placed in prison whose messengers must carry his word to Jesus and his disciples. Last Sunday, John was the powerful instrument of the conversion; this week he is a lasting symbol of hope. Indeed, the drama of John imprisoned suggests the Christian community at prayer, longing and waiting for the Messiah to set all creation free; the Christian assembly listens and is attentive to God's works, the greatest of which is about to unfold, all the while reaching steadfastly for the appearance of the Promised One.

Connecting the Bible and the Liturgy

The relationship with the eucharistic assembly and John the Baptist is strengthened by the liturgy for this Sunday. The first phrase of the **Collect** attributes to God a kind of eyewitness function over the activity of the people. The Latin verb *conspicere* refers to one who literally "catches sight" of his faithful at prayer. The **Collect** reminds the Lord that his people steadfastly await the coming of the Lord and long for his appearing. The effect here deliberately calls God into testimony over the church's celebration of the previous weeks of Advent and to see those who have gathered under its celebratory and vigilant wings. "O God, who see how your people faithfully await the feast of the Lord's Nativity, enable us, we pray, to attain the joys of so great a salvation and to celebrate them always with solemn worship and glad rejoicing." Like John, the people of God have not been dormant but vigilant. Those who have waited have done so faithfully, despite hardships and even suffering. We ought not to miss the bit of bartering going on here between the presider and God during the **Collect**, asking the Lord to act because of what he has seen. Interestingly enough, if John has been literally reduced to a voice, seeking to verify the coming Messiah, the church also pours forth its prayers in similar, heartfelt yearning for that same Christ Jesus. The joyful anticipation only increases as the faithful hear the presider remind the assembly of the coming of "the Lord's Nativity."

But this powerful longing is mixed with celebration and rejoicing. There is an enticing connection in the presidential prayers with Isaiah's entrancing vision in chapter 35—particularly in the **Collect**, which encourages the congregation to celebrate "with solemn worship and glad rejoicing." With hearts on fire, the hearts of the Christian people discover their salvation blended with Isaiah's flowering desert and the Baptist's waters of hope. Once again, there is an echo of anticipation on this Sunday, most vividly and iconically rendered in John the Baptist's question put to Jesus about his messianic identity. With both the Scriptures and liturgy so marvelously intermingled, worship on this Third Sunday of Advent serves to bring the congregation to a joyful, heartfelt conversion. At the end of the day, we might realize that before we celebrate the Lord's nativity, we will find ourselves purified in the glad and happy fire of our worship before the living God. The **Prayer after Communion** begs the Lord's mercy, "That this divine sustenance may cleanse us of our faults and prepare us for the coming feasts." It is as if Isaiah's dry desert is just waiting to see even more abundant flower; that those feeble hands and weak knees and frightened hearts are even now being steeled to be strong and fearless. This is the eucharistic assembly that lives inside divine promise at the edge of glimpsing the messianic king. As the psalmist reminds us, "the Lord God keeps faith forever." What better reason to hope?

Strategy for Preaching

The homilist on the Third Sunday of Advent would do well to attend to the hopeful signs present in both the biblical and liturgical texts. One thing to keep in mind in this regard, is Second Isaiah's abundant use of visual images deployed to show the enormous release that is about to occur for those in exile. Not unlike the images Isaiah deploys for those present on God's holy mountain, these are transformations of nature that signify God's breaking into history and reversing the fortunes of the oppressed. Israel will own a new springtime. Restoration of those who are weak or disabled; they are showcased as an example of God's curative powers.

If Isaiah demonstrates the prophetic restoration of Israel in a reimagined and reconstituted land, Jesus promises the same to John when he tells Baptist that "the blind regain their sight, the lame walk, lepers are cleansed, the deaf hear, the dead are raised and the poor have the good news proclaimed to them." These are concrete and specific demonstrations of God's activity in the world, implicating the full restoration that is to come.

The Christian assembly will need to hear the same. The homiletic text this Sunday could not be too vivid or too visual. The congregation longs to hear and see and feel the disclosures of the Holy in their midst every Sunday, but on *Gaudete* Sunday in particular these revelations are key to unlocking the prophetic hope that undergirds the Scriptures and the liturgy. The Lord's nativity is coming, perhaps in ways we are not anticipating. In a certain sense, the homilist is asking the question: "What did you come to the desert to *see*?" The answer is, of course, the workings of God in Word and Sacrament. So by unfolding the deeds of the Lord in visual imagery, the preacher is able to deepen the faith, hope, and love of the assembly. The whole liturgy, of which the homily is a part, will prepare the congregation for the coming feast.

In addition to using visual images, this is a particularly good Sunday to use a story that would reveal reasons for hope. I am thinking here of a contemporary story of someone who has done an extraordinary work of charity or maintained hope in a time of adversity. These examples should be drawn from ordinary people who do extraordinary things with great love. These kinds of stories are illustrations of God's activity among his people, a variation of the kinds of instances Jesus recommends to John. Therefore the homiletic core idea might focus on God's gift of hope to those in exile and then show through visual storytelling how such hope is disclosed. What are these images Isaiah uses? During *lectio divina,* try making a list and finding contemporary parallels. What are examples of God's activity in the world? The parish community? Lastly, the Eucharist itself remains the sacrament of rejoicing, the ultimate disclosure by Christ of his presence and love in the world. Is the presider enabling the congregation to worship in praise and thanksgiving, which itself points to God's presence in the world?

Fourth Sunday of Advent

Isa 7:10-14; Ps 24:1-2, 3-4, 5-6; Rom 1:1-7; Matt 1:18-24

A convenient way of thinking about these readings might be sub-sumed under the title of something like "Those Who Trust in God and Those Who Fail to Do So." The passage from Isaiah seems devout enough—but I would suggest that we draw deeper from this well. In a certain way, Isaiah 7:10ff. is an inversion of the annunciation, or a refusal of a divine invitation. Indeed, the dark side of Ahaz and his relationship with the Lord is that the Bible records this monarch as one of Israel's worst kings, one who was willing to sell the northern kingdom as a kind of biblical fire sale to the Assyrians, and even take on the worship of the gods of that nation. Although he preserved the southern kingdom, Ahaz's actions eventually led to the destruction of the northern kingdom in 721 BC. The current selection reveals only a part of Isaiah's intrepid attempts to get Ahaz to change his mind. Despite the turning away of God's offer, the Lord says that there will be a sign nevertheless. Thus, even in the midst of betrayal and sin, the ways of God reveal wonders and newness; it is a both a promise and a disclosure that God is with us, "Emmanuel."

The gospel is meant to be an answer to God's promise, as well as its mirror. We have Matthew's famous rendering of the scenes leading up to the birth of Jesus. There is a clear connection with the first reading with the quotation, "Behold, the virgin shall conceive and bear a son, / and they shall name him Emmanuel." But the gospel is more than a gloss on the Hebrew Scripture. In some sense, we should read this account of Mary's being found with child by the Holy Spirit and Joseph's response and dream as a foil to Ahaz's failure to trust God. Indeed, "Joseph's annunciation" is a revelation through a dream of what the Lord has done and intends to do. This is the sign from God as "deep as the netherworld, or high as the sky" that was fully embraced. Far from selling out his people like Ahaz before him, Joseph's cooperation with God's plan enables a new world and a new nation to come into being, a Savior who would break the cycle of sin and death and establish God's kingdom.

Paul is quick to acknowledge his own ascent to the divine plan in his letter to the Romans when he says that he interprets his own apostleship based on what God "promised previously through his prophets in the holy Scriptures." Such a call is designed precisely to "bring about the obedience of faith." When Paul refers to himself as "*doulos Christou Iesou,*" he is not referring to himself as a "slave" in the traditional sense. In fact, some prefer to translate "*doulos*" as "bondservant," that is, one who is completely and utterly devoted to the service of the master. This relationship is not one of captivity, but *love* propelled by a single-minded surrender of the ego for the sake of the other. Paul's parallel with Joseph and the contrast with Ahaz could not be more obvious.

Connecting the Bible and the Liturgy

This Sunday stretches out the promise of the incarnation and its fulfillment in Christ's passion, cross, and resurrection by witnessing its rehearsal in full bloom: we see that in a drama played out between the Old and the New Covenant, particularly by its foreshadowing with the prophet Isaiah and his encounter with Ahaz. Later we encounter both its completion and its foil in the gospel's recounting of Joseph's response to God's Word. The Scripture and the liturgy invite the congregation into the contemplation of what God is about to do. Clearly, the work of the Spirit links the readings and the presidential prayers together. Indeed, the **Prayer over the Gifts** immediately invokes the Holy Spirit when the presider prays, "May the Holy Spirit, O Lord, sanctify these gifts laid upon your altar, just as he filled with his power the womb of the Blessed Virgin Mary." This is an echo, of course, of the **Collect**, which encapsulates the incarnation in the use of the "Angelus Prayer." Additionally, the eucharistic assembly is drawn into the mystery of God's invitation on an active, participative level as well. Joseph and Mary, together with Paul, held up as models for responding to God's promise, the congregation becomes part of that same divine dialogue. "Having received this pledge of eternal redemption," the people of God ask for the grace "to press forward all the more eagerly" (**Prayer after Communion**).

The role of the Holy Spirit in the drama of the annunciation suggests that God's plan extends well beyond our own limited vision. Yes, we look forward with eager expectation to the mystery of the nativity. Yes, we continue to celebrate these coming days before Christmas in special proper prayers in the liturgy from December 17–24. Yes, the "O" antiphons and the church's Evening Prayer will pay homage to the special attributes of the coming Messiah. But there is more: the coming of Emmanuel, fulfilled by human cooperation, sets in motion God's divine plan for redemption, culminating in the paschal mystery. The **Collect** affirms this broad history of salvation when it asks that we who have been witnesses to this message of the angel to Mary may be brought *"per passionem eius et crucem ad resurrectionis gloriam."* The sweep of God's will finds its perspective as we are taken up into Joseph's dream: "She will bear a son and you are to name him Jesus because he will save his people from their sins." This encounter with the future destiny of the coming King only intensifies the magnitude of God's promise and the longing for its fulfillment in Christ newly born.

Strategy for Preaching

The homily this week might take is clue from the Responsorial Psalm: "Let the Lord enter, he is the King of glory." This refrain is both a petition and a challenge for the congregation, allowing the faithful to ponder aloud their own capacity to welcome the Word. It is the preacher's task to reveal the *dynamics of desire*—emotional, spiritual, and theological—of God's yearning for his people and the Christian faithful's own response to that divine yearning. Images of a deep netherworld, an endless sky, together with aggressive angels and intrusive dreams help us to reimagine ways to discover God asking us to partner with us in grace.

Clearly, the interplay between the conniving Ahaz, on the one hand, and the virtuous cast of New Testament characters who co-operate with God's will, on the other, play to the preacher's narrative advantage in constructing a homily. We see the model of how to respond to God portrayed in sacred story. Rather than simply retelling the gospel (never a wise strategy), the homily might lay a more basic subtext to approach a homiletic core idea, beginning with such a probing question as "Why did Ahaz refuse God's invitation?" And again, "How did Mary, Joseph, and Paul become bondsmen, or single-minded in God's service?" The answer to such questions, of course, is love, which reorients everything we do and fashions us as righteous people of God. In light of the incarnation, then, what are my priorities, and why do I do what I do? That final question becomes a potential homiletic core idea used to motivate the congregation into a deeper mystery and faith.

In articulating such a faith challenge, it is worth constructing a tight (but brief) theological conversation partner to accompany the challenge to the eucharistic assembly. *The Catechism of the Catholic Church* (1997) is a handy guide for theological reflection, as well as the *New Catholic Encyclopedia* (2002); these resources could well serve as a primary focus for disclosing concepts that are difficult to grasp, but to which the assembly can only give thanks and praise and an abiding wonder. Needless to say, the incarnation is, well, a mystery, but homilies should avoid abstraction. God in the flesh could not be any more concrete. Thoughtful analogies and biblical examples of God's entry into history would serve as viable illustrations to a complex dogma. Additionally, I would suggest that this Fourth Sunday of Advent is the best time to handle a theological or catechetical reflection on the doctrine of the incarnation because it will prepare the congregation for its liturgical unfolding in just a few days. Later I will suggest a further opportunity for theological reflection on this dogma on the Second Sunday after the Nativity.

Lastly, before the homily asks the congregation to do so, the preacher will need to explore prayerfully some basic questions concerning priorities in the light of the coming Lord. Have I let the Lord into my life, especially when I want to be in control? If so, where? What did this encounter with the holy look like, specifically? If I have not let the Lord enter, why not? What is that resistance about? Based on these experiences, am I willing to realign my life structures in order to apportion my priorities accordingly? These are questions that will be asked of the thoughtful listener, as well. A prayerful reading of First Isaiah's vocational call in 6:1-13 might prove fruitful in *lectio divina* as well as an extended meditation on the Responsorial Psalm.

 # CHRISTMAS TIME

The Nativity of the Lord

Mass during the Night (Years ABC)

Readings from the Ambo

Isa 9:1-6; Ps 96:1-2, 2-3,11-12, 13; Luke 2:1-14

Many scholars believe that Isaiah's oracle belongs to a kind of festival celebrating the king (most likely the commencement of Hezekiah's reign in 715 BC). Consequently, the images in this extraordinary passage harbor aspects of divinity that have been long associated with monarchical power from the time of antiquity. Notable among these tropes is the youthful aspect of this new reign, "a son is given us; / upon his shoulder dominion rests." A new springtime has come for Israel and therefore those "who walked in darkness / have seen a great light." Isaiah could not be clearer about a naissance emerging in his midst, granting prosperity to a nation now "multiplied," and freedom to a land no longer under "the rod of their taskmaster." A new order has been unleashed that has attached itself to the Davidic kingship, a line associated with justice and with righteousness.

Most important, the new kingdom has been initiated by the "zeal of the LORD of hosts." That final attribute of a God who leads armies into battle should remind us that although this passage may be celebrating the beginning of Hezekiah's kingdom, it is God's power that trumps all earthly kingdoms. It is worth considering the freight of the word "zeal" and its connection to God's activity in the world. Israel's passage into newness is made possible by a divine will that sustains and animates secular power because of the Lord's own righteousness and justice.

The Christ event recorded in the gospel discloses God's same zeal at work. In Luke's account of Jesus' birth, it would be hard to miss the reordering of secular power into sacred time and history. Indeed, the decree going out from Caesar Augustus that "the whole world should be enrolled" suggests an attempt to bring all things within the scope of a Roman imperial horizon. Yet simultaneously, a parallel history of salvation is also unfolding that is subverting a secular census: this is God's Son about to be born, which will go unrecorded by secular authorities, and who will break the cycle of sin and death passed on from one generation to the next. God's new empire is for all people, beginning with the lowly shepherds and proclaimed by heavenly hosts, who themselves become the first preachers of the Gospel of Christ at the moment of his birth.

Paul interprets the coming of God in the flesh as an opportunity to "reject godless ways and worldly desires." As the letter to Titus explains it, God's coming in the flesh demands a moral conversion, a turning away from sin and becoming a people who are "eager to do what is good." Key to understanding this process of conversion is God's own generosity, not our ability to accomplish good works. As Paul will make clear in chapter 3, it is by grace that we are justified, not our own works. If we can grasp that Jesus Christ "gave himself for us to deliver us from all lawlessness," then we can live in "blessed hope" and truly desire to be children of God. Therefore the Incarnation, or "the appearance of the glory of our great God" is reason to celebrate because of the freedom it grants us to unbind us from "*pases anomias.*" Some may translate this as "all wickedness," but the Lectionary says more accurately, I think, "all lawlessness," which connotes a disregard for either civil or moral law. This translation is especially appropriate in reference to the deliverance promised by God: it is not we who free ourselves from such "*anomias,*" but God who delivers us as a free gift within a new empire of peace and justice.

Connecting the Bible and the Liturgy

The reading from Isaiah and the **Collect** for this solemnity are inextricably linked by the common attention to the time of day of the celebration itself: it is night. Most obviously, when experienced from the lens of First Isaiah, the congregation has been placed in an atmosphere not unlike the people of Israel. We cannot help but notice the parallel with the Lukan narrative as well, with the travelers searching for a refuge in Bethlehem. The dynamic that unfolds is quite physical in its most basic sense: those who have come in from the darkness are now gathered into an ecclesial space, waiting for the light to shine. While Isaiah trumpets Israel's rescue from the darkness into light and Luke records the journey of Joseph and Mary from their own exile thanks to the workings of empire into sacred time and God's deliverance. The liturgy, then, calls the assembly's attention to the God who has made "this most sacred night radiant with the splendor of the true light." The only other formal liturgical time that the church will gather during the night will be at the Easter Vigil, which will once again be a celebration of the light in the midst of darkness. We share this place of light with the shepherds as well, who are keeping watch in the night and behold the glory of the Lord all around them. On a symbolic level, moreover, the recognition of the gathered assembly of the church, the Body of Christ, as a place of sacred light, suggests a petition for divine illumination. And so the **Collect** also asks God to grant the faithful a participation in the very life of the Christ who has come among us as light itself, even as we ask for a sharing in his eternal life in heaven: "grant, we pray, that we, who have known the mysteries of his light on earth, may also delight in his gladness in heaven."

Additionally, it is well to remember that this day is asking for a response from the eucharistic assembly to God's great gift in Christ. The **Prayer over the Offerings** retains in English the Latin equivalent of offering, "oblation," which has its roots in St. Jerome's Vulgate translation of the Hebrew Scriptures. The law of Moses, for instance, allows for a "meal offering" an *"oblatio"* to the Lord. Therefore the congregation's offering at the Eucharist becomes a "most holy exchange," a mirror of the mystery of the Incarnation because of our sharing in divine life and Christ taking on human flesh: we pray that "we may be found in the likeness of Christ, in whom our nature is united to you." In this same way, **Preface III of the Nativity of the Lord** proclaims, "For through him the holy exchange that restores our life has shone forth today in splendor: when our frailty is assumed by your Word not only does human mortality receive unending honor but by this wondrous union we, too, are made eternal." These prayers underline Paul's insight to Titus in delivering us from *lawlessness*, and ask God "to cleanse for himself a people as his own." For Paul, this very sacred exchange was "training us" for a response, "to reject godless ways and worldly desires." That response is the congregation's *oblatio* on this night and throughout the year. And so the eucharistic assembly prays for the grace to accomplish such conversion when the presider prays those who are "gladdened by participation in the feast of our Redeemer's nativity, may through an honorable way of life become worthy of union with him."

Strategy for Preaching

There are several things for the homilist to keep in mind for preaching at the Mass during the night on Christmas. Of all days, it is critical this day to exegete the assembly. "Midnight Mass" is a cultural as well as a religious event in many parishes throughout the States. For some, it is a long family custom that involves a meal before or after the liturgy, opening gifts and sharing of familial stories with friends and relatives. As is well known, there will be several who might be described as marginal churchgoers present at the Mass during the night. This group remains an important reality, and may be evangelized on this day in particular precisely because of their status living in a kind of secular diaspora seeking the light. It is up to the preacher to discover the images and symbols that will enable a large net to be cast in order to gather those who cling to the edges of the parish into the folds of God's mercy. I hasten to add at this point that this is certainly not the time to begin to chastise people (it is *never* a good time for that) for not attending Mass and just showing up on Christmas. That is contrary to the very intention of the Word on this most sacred of nights. Rather, the wise preacher will recognize that all of us walk in darkness to some degree and need the light of Christ to illuminate our hearts. The Good News is that at the very least some see the light shining in the darkling sky, even if it is only once a year! Can the homily work to increase the faith, hope, and love present in the congregation to respond to God's generous gift?

A core homiletic idea should be focused on God's astonishing reach of grace. It is up to the homily to unfold what that looks like, with Christmas as a kind of sacred touchstone. The visible signs of God's presence in Christ are available when the preacher begins to "name grace," as *Fulfilled in Your Hearing* (USCCB, 1982) puts it. To be sure, the readings name the grace of a God who dispels the darkness into light. Where else in Scripture can we see a God who delivers us from the night? What comes to mind here immediately is the Creator who separated light from darkness and delivered Israel out of the "darkness of Egypt." Is there more to say about this? Certainly. Secondly, grace is named in the liturgy by the very texts in *The Roman Missal*, with its petition (after Communion) to make the congregation a participant in divine light and so enable those gathered to act in the future "in an honorable," righteous, and moral way. Lastly, grace is named in the historical circumstances of the community itself. What has surfaced in the course of the Christmas season that might avail itself to a worthy and edifying communication of divine activity for the faithful? There are plenty of examples of self-giving and generous acts of kindness in parishes and communities. These are instances of selfless giving that have their origin in God's self-communication in Christ Jesus on this Holy Night.

Holy Family of Jesus, Mary and Joseph

Readings from the Ambo

Sir 3:2-6, 12-14; Ps 128:1-5; Col 3:12-21; Matt 2:13-15, 19-23

To understand the implications of the first reading, it may be help-ful to say something about its origins. The book of Sirach (sometimes called Ecclesiasticus—or the "Church Book") gets its name from its well-educated and pious Jewish author living in the second century BC. Ben Sira concerns himself with a kind of protracted meditation on the Jewish tradition, seemingly then at odds and increasingly threatened by Greek politics, culture, and religion. The author's strategy is to remind the Jewish community of their own tradition and to resist the creeping Hellenization of their contemporary cul-ture. "The Instruction of Ben Sira" contains advice drawn from the author's wide knowledge of Hebrew Scripture and other traditions, together with an extended application of the law of Moses. An ex-ample we have in the First Reading is a kind of descant on the fourth commandment. In some sense, the passage suggests a reason for the importance of the command to honor one's father and mother in the first place—and, quite literally, the exacting weight owed to parents. The Hebrew word that is used in the Torah in the fourth command-ment is *"kavod,"* which means "to glorify" or "to weigh with heavy honors." The honorific weight that the book of Sirach accords to fathers and mothers is not only cultural but deeply religious: the behavior of honoring parents keeps the law of Moses and therefore, "Whoever honors his father atones for sins, / and preserves himself from them. / When he prays, he is heard." This sanctification of sin by good works is well in keeping with the pious precepts contained in the Scriptures, which instruct that mercy covers a multitude of sins. Interestingly, the author deploys a domestic image as a reward for respecting parents and regards it, perhaps somewhat shrewdly, as something of an investment for the future, even a building project of sorts: "[K]indness to a father will not be forgotten, / firmly planted against the debt of your sins / —a house raised in justice to you."

Paul wants to extend the honoring of parents to the entire Christian community, or "God's chosen ones," and does so with some practical adages about living an upright life. We might understand the Pauline teaching here as emerging from a larger theological understanding of the Body of Christ when he tells the Colossians that they are to forgive "as the Lord has forgiven you, so must you also do." The debt here obviously extends well beyond familial obligations in the traditional sense, but extends the *"kavod,"* or the weight of heavy honors to the offending neighbor. A life of peace in Christ "in one body" lives in the context of thanksgiving—and ordered love. The last portion of this passage will strike many contemporaries as uncomfortable, but in Paul's mind, the One Body is modeled on a familial structure as he understood it within his own cultural horizon.

Such order and harmony depend on mutual love and submission, clearly witnessed in the colorful gospel passage. Once again, Joseph shows himself as an obedient and righteous lover of God and his family. It will not be the first time that (another) Joseph found himself in Egypt living out God's providential plan for the sake of his people. Nor is it the first time that God will deliver his beloved in an exodus from Egypt. The overall intention of the story rests on the providential nature of God's plan, which is testified to in the prophetic writings (although there is no known canonical reference to the quotation "He shall be called a Nazorean"). Rather than read this for an exacting parallel, we should understand it as Matthew's faith experience of God's will being fulfilled. Finally, it is hard to miss the subversion of the political will occurring at the same time and which God also undermined in the deliverance of Moses from Pharaoh's genocidal plan against the firstborn males of Egypt.

Connecting the Bible and the Liturgy

The **Collect** creates something of an imaginative bridge between the first two readings. *The Roman Missal* translates the Latin phrase used in the **Collect**, *"dignatus,"* meaning esteemed or honored, as "shining." The word picks up rather strongly on the Hebrew word (*kavod*) deployed in the first reading for honoring one's parents in a visual sense. It is not too much of a stretch to say that the Holy Family is to be weighed heavily, even glorified as a dazzling example. At the same time, this exaltation is not some ideation outside human experience or, still more strange, a religious fantasy of "the first family." Rather, the Holy Family is the model of perfect charity as Paul himself imagines the Christian community to be at its best. The Holy Family is the celebration of the virtues of "heartfelt compassion, kindness, humility, gentleness and patience." It is clear that these qualities also play themselves out in the Matthean account of the aftermath of Jesus' birth and the courageous family drama that ensues. Therefore, the **Collect** asks God to "graciously grant that we may imitate them in practicing the virtues of family life in the bonds of charity."

The liturgy also points the congregation toward a future domestic dwelling, a place where we may inhabit "the joy of your house" (*in laetitia domus tuae*). There is an echo here of the promise of a future dwelling made to the righteous from the book of Sirach where the debt of sins will be wiped away because of the kindness shown to a father; the memory of such good will shall figuratively construct a "house raised in justice" to the righteous observer of God's commands. Moreover, the expectation of the Christian community living in God's house recalls the well-ordered love for which Paul enjoins the Colossians to strive, a society made perfect by mutual obedience and love. Undoubtedly, the promise of the joy of God's house finds a foothold in Jesus' own promise in John 14:2-3: "In my Father's house there are many dwelling places. I there were not, would I have told you that I am going to prepare a place for you? And if I go and prepare a place for you, I will come back again and take you to myself, so that where I am you also may be." Therefore the **Prayer after Communion** prays that we may "imitate constantly the example of the Holy Family" (in striving for Christian virtues) in order that "we may share their company forever." The promise of dwelling in the House of the Lord comes from righteous behavior, or as the Responsorial Psalm puts it so well, "Blessed is everyone who fears the Lord, who walks in his ways!"

Strategy for Preaching

The Feast of the Holy Family holds a great potential for preaching, especially in dealing with the pastoral realities and Christian demands of the recently celebrated Solemnity of the Lord's Nativity. The readings speak to us of familial commitments as a doorway into righteousness; for Paul such blood connections are extended into the whole Christian community. The Word dwells among us in very substantial, concrete ways. Therefore a homiletic core idea might be a challenge to the congregation to examine their family relationships on every level of their commitment, including the invitation to push beyond the walls of domesticity and move into the arena of fellowship with the human family, with whom we will one day share "the bonds of charity" in the joy of God's eternal dwelling forever.

In order for the eucharistic assembly to receive the focus point of the homily, I suggest a simple parsing of the Hebrew word *kavod* as an entry point into the world of familial and global *caritas*. Along these lines we might take *kavod* as meaning (in some sense) glorifying—as well as honoring and esteeming our parents and loved ones: the freight of this attribute attached to one's relatives, embedded as it is in the fourth commandment, will weigh quite significantly on the Christian faithful. In this regard, some may need to be challenged from simply tolerating their parents in their advanced age to placing them in the highest regard. In the busy world of making a living, is there room in the Christian household for aging bodies and a faltering mind? In an American culture obsessed with youth and appearance, is old age an invitation to grace and wisdom? Can the congregation see their diminishing father or mother as a blessing, or perhaps something like the Holy Family whom *The Roman Missal* describes as a "shining example?"

God's own care for those who protect and love their parents by drawing them into his dwelling is certainly an image for the preacher to explore. To point to only a few examples: there is the obvious instance of a mother protecting her newborn, or a father looking for shelter (fitting for both the readings and the season). Yes, God is like that. And we might consider the way in which God has realigned the machinations of earthly tyrants like Herod, by intervening in human history and finding a place to thrive. The Holy Spirit itself becomes an image of the dove protecting her chicks from the storm and nurturing them in love. Jesus shows us his own lament for a Jerusalem he desires to save: "how many times I yearned to gather your children together as a hen gathers her brood under her wings" (Luke 13:34). These images of a protecting God are ripe for a poetic unfolding to help the congregation see—really see—what the demands of love look like. Poets can be instructive at every turn. I am thinking here of Gerard Manley Hopkins' magnificent line in "God's Grandeur," which reads: "Because the Holy Ghost over the bent / World broods with warm breast and with ah! bright wings." Hopkins triggers in most of us the reality that it is the Spirit who comforts, motivates, and draws the church and its members together as one and into the Father's House—both on earth and in heaven.

Solemnity of Mary, the Holy Mother of God (Years ABC)

Readings from the Ambo

Num 6:22-27; Ps 67:2-3, 5, 6, 8; Gal 4:4-7; Luke 2:16-21

The choice gleaned from the book of Numbers occurs at the end of a section in that book dealing with the Nazirites, particularly the laws governing Naziriteship, the most familiar of which to us is Samson's promise to not cut his hair. But the benediction at the end of the chapter 6 seems fairly unconnected to the rest of the text and functions something like a coda just before a description of the leaders' offerings commences in chapter 7. In a certain sense, the prayer of blessing is not so much an instruction on proper behavior (contrasting with the specific ones that we have been seeing in the instructions to the Nazirites) than it is God's own promise for a benediction when his name is invoked. Here we might recall the importance of the name in ancient Israel, particularly how YHWH or the Lord was so transcendent and wholly other that this "G-d" could not be represented, and then only obliquely, in an unutterable, unpronounceable symbol. As far as antiquity is concerned, knowledge of the divine name implies ownership and control. This episode recorded in the First Reading is an interesting development when the life of Moses is examined from our own horizon. Indeed, when Moses first encountered the Lord on Mount Horeb in chapter 3 of the book of Exodus, God told Moses that he would not give him his name (*shem*) in a parlance of what is really the Semitic equivalent to "It's none of your business." In the current passage, though, the Lord is telling Moses that the priestly lineage connected with Aaron (and Moses himself, also traditionally reckoned as a Levite) has access to the name, suggesting the sacred character of the Levitical priesthood (cf. Exod 28:1) and its zeal for God. Additionally, God's granting access to his name for the purpose of a blessing guarantees a future cultic legacy for Israel in its covenant with the Lord. We might speculate that this movement on God's part to grant Moses and Aaron a certain amount of ownership when it comes to invoking the Lord's name suggests a divine willingness to enter even more deeply into a covenant of love with his people.

That sacred bond becomes definitively expressed in the incarnation, of course, a promise that is sealed with the name Jesus. The Gospel of Luke here recollects "the name given him by the angel / before he was conceived in the womb." The circumcision of the child itself resonates with Israel's covenant with God and so plunges into our humanity at its deepest level by taking on flesh and being subject to the law of Moses. Mary is the witness of all of these things, "reflecting on them in her heart," and so, in some sense, she is the holder of memory of the sacred pact precisely because of her own motherhood. The name given by the angel at the annunciation was whispered to her at the most intimate of maternal moments, a mystery she alone would hold claim. Undoubtedly, in this early reference to the Mother of God, Paul's letter to the Galatians ratifies the maternity of Mary in the Second Reading, when he recalls God's pact with humanity and its ripening through the very act of birth: "*genomenon ek gunaikos, genomenon upo nomon,*" or "born of a woman, born under the law." Furthermore, the connection with the Christian community is clearly evident, since we have received the Spirit of God's Son in our hearts, "Crying out, 'Abba, Father!'" Thus Mary makes possible our own adoption as God's children, "an heir, through God," even as the church initiates its own children into the maternal womb of baptism.

Connecting the Bible and the Liturgy

The **Preface I of the Blessed Virgin Mary** that is to be used on the Feast of the Mother of God is a bit more biblical (and darker) in its references than the previous translation. *The Roman Missal* uses a more direct reference to the annunciation with "the overshadowing of the Holy Spirit," which reflects Luke's use of the verb *episkiazo*, meaning to cast a shadow upon. The emphasis clearly suggests a potential heavy burden, possibly hinting at Mary's future contemplation of these mysteries in her heart, or the passion of the Lord, which the angel Gabriel fails to mention. The *Sacramentary* used the expression "the power of the Holy Spirit," also present in Luke, but that rendering lacks the haunting encumbrance implied by the Spirit's power "to overshadow." Moreover, the new translation of the **Preface** demonstrates, in miniature, Mary's role as mother and an instrument of the incarnation: "For by the overshadowing of the Holy Spirit she conceived your Only Begotten Son, and without losing the glory of virginity, brought forth into the world the eternal Light, Jesus Christ our Lord." The singing of the **Preface** places the celebrant and the congregation in the same arena as the shepherds, who are also witnesses to the Christ-event; all return, "glorifying and praising God." Therefore the **Preface** underlines the praise and thanksgiving of the eucharistic assembly in a very powerful way by invoking the unseen witnesses to the nativity, the heavenly hosts. "Through him the Angels praise your majesty, Dominions adore and Powers tremble before you. Heaven and the Virtues of heaven and the blessed Seraphim worship together with exultation." These are the same vocal instruments of praise, the angels and shepherds, who, at the birth of Jesus in Luke 2:1-15, some lines earlier than the gospel for this Sunday, became the first evangelists with "Glory to God in the highest and on earth peace to those on whom his favor rests." **The Prayer after Communion** emphasizes the congregational response in praise and exaltation when it says that "we rejoice to proclaim the blessed ever-Virgin Mary Mother of your Son and mother of the Church." I read this praise not as a slave crying out to its master, but as a child by adoption speaking its first words of love, "Abba, Father." The Body of Christ, then, expresses the Spirit of Jesus in its heart in praise with the angels and all the heavenly hosts. On the Octave of Christmas, we are onlookers and witnesses of the Son, "born of a woman, born under the law" for the sake of our salvation, which made us children of the living God. That is the New and Eternal Covenant that allows us to call upon God by name, "Abba, Father!" and made possible by the Mother of God.

Strategy for Preaching

This feast figures within a range of Marian celebrations, but its position in the Christmas season guarantees it special prominence. In this celebration of the Christmas Octave, the eucharistic assembly has come prepared and visually catechized to ponder these things in their hearts. Images of Mary as Mother abound during the Christmas season on postage stamps, Christmas cards, and in mangers large and small. The Mother of God remains without doubt the most represented face in Western art, with the exception of Jesus himself. The reason for this extraordinary phenomenon may well be that the sharing of divine life has reached into the most basic and essential aspect of humanity: motherhood. It may be too obvious to point out, but everyone in the congregation will be touched in some way by a maternal relationship. This most common of experiences draws the assembly intrepidly close to this solemnity. The question for the preacher is how to lend this most sacred image a new life and meaning.

The day is marked also by the secular calendar, which is one of the few times that the liturgical season is underlined by a popular cultural event. Millions of people have celebrated the New Year, and the preacher should work this reality into the homiletic arc as a way of unfolding the praise and thanksgiving before us in contemplating the motherhood of God. Indeed, a core homiletic idea could focus on the new life that greets us always as a grace, always in mystery, always in blessing. These three areas could be unpacked as we see them marvelously disclosed in the Christmas season: the grace of God's intervention in history, which granted to Mary, as it does to us, an opportunity to cooperate with God's will, even under potentially difficult circumstances; the mystery of understanding that gift (maybe something like a single mother trying to deal with the difficulties of raising a child alone); and the blessing that may lie underneath whatever God places before us, a blessing because even in the most trying of circumstances God has whispered his name to us in the darkness and is with us in the presence of his Son.

The congregation should leave the Eucharist with a sense of God's continued activity in their lives, something that they share with the Mother of God herself. This is grace in action. As the mystery of the incarnation expresses itself in the **Prayer over the Offerings**, "grant to us, who find joy in the Solemnity of the holy Mother of God, that, just as we glory in the beginnings of your grace, so one day we may rejoice in its completion."

Second Sunday after the Nativity
(Years ABC)

Readings from the Ambo
Sir 24:1-2, 8-12; Ps 147:12-13, 14-15, 19-20 (John 1–4);
Eph 1:3-6, 15-18; John 1:1-18

The magnificent beginning of chapter 24 in the book of Sirach sets the tone for this Sunday, which is one of awestruck wonder at the power of God. Psalm 147 is a festive response to the celebration of Wisdom, the mysterious presence at God's right hand. The author's exultation of the Wisdom tradition in Israel and its relationship with God reflects the overall concern of Ben Sira in developing a school of thought to wean the Hellenistic Jews away from their Greek neighbors and their growing influence on God's chosen people in the Near Eastern world. In a certain sense, the personification of *Sophia* as a kind of companion to the Most High suggests the intimate relationship that the transcendent Hebrew God has with the depths of wisdom. That chaste companionship stands in sharp contrast to the mischievous and carnal behavior of the Greek gods. The passage we have here should be read in the larger context of chapter 24 in order to grasp the full force of Wisdom's place as a ubiquitous, abiding presence who announces that "Before all ages, in the beginning, he created me, / and through all ages I shall not cease to be. / In the holy tent I ministered before him, / and in Zion I fixed my abode."

Christians might read Jesus as the personification of wisdom, with some important differences, which will be clarified in the Prologue of John's gospel. The *Logos* was present (though uncreated) at the dawn of time, collaborating in fashioning creation with the Eternal Father and, though like Wisdom dwelling in highest heaven, became flesh. The Word has made his home with humanity. A haunting line in this regard is in verses 6-7 from the book of Sirach: "Over waves of the sea, over all the land, / over every people and nation I held sway. / Among all these I sought a resting place; / in whose inheritance should I abide?"

If we think of the Prologue to John's gospel as a hymn, its contours become more lucid, its insights more penetrating. Clearly, the language in John allows for a kind of resplendent praise augmenting the creation narrative itself in Genesis, one that is now informed by the Word becoming flesh. In contrast to Ben Sira, John substantiates not ethereal Wisdom, but the Word become Light in the world. Moreover, the presence of the Word engages testimony (from John the Baptist), which then lives among us in proclamation even though "his own people did not accept him." The plea from Paul to the Ephesians, then, is for "a Spirit of wisdom and revelation / resulting in knowledge of him."

Connecting the Bible and the Liturgy

Like the Scriptures, the liturgy for the Second Sunday after the Nativity emphasizes the sublime mystery of the Incarnation and offers the congregation an opportunity to delve into its richness. The **Entrance Antiphon**, even if it is unused in the liturgy itself, is especially evocative for reminding us of the connection between the Eternal Word leaping from heaven's royal throne down to earth at midnight. The **Collect** picks up on the presence of the Eternal Word becoming flesh in our world precisely as light, revealing to the world the glory of God "to all peoples by the radiance" of his "light." But perhaps the most available liturgical language for drawing out the scriptural readings remains any of the three **Prefaces for the Nativity of the Lord**. For instance, **Preface I**, though rather brief, picks up very nicely on the "mystery of the Word made flesh" by echoing John's Prologue and its imagery of light when it says that "a new light of your glory has shone upon the eyes of our mind (*nova mentis nostrae oculis lux tuae claritatis infulsit*), so that, as we recognize in him God made visible, we may be caught up through him in love of things invisible." There are notes here of the recognition (*cognoscimus*) and discernment enlightening the mind, which, we might remember, Paul emphasizes in his letter to the church at Ephesus, and a homage to the place of wisdom in gaining understanding. Similarly, **Preface II** emphasizes the Word becoming flesh and dwelling among us and our response "on the feast of this awe-filled mystery." In fact, most of this **Preface** might be considered as a theological commentary on the Christmas event, certainly one that fits neatly as a companion to the Prologue. "Though invisible in his own divine nature, he has appeared visibly in ours, and begotten before all ages, he has begun to exist in time." Yet the **Preface** does not end there but suggests the work of redemption and, as the Prologue puts it, makes us the recipients of his fullness, "grace in place of grace." Our nature has been thus taken up in Christ, "so that, raising up in himself all that was cast down, he might restore unity to all creation and call straying humanity back to the heavenly Kingdom." This last section, in particular, discloses the mission of the Word made visible, not simply for our edification but for divine reconciliation. Lastly, **Preface III** focuses on "the holy exchange" implied in the Prologue and in Paul's letter to the Ephesians, the latter of which says that this exchange "destined us for adoption to himself through Jesus Christ." The **Preface** affirms the same since, "when our frail humanity is assumed by your Word not only does human mortality receive unending honor but by this wondrous union we, too, are made eternal," or as Paul might say, we receive "the riches of glory in his inheritance among the holy ones."

Strategy for Preaching

With Christmas only a few days beforehand, the homily on this Second Sunday after that solemnity should focus on a concrete theological expression of the incarnation. Most congregations are really waiting for a more searching interrogation of the mystery of God made flesh. That task is not easy, since all the readings, beautiful as they are, speak rather abstractly about Wisdom and its place before all ages, together with the Word present from the beginning and its appearance among us as Light. Even Paul seems a bit like a systematic theologian at times in the letter to the Ephesians. How can the preacher make the Word made visible, really *visible* to the Sunday assembly? Of all days, it would seem that our task as homilists remains, to paraphrase novelist Joseph Conrad out of context, "to make them see."

That said, I might recommend a combination of catechetical and practical rhetorical strategy for the homily. A prime resource to keep in mind here and elsewhere is *The Catechism of the Catholic Church* (chapter 2, article 3), which deals with the creedal affirmation: "He was conceived by the power of the Holy Spirit, and born of the Virgin

Mary" (456–83 might be particularly useful in addressing that state-ment). Now the assembly will not hear a tissue of quotations strung along without any force or context, but a homiletic core idea could be posing the question simply as "Why did God choose to dwell among us, and how is he re-creating us day by day?" The readings and the liturgy help to fill out this theological query because they are full of images of light, "wisdom sings," "opens her mouth," and ministers before God "in the holy tent." Ironically, John's Prologue seems much removed from the common experience where men and women toil and love, but it is the preacher's responsibility to be what *Fulfilled in Your Hearing* calls, "the mediator of meaning" for the assembly and unfold the Word made visible.

So then the issue to confront is simply this: what does John's Prologue look like? Are there appropriate windows into the text? Yes, undoubtedly. The coming of the Word is like opening the window in a dusty attic on a brilliant spring day, or a sudden yank of some heavy and dusty drapes in a room filled with decay. (A good reference might be the closing chapters of Charles Dickens's *Great Expecta-tions* in which the protagonist, Pip, lets in the sunlight on old Miss Havisham's frightful room, where, with mice as her companions, she has sat for decades with her rotting wedding cake for a day that never came.) The coming of the Word is also like a wonderful secret that was first whispered in the dark but now takes on new life when it is proclaimed. We know the negative side of spreading gossip and rumors, the useless words we throw away every day on our mobile gadgets, but what about good news that travels? This witnessing was what John the Baptist did, even though he was not the Light. His testimony and ours can multiply the presence of the Word among us. The coming of the Word is also like the Word we speak back to God through Christ in the liturgy. This suggestion encourages the as-sembly to intentionally embrace the language of praise and live inside faith, hope, and love. Since the **Preface** will soon follow, getting the congregation to listen closely to that text and to own the responses at the **Preface Dialogue** as well as other congregational responses, such as the Mystery of Faith, is an unfailing homiletic tactic that blesses the faithful with the same thoughtful intention contained in the words of Paul: "May the eyes of your hearts be enlightened, that you may know what is the hope that belongs to his call, what are the riches of glory in his inheritance among the holy ones."

The Epiphany of the Lord (Years ABC)

Readings from the Ambo

Isa 60:1-6; Ps 72:1-2, 7-8, 10-11, 12-13;
Eph 3:2-3a, 5-6; Matt 2:1-12

The inspiring selection from the book of the prophet Isaiah to celebrate the solemnity of Christ's manifestation among the nations belongs to the larger frame of Isaiah 56:1–66:24, often referred to as "Third Isaiah." The scholarly community generally dates the text somewhere around 520 BC, marking this section as contemporary with the return of Israel from the Babylonian exile. Generally speaking, Third Isaiah shares some common features with Second Isaiah (some believe the author to be a disciple of his forerunner) and is informed by a somewhat disillusioned reality because the jubilant expectations of Israel have not come to pass. Chapters 56–59 are strikingly strident in their admonitions to Judah after their return from exile in 539 BC, which include warnings about idolatry, false worship, and injustice.

The current passage, however, shows itself to be a bit of an exception to the content and the tone present earlier in Third Isaiah and even includes a promise for rebuilding by foreigners, which is not part of this selection (v. 10). Notable from the first verse is an address to Jerusalem itself and the promise to become the carrier of light. We might mention the importance of the corporate salutation, a feature of community joy and responsibility that will run through all of the readings. Third Isaiah is here paying special attention to the homage of earthly powers to God's kingdom of light: "Nations shall walk by your light, / and kings by your shining radiance," specifically Midian, Ephah, and Sheba, all of them from eastern Arabia. From the point of view of the present solemnity, these tributes from the diverse nations become especially evocative, right down to the bearing of "gold and frankincense" imagined in the Isaiah text, an echo of the gifts of the eastern visitors in Matthew's gospel. These two texts reveal an interesting little intertextual dynamic at work, but the parallel should not be overdrawn. There is more to tell, especially when it comes to the corporate share of responsibility. Where Third Isaiah represented Jerusalem as the splendor of the Lord, that city is implicated in the gospel by resisting the new light in the heavens, together with its king, Herod, who was "*etarachthe kai pasa Ierosoluma met autou*" (greatly troubled / and all Jerusalem with him). I think Matthew is reminding his hearers that corporate opposition has its associations with the remarkable global call of "the wealth of the nations" brought to the poor. Bethlehem of Judea, then, the least of cities, eclipses Jerusalem as the city of light because God has rested beneath the light; it is now the new light of nations and owns a child as its king.

Meanwhile, Paul is at work with his own reversals as his letter to the Ephesians and begins to sketch out what he reads as God's revelation to the Gentiles, a theological insight that will become one of the dominant threads in the unmatched preaching tapestry. This mission to the Gentiles highlights yet another significant color in the Pauline theological weaving: unity in Christ. A few verses earlier, at the end of chapter 2, for instance, Paul speaks of Christ as the cornerstone that holds the whole dwelling together and into which we are all drawn into participation. So Paul sees the Gentiles as "coheirs, members of the same body, / and copartners" and "*sugkleronoma kai sussoma kai summetocha*" in God's unfailing promise in Christ. The call to unity in "*sussoma*," the same body, sets up a wider discussion of the unity of the Body in chapter 4 to follow.

Connecting the Bible and the Liturgy

This liturgy occasions a Vigil Mass as well as a Mass during the Day; the readings are the same for both. The solemnity is unusual in that it is well integrated in terms of the symbolic structure present in both Word and sacrament, even in its cultural ambiance. As with the Mass during the Night at Christmas, the Vigil Mass for the Epiphany already presents the Christian community with the natural symbols to be accessed for the solemnity: darkness, light, and, of course, the stars. The texts themselves highlight each other as well. The **Collect** for the vigil implores the "splendor" of the Lord's majesty to "shed its light upon our hearts that we may pass through the shadows of this world and reach the brightness of our eternal home." The coming of the Lord makes this day like a New Jerusalem, where God's light is shining in Christ.

A very interesting (and hard to avoid) parallel exists between the liturgy and the action of the gospel registered in the **Prayer over the Offerings** for both the vigil and the day Masses. "In honor of the appearing of your Only Begotten Son," the presider asks on behalf of the congregation that the Lord accept "the first fruits of the nations" (Vigil). The allusion here is to the corporate body, the nations bringing tributes from afar in Third Isaiah, but also the *ethnoi* in Paul who are now incorporated into one Body, one partnership. The presidential prayer and the gospel fit nicely together here. Along these lines, the **Prayer over the Offerings** in the Mass during the Day transforms this parallel action of the magi and the congregation into a theological statement about the work of Christ: "Look with favor, Lord, we pray, on these gifts of your Church, in which are offered now not gold or frankincense or myrrh, but he who by them is proclaimed, sacrificed and received, Jesus Christ." The sentence structure is a bit awkward here, but the christological moment should not be lost. Christ is the new gift being offered, who, in receiving them, also proclaims our redemption. The prayer recalls Christ's grace of reconciliation, which fully takes up all gifts preceding it, even as the nations come toward the Light. The **Preface of the Epiphany of the Lord** picks up on this mystery when it says that "when he appeared in our mortal nature, you made us new by the glory of his immortal nature." That *"nova nos immortalitatis eius Gloria reparasti"* of the great exchange between God and humanity reminds us that the Lord is the true giver of gifts, transforming our own.

Strategy for Preaching

With the Solemnity of the Epiphany of the Lord, the readings and liturgical prayers shift the axis of the congregation's worship from contemplation to action. The days after Christmas, including the Solemnity of the Mother of God (as well as the Second Sunday after the Nativity), are continued reflections and deep ponderings of the mystery of the nativity. Now the church has hardly ceased its meditation on the incarnation, but the Scriptures for today bring into focus the implications of God taking on human flesh in a public, and indeed, global, way. In this regard, the liturgical pattern from the Nativity to the Epiphany follows Paul's own movement in the Spirit, who tells us that he first received the mystery "by revelation" but has now become a promise to all. The Light that has dawned will not and cannot be incased in darkness. So God's outreach shines even to the ends of the earth, where nations will come streaming. That same light shatters distinctions between Jew and Gentile for Paul.

Preaching on this solemnity, then, has global signification, and its symbols have a very contemporary feel. With our instant communication, our own world is itself becoming more and more like a large village. Moreover, this solemnity's corporate emphasis raises the issue of national boundaries, which God has erased. The social implications of following the gospel become clear from the trek of the magi who "departed for their country by another way." Some, like the magi, may choose to follow the light; others, like "all Jerusalem" may find themselves allied with earthly powers instead of God's kingdom.

A core homiletic idea might consist of challenging the congregation to consider the social realities of God taking on our human flesh. If we are to take the **Preface of the Epiphany of the Lord** at its word, or that we have been made "new by the glory of his immortal nature," then a new star has appeared in our horizon implicating us in God's splendor. Are we willing to see the transformation of our earthly reality into the gift of witness to the incarnation? And if so, what would that testimony look like in the public square? Here, the homily might start to name the contemporary gifts all of us bring to be unwrapped by grace. Needless to say, the more specific we can be in the homiletic text, the better the hearers of the Word will be able to become copartners with the preacher. Some bring gifts of diversity that are golden in their poetic expressions of Hispanic song and praise. Others offer the frankincense of their hard work, after a long day at the accounting firm; they come to offer their time by helping with parish bookkeeping. Still others bring the myrrh of bereavement ministry to their brothers and sisters, by cooking dishes after funerals or spending time with the children of loss. All of these gifts are testimony to the global reach of the incarnate Word into which the Christian faithful have been drawn this season. That witness will have public consequences in and out of the parish. These are specific challenges to ratify the promise God made in Christ, an invitation to enflesh what has already been made Incarnate.

The Baptism of the Lord

Readings from the Ambo

Isa 42:1-4, 6-7; Ps 29:1-2, 3-4, 9-10, (11b);
Acts 10:34-38; Matt 3:13-17

The text presented in the Hebrew Scriptures is the first of the four celebrated "Servant Songs," the place of which in the overall corpus of Second Isaiah has been disputed. Depending on whether or not they function independently or are part of the larger context of the text will determine their meaning. Those who see Isaiah 42:1-9 as independent from the context of the rest of the text often read the servant as referring to an individual; those who see the song fitting into the larger contours of text usually prefer to understand the servant as a corporate body, specifically, Israel. Since the present passage in the Lectionary has already isolated the Servant Song by removing it from its context, we are able to see that isolating the text lends itself to think of the "servant whom I uphold, / my chosen one with whom I am pleased" as referring to an individual, messianic presence. On this feast of the Baptism of the Lord it seems clear that the Christian community has appropriated this passage as a way of understanding the mission of Jesus, who now turns to his public ministry. From the perspective of the liturgy, the Servant Song is about Christ and his mission.

It is notable to consider the shift in point of view of Isaiah's text, which lends a dynamic of personal intimacy with God as the protagonist. Verses 1-4 are divine testimony over the unique messianic anointing that has come upon the servant who has been engaged for justice and teaching. But then verses 6-7 become astonishingly personal: "I, the LORD, have called you for the victory of justice, / I have grasped you by the hand." This personal encounter is a peerless transition to the theophany occurring in Matthew's gospel that takes the Isaiah text one step further: "This is my beloved Son, with whom I am well pleased." We see here a brilliant collusion of the fulfillment of Isaiah's servant text together with an expression of the Trinity expressed in Matthew's account of the baptism of the Lord. Indeed, at the very moment when the voice announces itself from heaven, Jesus notices that "the heavens were opened for him, and he saw the Spirit of God descending like a dove and coming upon him." The Matthean rendering of Jesus' encounter with the Spirit deserves special attention in Year A, especially when that moment is contrasted with Luke (Year C), which does not account for Jesus' own point of view in the descent of the Spirit. Needless to point out, the trinitarian moment has been observed at the moment of baptism by the Son himself, who has now claimed the role of the servant expressed by Isaiah.

The Second Reading from the book of Acts recalls that this kind of trinitarian theophany echoed in the Lord's baptism formed an essential spine in the Church's early preaching: "how God anointed Jesus of Nazareth / with the Holy Spirit and power." Indeed, the very messianic threshold of divine anointing becomes the occasion for the acclamation and acceptance of all the nations since, "God shows no partiality." All of us become the beloved. All are called to partake of that same divine reality, brought to us by Jesus. Since "God was with him," Jesus was an agent of healing and restoration that transcends national boundaries, making himself a "covenant of the people, / a light for the nations."

Connecting the Bible and the Liturgy

The **Collect** immediately introduces a trinitarian image when it recalls the scene in the Jordan: "Almighty ever-living God, who, when Christ had been baptized in the River Jordan and as the Holy Spirit descended upon him, solemnly declared him your beloved Son." Further, the prayer links the congregation's participation in this trinitarian mystery by recalling the life of the baptized who become "your children by adoption, reborn of water and the Holy Spirit." The *Sacramentary* translated this passage as "your children born of water and the Spirit," which, although it certainly maintains the essential character of the meaning of baptism, lacks the theological and Pauline force of *filis adoptionis tuea*. Moreover, the earlier translation also asks that these same children born of water and the Spirit remain "faithful to our calling." But *The Roman Missal* chooses to use the expression "be well pleasing to you" (Latin: *beneplacito*), a more formal rendering of the text, to be sure, but also an intertextual convergence of the baptism of the Lord in which the voice from heaven proclaims that Jesus is the "beloved Son, with whom I am well pleased" (Greek: *eudokesa*). The prayer's petition to almighty God imploring that we be well pleasing may sound a bit awkward and even more difficult to sing, but its articulation follows a biblical lead and allows the congregation to share in the Lord's baptismal event and become renewed in the life of the Beloved.

Both the **Prayer over the Offerings** and the **Preface: The Baptism of the Lord** remind us of the "servant" who has been baptized in the Jordan and his intended mission. When the **Prayer over the Offerings** says that the "beloved Son . . . willed in his compassion to wash away the sins of the world," it is suggesting that Christ's very mission "to fulfill all righteousness" in his baptism was an avenue, a conduit for our remission of sins. This last prayer allows that the baptism of the Lord is the beginning of a transformation not only for the eucharistic assembly but "the world." Thus did Peter proclaim to the house of Cornelius in Acts saying, "In truth, I see that God shows no partiality. Rather, in every nation whoever fears him and acts uprightly is acceptable to him." The acknowledgement of Christ's mission to the whole world ratifies his position as Isaiah's Suffering Servant who "shall bring forth justice to the nations . . . a covenant of the people, a light for the nations." Indeed, the link with Isaiah is further acknowledged in the **Preface** when it says that "By the Spirit's descending in the likeness of a dove we might know that Christ your Servant has been anointed with the oil of gladness and sent to bring the good news to the poor." With a biblical allusion of the Servant stretching back to the exile, the eucharistic assembly can celebrate the sanctification of the waters in the Jordan as the cleansing of their own sins in the righteousness of Christ. The congregation can only respond joyfully in thanks and praise.

Strategy for Preaching

The celebration of the Baptism of the Lord initiates the First Sunday in Ordinary Time and sets the table for both the mission of Jesus as Servant and the people of God as witnesses of the life of the

Beloved. Preaching this day will benefit greatly from the dominant image of water, which could be accessed in any number of ways: many of these might be drawn from successful stories or historical recollection. Flannery O'Connor's short story, "The River," is a moving and rather frightening account of what happens when we take baptism seriously, as a real death to sin. Arthur Penn's *The Miracle Worker*, a 1962 film rendering of Anne Sullivan's indelible educative work with Helen Keller, contains a magic moment when the blind and deaf child suddenly speaks a word after numerous and very dramatic efforts on the part of her teacher to communicate to her. With her hands and face under an outdoor spigot, Helen finally utters the fateful word, "water." Both stories occasion the visceral recognition of symbol, a commonality that water is simultaneously a death-dealing and life-giving encounter. Baptism is destruction and rebirth as well.

A core preaching idea on this feast might be something like this: if Jesus himself has been called into mission by his own baptism, we are invited to do the same and live out our vocation through healing and proclamation. The preacher could organize the homily around water as a wake-up call to service—the kind of wake-up call that allowed a blind and deaf child to discover a new language because a servant teacher plunged her into a new experience. This servant model of Jesus invites us all to share in that richness, "to open the eyes of the blind, to bring out prisoners from confinement, and from the dungeon, those who live in darkness," according to Isaiah. That text is further echoed in the **Preface of The Baptism of the Lord**, which could be emphasized as the call to Christian service in likeness to Christ: "By the spirit's descending in the likeness of a dove we might know that Christ your Servant has been anointed with the oil of gladness and sent to bring the good news to the poor."

The overall homiletic task, then, is to allow the assembly to know that they are *already* the Beloved but are also called into mission as well. Being "well-pleasing" in God's sight may be a matter of claiming our fellowship with Christ, a profound recognition that our ordinary Christian life is a matter of indwelling with the Trinity through our service to the church, the world, and one another. Our call to be servants, then, is modeled on Christ's own journey and we are, above all, asked to imitate him in fulfilling "all righteousness" by our own commitment in baptism. This day is an opportunity for the assembly to reflect on the meaning of their own baptism, and so I think the homily should strive to get the congregation to reach for a new future in Christ, an exciting renewal of their baptismal promises to reject evil and live in justice and goodness. From the start of the day, the assembly all moves into Ordinary Time with optimism and a sense of purpose that the Lord has grasped them by the hand and formed them in mutual love "as a covenant of the people."

LENT

First Sunday of Lent

Readings from the Ambo

Gen 2:7-9; 3:1-7; Ps 51:3-4, 5-6, 12-13, 17;
Rom 5:12-19; Matt 4:1-11

The Yahwist account of the creation of humanity in the book of Genesis represents an iconic episode that takes us back to origins, appropriate enough for the First Sunday of Lent. The story is meant to disclose how the Giver of Life is betrayed by creation and what the consequences of that sin entails. From a strictly literary reading of the passage, the Fall story might be construed as a drama of contamination and transgression in which the crafty serpent gains access to the pristine land of Eden and seduces the innocent. The hearer's sympathy is allied with the Creator who appears to be exceptionally trusting with this creation and, more to the point, generous with the gifts of freedom for the man and woman. The story of the Fall seems to embody the quality of a fairy tale, with its talking snake and dramatic punishment, but these colorful qualities make the account all the more indelible and, justifiably, arguably the most famous single incident in all of the Hebrew Scriptures.

This familiar and almost surreal quality of the Fall in the second story of Creation should not lessen the gravity of this seminal portrait of the first sin. The full picture of the event (until Gen 3:24) should be read in its entirety, but even the selection here reveals the essential dynamics of the story and its dreadful consequences. Indeed, in a matter of only a few paragraphs, we see the Lord God shaping the first human being out of clay, raising him to the steward of Eden, and Adam only then falling the hapless victim to the rejection of God first by disobedient betrayal then by lying. There is, however, an important "afterward" of sorts that should not be neglected and occurs almost at the end of chapter 3: "for the man and his wife the

LORD God made leather garments, with which he clothed them." In a comic sort of way, this seems to be the alternate apparel available for the couple who have recently fashioned for themselves rather skimpy underwear out of fig leaves. I think the point here is that God's punishment cannot erase the love he maintains for Creation; although Adam and Eve are banished, their shame has been covered, surely a hint at the enduring love that will follow this story of salvation from the tree of life to the cross on Calvary.

Paul makes the transcendent connection between the first transgression of sin (and its echoes throughout history) and God's own gift of restoration abundantly lucid in his letter to the Romans when he says that "the gift, after many transgressions, brought acquittal." Central to Paul's theology is what he takes from this free gift of God: "just as through the disobedience of the one man, / the many were made sinners," so through the obedience (*upakoes*) of one will the many be made righteous (*dikaioi*). Coursing throughout this passage and throughout Romans, of course, is the doctrine of grace. Earlier in chapter 5, Paul says that "for Christ, while we were still helpless, yet died at the appointed time for the ungodly" (6), a kind of refrain to the overall argument that we are justified, like Abraham, by faith since we do nothing to earn our redemption.

To this end, Matthew's account of Jesus' temptation in the desert serves as an illustration of the One Man succeeding in obedience with three of the most basic sins: appetite, pride, and vainglory. The focus in the narrative is on Jesus' resistance to these most basic of temptations, as well as his strategic combat against the devil, answering the demon not only with a refusal to sin but effectively banishing him, first by Scripture and then his own command. In the background here remains the ascetical undercurrent of fasting forty days in the wilderness and the force of the Spirit that leads Jesus into the wilderness after his baptism in the Jordan.

Connecting the Bible and the Liturgy

When the **Collect** prays that "we may grow in understanding of the riches hidden in Christ," it is acknowledging what Paul refers to as "the gracious gift of the one man Jesus Christ overflow[ing] for the many." *The Roman Missal* enjoins that *"ad intellegendum Christi proficiamus arcanum"* and sets the tone of this Lenten season, which is not about our work, but Christ's. To be sure, there is a plea at the **Prayer over the Offerings** for the "right dispositions" to be able "to celebrate the beginning of this venerable and sacred time." But the focus of the Scripture and the liturgy remain a petition to deepen the faith of the congregation to understand the work of God in Christ.

That understanding certainly unfolds in Matthew's portrait of Jesus' temptation in the wilderness, an obvious mirror to the Fall in Eden, which Paul weaves into a crucially important theology of justification and sanctification that will receive, famously, responses ranging from St. Augustine to Martin Luther and Karl Barth. The **Preface for the First Sunday of Lent** underlines the connection between the disobedience of one man and the obedience of another when it says that "by overturning all the snares of the ancient serpent, [Christ] taught us to cast out the leaven of malice." Worth attention in the **Preface** are at least two expressions that capture the relationship the congregation has with Christ's own work. The first is: "by abstaining forty long days from earthly food, he consecrated through his fast the pattern of our Lenten observance." Therefore Jesus becomes not only a model or teacher for the assembly but his very act of obedience and resistance to sin was a "consecration" of the days of Lent. Secondly, "he taught us to cast out the leaven of malice, so that, celebrating worthily the Paschal Mystery, we might pass over at least to the eternal paschal feast." In my reading of this **Preface**, I suggest that this *fermentum malitiae* (leaven of malice), which should be rejected in a kind of fast from sinful behavior against charity—so that we might be prepared *"ad pascha demum perpetuum transeamus"*—is directly related to the temptation scene itself: Jesus refuses to turn the stones into bread—or, we might read, partake of the leaven of malice—and prefers instead to live by the Word that comes from the mouth of God until that final Passover. Here, I think that the liturgy picks up on the vital importance of understanding that sin attacks our relationships, quite evident in the serpent's skillful malice in Eden and even more visible with the devil's attacks on Jesus in the wilderness. The Bread to be lived on, then, is the Word of God, which nourishes and builds up in the virtues. Therefore, the **Prayer after Communion** then celebrates the true bread of Christian unity, the "heavenly bread, by which faith is nourished, hope increased and charity strengthened . . . [so that we might] strive to live by every word which proceeds from your mouth."

Strategy for Preaching

The First Sunday of Lent is a time for intense soul examination, a recognition of the limits of our mortality and the acknowledgment of "one man's obedience" that redeems us. This is also the celebration of the Rite of Election in which those catechumens seeking full participation in the church at the Easter Vigil will be admitted with proper prayers and intercessions. If the story of the Fall appears to be something from the distant past, it is up to the preacher to make the first sin vivid and to let the eucharistic assembly lay claim to its mortal ramifications. Without a sense of personal and corporate sin, the congregation will fail to grasp the necessary place that Christ holds as the Redeemer of the world; gratitude will slip and the very zeal that propels the Christian faithful toward the celebration of the paschal mystery will flicker very low indeed.

I do not recommend a "fire and brimstone" sermon but one that mixes the reality of sin with the covenant of grace that redeems it. The Scriptures themselves as well as the liturgy celebrated this day illuminate Christ Jesus and his triumph over sin in the wilderness, a preview of the obedience that will take the Lord from the desert to Jerusalem and finally death and resurrection. So a core homiletic idea might be this: although we share the sin of all humanity, God's free gift in Christ has bought us the grace of everlasting life. The key allowing the assembly to unpack this idea will be establishing a visual vocabulary to support it. So what does this homiletic core really *look* like? Since we are an affluent American culture in the midst of late capitalism, one tactic might be to use a visual economic analogy. For instance, we are all used to trading something for an equal amount. We did it when we were children when we flipped our baseball cards and traded a pitcher from the Yankees for a pitcher from the Mets; we did it in college when we swapped clothes with our roommates; and we do it today when we trade in our automobiles. Nobody wants to take a loss—except God. Trading divinity for humanity, swapping Christ for Adam, redeeming sinners with coupons they did not even own: all that seems unequal. And guess what? It is. An acknowledgement of this very inequality that purchased our eternal life through grace leads to genuine sorrow through gratitude.

Lastly, as with the First Sunday of Advent, preachers who are pastors should ask themselves if they have a pastoral preaching plan for the season at hand. The catechumens are being led to the sacred waters, but the baptized are encouraged to "grow in understanding of the riches hidden in Christ." I might suggest that the preacher also consider a reading plan for the season as well, something to help strengthen the reflective powers so vital to producing good homilies. What comes to mind immediately is Dante's *Purgatorio*, of which there are numerous translations. Of the three books in the *Divine Comedy*, *Purgatorio* is perhaps the most theologically interesting and, I think, helpful during this season.

Second Sunday of Lent

Readings from the Ambo

Gen 12:1-4a; Ps 33:4-5, 18-19, 20, 22; 2 Tim 1:8b-10; Matt 17:1-9

The call of Abraham in the book of Genesis represents God's first invitation to those who have been reckoned as Israel's patriarchs. The contrast with the Fall story used in the Year A Cycle last week could not be more obvious. Original sin and betrayal of God's trust yielded shame, pain, and death for Adam and Eve; but the Lord's outreach to Abram is a promise for fertility, a new land and an endless blessing. From the perspective of salvation history, a benediction has replaced a curse as we follow the father of the chosen people into a horizon unknown to him. We know that this story was assembled during the monarchical period in Israel, and so the account of the *berakah* or blessing to Abram's progeny tells us something about a kingly culture that has itself discovered a benediction from God. In a sense, for a later society to read back retrospectively into its history the noble character and deeds of its founding father is a common feature in many cultures; Americans still write histories of George Washington and admire his portrait, which, in turn says something about contemporary values. A present-day civilization will only be as good as they understand their past origins.

Clearly, the biblical author values the kind of trust in God that eluded the first man and woman and wants to establish a genealogy rooted in a worthy patriarch. "Abram went as the Lord directed him," suggests an immediate response to God's plan and benediction. What did he have to reject if Abram followed God's call? God asked Abram to leave the familiar homeland of Haran in Mesopotamia, together with its polytheism and temple cultic practices such as those that involved worshiping Nanna (the moon) and Utu (her son). To understand the vocation of Abram is to see Israel's highest value inscribed in the first commandment: Love the Lord God alone and have no strange God's before him. Christian hermeneutics in later generations will read Abram as a "Father in faith," as Paul does. Paul reiterates his contemplation of Christ's work of redemption in 2 Timothy when he says that God called us to a holy life, "not according to our works but according to his own design and the grace bestowed on us in Christ Jesus before time began." And we can see the early Christian community working out this call to a singular, personal relationship with God in the transfiguration story in Matthew's gospel. With their ascent up Mount Tabor, Peter, James, and John are also being "taken up," (from the Greek verb *anaphero*, which can mean either literally or figuratively taken up) or called into an ecstatic blessing, mediated by Jesus who fulfills the covenant promised to Abram. This transfiguration narrative will occur on all the Second Sundays of Lent in the Lectionary cycle, but its connection with Abram in Year A necessarily associates the transfiguration of Jesus with discipleship and its inevitable departure from the familiarity of household gods: the call from the Most High God himself, hidden in a cloud of unknowing, and life in relationship with his Son, the Beloved, *o agapetos*, and putting away the foreign idols from among us and living attentively on our own journey to the Promised Land. It is the beloved Son to whom we should incline our ears in trust and love, even as he takes us up into a new and eternal covenant.

Connecting the Bible and the Liturgy

Like the First Sunday of Lent, this Second Sunday is endowed with a gospel narrative that varies only by authorship with the Synoptics and presents multiple connections with the liturgical texts. The transfiguration has presidential prayers and a **Preface** all its own. With the coming of Lent, a restored feature with the new *Roman Missal* is the **Prayer over the People**, which also accentuates the gospel for the day. To this end, the **Collect** helps us gain access to the point of view of the transfiguration story. That perspective is clearly centered on Jesus' closest companions, Peter, James, and John. "O God, who have commanded us to listen to your beloved Son" reinforces our kinship with the disciples who are being taken up the mountain; their vision becomes ours, and God's command to them has been made to us as well. In a parallel instance, this call to listen could also be extended to Abram who was asked to depart from his strange polytheism into relationship with a singular God who will demand everything as the patriarch enters into unknown territory. Both calls are infused with promise and blessing, Abram with a "great nation" and Jesus' disciples with the haunting specter of future proclamation that must wait until "the Son of Man has been raised from the dead."

A promise is also given to the eucharistic assembly as well, since we pray to God "to nourish us inwardly by your word, that, with spiritual sight made pure, we may rejoice to behold your glory." The congregation's connection with Abram and his children surfaces in the **Prayer over the People**, appropriately enough. "Bless your faithful, we pray, O Lord, with a blessing that endures forever, and keep them faithful to the Gospel of your Only Begotten Son, so that they may always desire and at last attain that glory whose beauty he showed in his own Body." The Christian faithful are again closely identified with discipleship in the **Preface** for the Second Sunday of Lent. Indeed, the parallel of Jesus' transfiguration with the resurrection remains a frightful puzzle to the disciples but manifestly explicit in the church's **Preface: The Transfiguration of the Lord**. "For after he had told the disciples of his coming Death, on the holy mountain he manifested to them his glory, to show, even by the testimony of the law and the prophets, that the passion leads to the glory of the Resurrection." Now the congregation's point of view extends over the more limited perspective even of Jesus' most trusted disciples. We have a chance to glimpse the presence of Christ's resurrection and glory even now in the celebration of the Eucharistic Liturgy where we proclaim in *Mysterium Fidei:* "We proclaim your Death, O Lord, and profess your Resurrection until you come again." That Eucharist is transfiguration, an absorbing and taking up of the baptized assembly by faith in Christ, a foretaste of future glory. As the **Prayer after Communion** says, "As we receive these glorious mysteries we make thanksgiving to you, O Lord, for allowing us while still on earth to be partakers even now of the things of heaven."

Strategy for Preaching

A sober theological reminder for the Second Sunday of Lent is that Pelagianism in its various forms is still alive and well today. The fifth-century heresy that saw humanity as essentially good and, therefore, having no need for God's grace has been a prominent feature in our post-Enlightenment, postindustrial Western society. The readings for today emphatically take us in the opposite direction: the human subject is saved by God's direct invitation and divine reversal. From a preaching perspective, it will be helpful to see the First and Second Sunday of Lent as intimately conjoined. Where last week laid out sin and its ramifications, this week provides its necessary antidote. That remedy comes utterly at God's own initiation. The call of Abram by God at the beginning of chapter 12 in Genesis seems so startlingly abrupt; there is nothing about Abram's character or righteous deeds that would owe him any particular favor with God. Chapter 11 is the story of Babel and then a genealogy, including the descendants of Terah, the father of Abram. So the position of the narrative itself, together with the obviously strong intervention of God into human history and the life of Israel, underlines this passage as an invitation to grace, a gratuitous blessing of abundance.

Preachers might attend to the inevitable tendency for their attentive and faithful hearers of the Good News to lean into a contemporary culture dominated by Pelagianism. What is the dominant myth that underlies the American narrative that is almost always at odds with salvation history? Certainly we can see the Horatio Alger mythology lurking in the background here, whereby an individual rises above his circumstances and gains in wealth and plenty. A version of this with a more "religious" undertone is this: We have (deservedly) found a new Promised Land and flourish monetarily because we do the right thing. This is the so-called Prosperity Gospel. These Pelagian or semi-Pelagian notions were combated early on by Paul—"not according to our works" are we called holy, he tells Timothy. So too with Abram and Jesus' disciples: they are called not because of their talents or virtue, but because God has freely decided to do so.

How does the preacher confront the contemporary congregation whose culture tells them that we survive by our works alone? I believe that a core homiletic idea could be the call to discipleship and an acknowledgement of both its source and its sustaining power. Homilists might remember those who have responded to God's call already sitting right in front of them at one of their liturgies: they are the members of the Rite of Christian Initiation for Adults (RCIA), who await full participation in the life of the church. Even if these folks are not present as hearers, they can be alluded to in a homily that begins to probe the congregation with questions about discipleship. Why would anyone want to be a disciple in this day and age? They are chosen not because of any special skills or talent or ability to earn a large salary, but because they heard God's voice whisper in their ears. Perhaps some familiarity with those in the RCIA group will help to gain access to a story or two about their own journey in faith. (By the way, it is important to ask permission if the preacher is going to say something about a particular individual. Not everyone is comfortable with a public retelling of their life, but some are perfectly fine with a brief recounting.) Outside of the RCIA group, it is often useful to cite short stories of individual faith experiences, but I think that I would steer away from extraordinary calls; these may be edifying but do not make crystal clear that God can call everyday people into holiness. In the end, preachers need to get the assembly to want and desire a deeper relationship with God: we are all called to leave our household gods behind us, and that is the challenge as we move toward Easter and the sight of Christ's glory.

Third Sunday of Lent

Readings from the Ambo

Exod 17:3-7; Ps 95:1-2, 6-7, 8-9; Rom 5:1-2, 5-8; John 5:42

The reading from the book of Exodus this week presents the faith community with a challenge to a variety of relationships that will come to a crisis in the desert: Israel's relationship with Moses; Moses' relationship with the people; and Moses' relationship with God. The first of these receives the author's attention immediately. The crisis is precipitated by a thirst for water, with the ensuing complaint: "Why did you ever make us leave Egypt?" The passage says that they "grumbled against Moses." From one point of view, the Hebrew word *rib* does mean "to complain" or "to quarrel," but it can also have another, more technical meaning. To bring a complaint against someone also means to bring a lawsuit to an offending party. Now the Septuagint translates the Hebrew word for complain, *rib*, into the Greek equivalent, *egogguzen*, and the Latin Vulgate says something similar with *murmuravit*. I am not altogether sure that we are getting the play on words here when we just see *rib* as grumbled, which is, more or less, a psychological state closer to what in Yiddish would be "kvetching." Does the biblical author want us to see that the people of Israel have a legitimate complaint against Moses and God? Read a different way, the people are bringing a *rib* or a lawsuit against Moses for bringing them out of Egypt, for breaking his promise to them. They will die in the desert, so they think, and not live as they were told. Indirectly, this is also a lawsuit against God, something like "God on trial," a kind of reversal of the test the Lord has challenged the people with on their way through the desert. In a way, such a trial might be called what the Scriptures say is really on the mind of the people in the desert: "Is the Lord in our midst or not?"

God defends himself by answering with largess. Indeed, God himself answers both Moses and the people with a sign of hope: water from the rock. The Lord's response addresses the people's question about God's presence and, in so doing, proves that he is innocent of any breach of the covenant he has with them. Ironically, the scene purported to put God on the witness stand to test him, but this scenario ultimately became a platform to test the people. Moses was both defense attorney and prosecutor.

Paul's answer to "God on trial" is a hope that does "not disappoint," or *"ou kataischunei"* that more literally may be stated as "does not make us ashamed." This indeed was the experience of the people of Israel in the desert, who were shamed and resisted but then redeemed through the renewal of a divine promise of hope. To this end, Paul articulates one of his most important theological arguments in this passage from Romans, *"dikaiothentes oun ek pistoeos eirenen echomen"*—we have then been justified by faith. The pouring out of the love of God into our hearts through the Holy Spirit is a poetic association of the water that comes to us gratuitously in the desert of doubts and deepest yearnings.

That free gift, again through a primal association of thirst and water, discloses itself with Jesus' encounter with the Samaritan woman at the well in John's gospel. Certainly, there are the natural associations with yearning for God and images of water to be mined with baptism on this Third Sunday of Lent and the celebration of the first scrutiny in preparation for the baptism of the catechumens. By contrast with Israel in the desert, Jesus has aggressively gone out of his way and sought out the Samaritan woman, a demonstration of grace at work to prompt a dormant faith experience. Jesus ignores Jewish conventions by getting to the heart of human desire, a reality of which the woman is blithely unaware until Jesus helps us to understand the meaning of "living water." The deepening awareness of the need for the water of eternal life leads the woman to an acknowledgement of Jesus as a prophet and then the Messiah, a role that the Lord himself affirms. In so doing, Jesus proclaims his role as the reconciler of traditions and factions, collapsing into himself the cultic traditions of the Jews and the Samaritans, which will be neither in Jerusalem nor on Mt. Gerizim.

Connecting the Bible and the Liturgy

Since this Sunday is also the occasion for the celebration of the first scrutiny, there is a valuable opportunity to expand the

connections between the Lectionary readings for this Third Sunday
of Lent and the liturgy. In the Third, Fourth, and Fifth Week of the
Mass of the Scrutinies, the gospels for the Woman at the Well, the
Man Born Blind, and the Raising of Lazarus will all be used, all of
which occur, of course, in Year A. (In Years B and C these gospels
should also be read if the scrutinies are to be celebrated.)

There are many associations to be made here. Consider, for instance, the way in which the **Collect** for the first scrutiny in *The
Roman Missal* addresses the catechumens: "these chosen ones."
They certainly are chosen, but so are the people of Israel who give
into grumbling (maybe even a lawsuit) against Moses and the Lord
in the desert. Chosen, yes, though contentious: that might describe
the relationship that God has with the people he has called his own.
A wise connection at this point is remembering that this time of
preparation before baptism may also be a time of intense conversation and trial, but it's also a place to understand God's free gift in
Christ about to be lavished on those to be baptized. The catechumens
come to the sacrament, then, in Pauline language, not by their works
but by faith. This longing and yearning for the deep waters that only
Christ can quench can be discovered if we allow the Lord to uncover
the desire within us. As the **Preface: The Samaritan Woman** reminds
us, "when he asked the Samaritan woman for water to drink, he
had already created the gift of faith within her and so ardently did
he thirst for her faith that he kindled in her the fire of divine love."

Based on the readings and the liturgy, therefore, this first scrutiny
is a time to discover the sin that lurks deep in us all and to understand
that we will often resist the gift of grace. But through God's efforts
and the Spirit's labor we are also able to recognize that this same
grace will seek us out and expand our faith if we desire it. The entire
eucharistic assembly might benefit from establishing a connection
between the biblical readings and the liturgy, the latter of which holds
sway in Lent with the language of scrutiny meant for catechumens;
this experience can only strengthen the commitment of the baptized
assembly. In fact, the presidential prayers for the Third Sunday of
Lent are particularly attentive to the "grumblings" or "murmurings"
of sin that face all humanity but are only raised up by God's mercy.
The **Collect** becomes the occasion for a "confession of our lowliness,"
since we are "bowed down by our conscience" and pray that we "may
always be lifted up by your mercy." And the **Prayer over the Offerings**

is a petition that "we who beseech pardon for our own sins, may take care to forgive our neighbor."

Strategy for Preaching

The readings and the liturgy more than hint at the direction preaching takes this Sunday, which could focus on faith in the midst of ongoing Christian discernment. Here, once again, the catechumens make natural symbols, since their very presence as those searching for living water provides the rest of the congregation with an invaluable witness to the journey toward the paschal mystery. If the RCIA group has been used as examples in previous Sundays in Lent, the preacher may not want to overburden them with too much symbolic freight for the sake of the whole congregation. Nevertheless, as I have suggested before, the presence of those who are actively discerning God's will in a public context provides a considerable witness value at the liturgy. In this context, the Pauline theology of faith leading to righteousness is in order and appropriate, but the preacher should avoid abstractions or simply dropping complicated terms without a catechetical preparation for whole congregation. Therefore, a concrete focus or homiletic core idea that has specific tactics attached to it might look something like this:

Core: All of us will find ourselves struggling in the desert of human suffering and longing, but Jesus leads us to the waters that alone will satisfy our thirst: himself.

Tactic one: Demonstrate the commonality of human longing and its biblical antecedents (the people of Israel at Massah and Meribah) together with a contemporary picture of people searching for meaning and finding no ready answers. An illustration for points of resistance might be Frank Cotrell Boyce's *God on Trial* (2008).

Tactic two: Jesus helps us discern our deepest desire. In baptism, we have all put on Christ as a garment and have been given a light in the darkness. We search for that same paschal flame at the end of this Lenten season to illuminate our hearts and renew our baptism. I judge that it is important to avoid a knee-jerk response such as "the answer is Jesus." Rather, it is the Lord who helps his people discern their relationship with him and brings us to awareness.

Tactic three: The catechumens are engaging in this very process in the RCIA. Christian community and reconciliation, the call to recognize our sins and engage in prayer, fasting, and almsgiving helps us to leave our selfishness behind and live for others. We are reminded of the need for the Lord's mercy as we come to the well of the church to drink and feed at the sacramental table. There, we will find a hope that will not disappoint us.

Fourth Sunday of Lent

Readings from the Ambo

1 Sam 16:1b, 6-7, 10-13a; Ps 23:1-3a, 3b-4, 5,6;
Eph 5:8-14; John 9:1-41

The passage taken from the first book of Samuel sets in motion a leitmotif present throughout religious experience in both East and West: the presence of the Holy in unlikely places and people. Again, the metaphor of blindness and insight is yet another universal way of capturing, oftentimes ironically, the ability to perceive the truth or not. The unlikely presence of God's hidden self and how it is disclosed is the subject of the two narratives in the Lectionary readings in 1 Samuel and the Gospel of John. Both selections implicate the hearer in a passage from darkness to light—or the failure to do so—causing us to affirm (or not) Paul's acclamation to the Ephesians, "You were once darkness, / but now you are light in the Lord."

A striking clue to the dynamics of recognition appears in the Lord's injunction to Samuel when it comes to choosing the anointed one. "Do not judge from his appearance or from his lofty stature, / because I have rejected him. / Not as man sees does God see, / because man sees the appearance / but the LORD looks into the heart." In other words, God sees more than we see; kingship in Israel will be based on a different set of criteria than, say, the kind that motivated an earlier popular affirmation of the tragic Saul, who was physically imposing. Moreover, that this chosen one is the youngest in Jesse's family underlines the divine motivation to anoint a king who is "rejected"—the least among his brothers. A similar emphasis on David's lack of conventional qualification occurs throughout the David cycle, most notably in his battle with Goliath, a triumph that has become emblematic of the underdog's ability to champion over fierce odds.

Who is in and who is out? That seems to be the question to which
the religious leaders in John's gospel seem to be able to answer without much trouble. As Jesus tells them at the end of the account of
the Man Born Blind, it is their very failure to understand the grace
underneath that keeps their blindness intact. The Pharisees cannot
reconcile that God's presence can exist beside human frailty. As they
ask about Jesus, "How can a sinful man do such signs?" Ironically,
the religious establishment fails to see the signs that are unfolding
right before them, while the young man, blind from birth, has gained
his sight and believes. "I do believe, Lord," he tells Jesus. John is
pushing us to consider the sense of sight, which also is now meant
to include the eyes of faith. Clearly, there is a baptismal image at
work in the restoration of the man to sight after he washes in the
Pool of Siloam. The only thing that the Pharisees are able to see is
a work performed on the Sabbath, which leads them to think they
are not blind at all. Once again, Jesus turns the table and says, "If
you were blind, you would have no sin; / but now you are saying,
'We see,' so your sin remains."

Paul, a redeemed Pharisee, wants no part of works of darkness
and urges the Ephesians to "[l]ive as children of light." Paul regards
a turning away from darkness toward light as a primary move to
live in righteousness and truth. We might recall that he himself
was subject to a period of blindness, having encountered the risen
Lord on the way to Damascus. Interestingly, in the first verse of the
passage taken from the letter to the Ephesians, Paul does not use a
primary preposition in relation to light and darkness, as if one could
be "in" darkness and move then "in" light. Rather it is *ete gar pote
skotos nun de phos en Kyrio*," or "you were formerly darkness and
now you are light *in* the Lord." Light and darkness seem to embrace
the whole person, which one either embraces or rejects. The primary
preposition rests in relationship with being "in the Lord," now that
this transformation has occurred.

Connecting the Bible and the Liturgy

The Fourth Sunday of Lent presents itself as a joyful and hopeful sign of things to come at the end of the Lenten season; it is also
the celebration or the second scrutiny for those in preparation for
baptism. The day also harbors some sobering images in the liturgy

that hint directly at the readings. The **Prayer over the Offerings** and the identical proper prayer used for the second scrutiny, for instance, allude to the healing of the man born blind when it says that "we place before you with joy these offerings, which bring eternal remedy, O Lord." Overall, the prayers and the **Preface** for this Sunday will capture the important imagery of light and its attendant relationship to discipleship with the coming of Easter. "By the mystery of the Incarnation, he has led the human race that walked in darkness into the radiance of the faith and has brought those born in slavery to ancient sin through the waters of regeneration to make them your adopted children." Consider how, like the man born blind, those who were in darkness now have new sight, the eyes of faith. Further, the man who was born blind symbolizes our own subjection to "ancient sin," one that was simply part of fallen humanity. That yoke has been broken by the water of baptism, which regenerates all who wash in its healing waters and makes them "adopted children," a term Paul uses (in Romans 8:15) to describe the new relationship we have with Christ as coheirs and heirs of God. We can now cry "Abba, Father" as children of adoption. In an interesting sort of way, although the parents of the man born blind figure in the story, his very cure seems to prompt them to surrender their son to another, more mature relationship. Will the young man acknowledge Christ? "For this reason his parents said, 'He is of age; question him.'"

This episode in the gospel is something like a "coming of age story" (echoed in David's anointing as well) and certainly suggests a prominent place for catechumens, who during this second scrutiny are making their way to acknowledging Jesus' own prominence in their lives. For this reason, the **Collect** (for the proper prayers of the scrutinies) says, "Almighty ever-living God, give to your Church an increase in spiritual joy, so that those once born of earth may be reborn as citizens of heaven." There is a little bit of a wordplay in the Latin text, which emphasizes the contrast between the earthly and the heavenly creature, the darkness and the light, as it were. We pray so that *"qui sunt **generatione** terreni* (born of earth) *fiant **regeneration** caelestes* (reborn of heaven)." We might be mindful of the broad contrasts of imagery that occur throughout the readings and the liturgy between darkness and light, earth and heaven, death and life. These contrasts reinforce the experience of a community— the catechumenate and the baptized assembly—not only moving but *awakening* to the Easter call: "Awake, O sleeper, and arise from the dead, and Christ will give you light."

Strategy for Preaching

With one of the most dominant images in literature at the disposal of the preacher, the homiletic task for the Fourth Sunday of Lent seems fairly clear. The homily should work toward moving the assembly from darkness to light. This prospect of illumination anticipates the Easter fire and the baptismal water at the Easter Vigil, so the preaching foreshadows that great liturgical event, preparing both the catechumens and the baptized for a passageway out of darkness into that wonderful light. The question is: what does this homiletic arc look like?

A homiletic core idea will tend to center around something like this: We are by nature familiar with darkness, but Christ has gone down to death for us to give us new life in water and the Holy Spirit. Preaching that acknowledges darkness will "name the demons" all too present in human blindness, to paraphrase *Fulfilled in Your Hearing*. That acknowledgement may start to focus specifically on the blindness all of us have as part of life's everyday condition. Preaching may also take shape around an exploration of what we are blind to in our lives. (This interrogation mirrors the scrutinies celebrated for the catechumens, which have considerable power for everyone for renewal and self-searching.) There are also ways in which our culture colludes with our blindness by covering up the truth; there is a lot of material to mine here, to be sure, including participating in a society that routinely empowers the powerful and disenfranchises the weak. Obviously, the key to the homily, though, will not be only naming the demons but also "naming grace," which *Fulfilled in Your Hearing* also registers as one of the key functions of the preacher for the liturgical assembly. The homily should motivate the congregation to *want* and *desire* the light, having now acknowledged their blindness (this is what the Pharisees cannot manage to do). It is as if the homily brings the congregation to a coming of age, much like the man in the gospel. Enkindling the desire for the light will be a matter of naming specific instances of grace underneath: how the youngest and most vulnerable (like David) hold the power to reveal the presence of the Lord; how those we consider sinful (the Pharisees' judgment on the man born blind) hold the key to our redemption; how Jesus, the man of sorrows, becomes the restorer of life.

Finally, it may be well to face the congregation with the reality that God's true power will be hidden in death and shame, but true vision is being able to see with the eyes of faith the God who has triumphed over death and restored life.

Fifth Sunday of Lent

Readings from the Ambo

Ezek 37:12-14; Ps 130:1-8; Rom 8:8-11; John 11:1-41

Like most of the selections in the Lectionary, the full force of the reading becomes clearer when the text is situated in context. In the case of the prophet Ezekiel, we might see chapter 37 as a whole, framed by his mission to the exiles of the deportation in Babylon in 597 BC. Broadly speaking, Ezekiel concerns himself with bringing God's message of destruction and renewal, and these are going to take shape around various addresses to different members of the Israelite community. His journey leads him to interpret the destruction of Jerusalem and the failure of its leadership, accusing these "shepherds" of abandoning their flocks. At the same time, the latter part of the book of Ezekiel (beginning with chapter 34) will deal with God's plan for transforming not only these false leaders but the whole nation as well into God's protective hegemony.

Our First Reading picks up the plan for restoration in a memorable and vivid way, using images of God opening graves and returning to Israel. Clearly, this is a promise to end the lethal and deadening experience of exile and an invitation to new life. The life to come emerges from the Lord's Spirit, the *ruah*, which will reanimate the land of Israel. It is interesting to note that this Spirit of life is a promise made not only to one but to many. "O my people, I will open your graves / and have you rise from them, / and bring you back to the land of Israel." There is a return to origins with an invocation of the spirit and the promise of new life. The first human being received the gift of life, but this Spirit will bring back an entire nation into the fold of God's leadership. The rest of chapter 37 deploys striking images of "dry bones" reassembled in a valley; they are then breathed into by

God's breath. Once again, there is a corporate image envisioned as part of Israel's return. Indeed, the very Spirit that has been evacuated from an exilic community and made them dispirited has now returned as a unified nation. In the end, this is not God reworking parts of a human being into a kind of Frankenstein's monster or a zombie; rather, God's life and Spirit become the source of life for a new reality and a new beginning. Living in that Spirit of God is Paul's advice to the Romans because the body is dead to sin. Paul is imagining a more personal and moral encounter with the Spirit than Ezekiel, because it is the Spirit of Christ that claims the life of those who are no longer *"en sarki"* or in the flesh.

The raising of Lazarus fits into a larger frame narrative, particularly from the point of view of plot. John 11:1–12:50 forms a connection between this climax of Jesus' "signs" and what the Lord names as his "hour." Chapter 10 ends with the Lord just escaping arrest, and then he flees across the Jordan. After this period, he and his disciples return to Bethany, having received a message from his friends Martha and Mary that their brother, Lazarus, was seriously ill. With the return to Judea, Jesus not only goes to visit the family but walks fully conscious and determined into this hour—his rejection and death.

Why did Jesus wait to visit his sick friend? The narrator himself seems surprised at this delay, which only becomes clear from hindsight: the raising of Lazarus is a sign that discloses God's glory and the power of the resurrection. In the process of waiting, Martha is provoked into the role of a spokesperson, a witness to Jesus' own role as a believer: "Yes, Lord," she tells him. "I have come to believe that you are the Christ, the Son of God, / the one who is coming into the world." So from the point of view of plot, the raising of Lazarus distinguishes itself from the various other moments in the Synoptics in which those who are dead are raised. Bringing the widow's son at Nain back to life (in Luke 7:11-17) is part of Jesus' overall mission of healing; and all three accounts of the restoration of Jairus' daughter (Luke 8:40-56; Mark 5:21-43; Matt 9:18-26) are coupled with the healing of a woman with a hemorrhage. By contrast, Jesus' call for his friend Lazarus to "come forth" from the grave is a direct provocation to the Pharisees. The reason? This man is performing many *"semeia,"* or signs that are causing people to believe. So it is the sign of the resurrection that is the real problem for the Pharisees in John 11:1-41, all the more so since Lazarus has now become "unbound" and is fully alive through Christ. Surely this crisis in the plot concerning the sign (in a gospel filled with them) is a prelude to that greatest of signs—the passion, death, and resurrection of Jesus himself.

Connecting the Bible and the Liturgy

In some dioceses in the United States, images, pictures, and crosses are covered (crosses until the end of the celebration of the Lord's passion on Good Friday; images until the beginning of the Easter Vigil). The covering of images underlines the Johannine emphasis on the raising of Lazarus as a sign and foreshadowing of the resurrection to come. This Fifth Sunday of Lent also celebrates the third and last scrutiny, with its presidential prayers highly evocative of the baptism that awaits those in the catechumenate. The **Collect** asks God that "these chosen ones" may "*renoventur fonte baptismatis.*" *The Roman Missal* translates this as "that they may receive new life at the font of Baptism," which is accurate enough. But "*renoventur*" can also mean that they may be *restored* to their original condition. In some ways, I think this latter meaning gets to the theological core of the sacrament of baptism: it is not only new life—it is certainly that—but it is also the restoration of what was dead into a new creation, a child of God by adoption. With baptism, all are brought out of the dark reign of sin and reinstated into a relationship with God, lost by sin. With Christian baptism, we are brought out of the kind of exile that Ezekiel describes, and re-created in the Spirit. Jesus returned the dead Lazarus to his original condition; that was a sign that the resurrection would restore humanity to its former condition through Christ. That original state also includes the community (here Mary and Martha) to whom Lazarus is restored. Therefore, the whole of humanity is being realigned into a world of grace, not simply reanimated. The **Prayer after Communion** gets at this complete transformation of those to be baptized when it refers to them as those who are "to be reborn," or "*regenerandis,*" a gerundive use of a term for those *about to be baptized* favored by patristic authors like St. Leo the Great.

I think we are meant to see the strong connection between the catechumens' impending rebirth in baptism, the restoration of Israel, and the raising of Lazarus. Indeed the **Preface**: Lazarus makes this very connection when it says that "For as true man he wept for

Lazarus his friend and as eternal God raised him from the tomb, just as, taking pity on the human race, he leads us by sacred mysteries to new life." Since Christ *"ad novam vitam sacris mysteriis nos adducit,"* we are reborn in water and the Holy Spirit. I think it is notable that the **Preface** would choose a very human moment in John's gospel—Jesus weeping for his friend—as a window into compassion for the whole human race. Here again, we see an important alliance being established between the tomb and the womb, the place of death and the pool of regeneration. The raising of Lazarus is a liberation, clearly imaged by the unbinding of the man by his burial garments. This raising to life is a sign that God will re-create lost humanity and restore it into the world of light.

Strategy for Preaching

With the obvious emphasis on the reality of the resurrection everywhere evident in the readings and the liturgy, this Fifth Sunday of Lent presents a number of options for preaching. Some of these will vary as to whether or not the homilist is preaching with the catechumens present or not. I would like to propose a homiletic strategy that would focus on three different areas in the Scripture and the liturgy.

Option 1. Focus on the celebration of the third scrutiny (using biblical and liturgical texts). The core homiletic idea centers on an anticipation of baptism (acknowledging the presence of the catechumens) and its power to re-create those about to receive it, recognizing our own deadness to sin. Drawing from the presidential prayers in the proper prayers for the third (C) scrutiny, the preacher demonstrates that we are helpless and bound until we hear God's call to come to life. Other sources are the Rite of Baptism itself and *The Catechism of the Catholic Church*, 1262–84. Scriptural images of darkness and dry bones will contrast with light, freedom, and new life.

Option 2. Focus on the Ezekiel text. The core homiletic idea centers on the corporate reality of sin as a kind of exile from God, but the presence of the Lord's Spirit makes a fallen nation his own. The emphasis here might be on corporate or social sin in the contemporary world but how God's power breaks through to give new life. The analogy of the exile presents a nice analogy of those who are lost, especially those caught up in a cultural or societal sin; God's Spirit brings these dry bones together for healing and restoration.

Option 3. Focus on John's gospel. The homiletic core idea is that the resurrection of the body will free us from our bondage to decay and bring us with Christ's intercession into the light of eternity. There are a lot of images to exploit when preaching on this passage on the raising of Lazarus (the weeping of the Lord, the darkness of the grave, the unbinding of the risen one). The **Preface** for the Fifth Sunday of Lent offers substantial references for a homily as well, since the prayer accesses the gospel very specifically. Support for this can be gleaned from the doctrine contained in *The Catechism of the Catholic Church* on the "resurrection of the body," specifically 988–1003.

HOLY WEEK

Palm Sunday of the Passion of the Lord

Readings from the Ambo

Isa 50:4-7; Ps 22:8-9, 17-18, 19-20, 23-24; Phil 2:6-11;
Matt 21:1-11 (at procession); Matt 26:14–27:66

The reading taken from Isaiah is the third of the so-called Servant Songs, the whole of which embraces Isaiah 50:4-9. We will hear the entire selection read again on the Wednesday of Holy Week, together with the other Servant Songs, which form a kind of mosaic for the holiest of the seasons in the church. This passage is a matchless, deeply reflective monologue of one who understands the demands of faith.

"A well-trained tongue" has been translated a number of ways: the King James Version (1611) says, "the tongue of the learned"; the New Revised Standard Version says, "the tongue of a teacher"; La Bible de Jerusalem says, *"une langue de disciple"*—"a tongue of the disciple." The last is probably closer to the Hebrew: "the one who has learned." Indeed, we would not want to confuse the Servant with a rhetorical specialist skilled in words. His tongue has not been educated in speaking fancy phrases. On the contrary, the implication of the disciple who has learned fits the rest of the passage, which rejoices in listening, not speaking: "Morning after morning / he opens my ear that I may hear; / and I have not rebelled, / have not turned back." This is how the tongue is taught—through listening to suffering. The overall sense of the passage is that suffering can be redemptive. That message of learning through suffering is especially applicable to Second Isaiah's address to those in exile, a mysterious twilight of loss and misery for Israel. The Servant submits to insults and beating because his faith is steadfast in the Lord, who comes to his help.

This suffering also engages and animates mission. The disciple's tongue has learned "how to speak to the weary / a word that will rouse them." The Servant's toil exists for the sake of others, to set them free from the shackles of exile. In the face of suffering, the Servant claims a liberation that becomes triumphantly defiant: "I have set my face like a flint, / knowing that I shall not be put to shame." Strongly linked to the Suffering Servant is Psalm 22, with its powerful refrain questioning God's very presence. The psalm follows the same pattern of anguish and lament but then ends on a celebratory note, vindicating the one who has been struggling with the pains of doubt and suffering: "I will proclaim your name to my brethren; / in the midst of the assembly I will praise you."

The famous selection taken from Paul's letter to the Philippians, which is rich in christological associations and dogmatic complexity, has obvious parallels with Isaiah's Suffering Servant. This passage (possibly an ancient hymn) celebrates the humble acceptance of Christ the Servant who embraces humility for the sake of proclamation for the weary and oppressed and the mission of liberating humanity from sin. Indeed, a solitary quality characterizes this Christ Jesus who emptied himself (*heauton ekenosen*), taking the form of a slave. The Greek word, *doulou* (in the genitive, it becomes adjectival) can also be translated as "servant," establishing yet a further connection to the Isaiah text.

The level of Jesus as the Suffering Servant and the one who did not cling to equality with God but emptied himself, is explored on various levels with all three Synoptic accounts of the passion narrative. Indeed, the Suffering Servant provides a lens with which to view these passion stories. Depending on the year, these perspectives develop a richness all their own. Matthew's Jesus seems more aware of his *kenosis* than Mark's portrait of the Lord when he says that "my appointed time is near." What are the christological implications of Jesus' self-knowledge in regard to his suffering? Isaiah's Servant learned from his suffering, and Jesus brings this awareness to the passion narratives to various degrees. Those contours of self-emptying become especially jarring when Matthew and Mark both cite Psalm 22, a kind of confirmation of the Suffering Servant: "My God, my God, why have you abandoned me?" Then again, Luke imagines one of the last statements of Jesus as liberation for a thief. Perhaps this last-minute confession was a Lukan version of another kind of *kenosis*, this one meant as a model for the Christian community in order to gain access to the kingdom by the Servant King.

Connecting the Bible and the Liturgy

The emphasis in the readings and the liturgy is on the Christ who suffers and our response. There is an interesting intersection that occurs in most parishes when the congregation is asked to play an active role in the reading of the Lord's passion by assuming the part of the crowd. The congregation's participation in the gospel allows the reading to become a dialogical rather than passive performance. In this case, the congregation absorbs the injustice of the crowd who welcomes the king with palm branches at the beginning of the liturgy but then asks for Jesus' crucifixion during the gospel. How can the assembly not see the self-emptying described in Philippians? The **Collect** sets the tone of a Servant model after the Solemn Entrance by referring to Jesus as "an example of humility for the human race to follow."

I think there is a very interesting aspect of this **Collect** for Passion Sunday, an ancient prayer taken from the late seventh-century *Gelasian Sacramentary* that centers on the phrase "Almighty ever-living God, who as an example of humility for the human race to follow: *caused our Savior to take flesh and submit to the Cross.*" The *Roman Missal*'s translation of *fecisti* names the Latin expression accurately enough in English, but we must be cautious about its subtleties: on one level, yes, we are able to say that almighty God "caused" the Savior to assume flesh and submit to the cross. But certainly, this "causing" is a much more nuanced way of saying "making," which is the way St. Augustine famously uses this verb at the beginning of the *Confessions* ("*Nos fecisti ad te et inquietum est cor nostrum donec requiescat in te*"—"You have made us and our hearts are restless until they rest in you."); that usage here would imply an unorthodox stance that Christ had no free will but was somehow "made" to submit to the cross.

That strict sense of "*fecisti*" implicating direct causation or compulsion is surely not the intention of *The Roman Missal* or the way "caused" is to be read in the **Collect**. Moreover, there may be some further confusion around the God who "caused" Christ to submit to the cross that betrays our understanding of the Suffering Servant. The previous translation in the *Sacramentary* avoided this problem by saying: "He fulfilled your will by becoming man and giving his life on the cross." On the other hand, the way *The Roman Missal* translates the verb *facere* in this instance asks us to see "cause" as something like "to accomplish," an indication of the Son cooperating with God's will. One of my colleagues, a fine Latinist and professor of systematics, suggested that "to establish" is another way of understanding this verb *fecisti* in the present context. In any case, there ought not to be any hint of coercion of the Father's relationship with the Son. To this end, Christ's self-emptying of Philippians must become absolutely and doctrinally lucid—he emptied himself, took on human flesh, and submitted to the cross, and that was accomplished (or established) by almighty God—even as we are more aware of Christ's intention to come to "his hour" of his passion and death. And the cooperation with God's will is further underlined in the **Preface for the Passion of the Lord** when it says, "though innocent, he suffered *willingly* [italics mine] for sinners and accepted unjust condemnation to save the guilty." With the careful parsing of the **Collect**'s complexity and read alongside the readings for the day, the community may now learn from the Suffering Servant's *kenosis* what it means to find redemption and almighty God's role in that work.

Strategy for Preaching

It is well known that Palm Sunday draws a lot of people into its doors. These folks are not all weekly Mass goers. Preaching can speak to them and the regular parishioners about the Lord's passion. If the Suffering Servant speaks to anyone, he does so to those who are marginalized or even lost. Nothing crosses human boundaries more profoundly than suffering and an understanding of personal and social sin.

A core homiletic idea could be that Christ was handed over as criminal for our offenses as God's merciful sacrifice of redemption. What this looked like specifically will be inflected by the gospel for the yearly cycle. Here is where a text of gospel parallels comes in handy. It is possible to pull out a salient and distinctive feature of Christ's servanthood illuminated by the account in either Matthew, Mark, or Luke. In Matthew's rendering of the arrest at Gethsemane, Jesus tells the man who had cut off the ear of the high priest's slave that he should "put your sword back into its sheath, for all who take the sword will perish by the sword" (26:52).

This is an example of the Servant emptying himself of earthly power and advising others to do the same. In Mark, after the arrest others fled, but a young man followed Jesus wearing nothing but a loin cloth. "They seized him, but he left the cloth behind and ran off naked." Here is an instance where all of us are called to self-empty if we are to follow the Servant himself. Similarly, one of two thieves calls out to Jesus on the cross saying, "we have been condemned justly, for the sentence we received corresponds to our crimes, but this man has done nothing criminal" (Luke 23:41). All of these are differing aspects of the same focal point and reveal a quality of the servant. The congregation should be challenged to see the Servant in Jesus as one who has allowed himself to be slain for our offenses and then understand its implication. As the **Prayer over the Offerings** puts it: "by this sacrifice made once for all, [may] we feel already the effects of your mercy."

Thursday of the Lord's Supper
(Years ABC)

Readings from the Ambo

Exod 12:1-8, 11-14; Ps 116:12-13, 15-16bc, 17-18;
1 Cor 11:23-26; John 13:1-15

The first half of chapter 12 in the book of Exodus deals with the Lord's instructions to Moses on the specifics of celebrating the Passover and the feast of Unleavened Bread. There is a little shift beginning in verse 21 when Moses tells the elders how to carry out these divine instructions. Although our passage is concerned only with what God says to Moses, the section in which Moses transmits God's orders to the elders suggests the emerging institutionalization of Passover: not as a private revelation to Moses, who was unique among men, but as a liturgical feast with which the elders were charged to carry out and repeat through *zikaron*, memory.

The keeping of Passover as a memorial of the passage out of Egypt cannot be emphasized enough, since its celebration clearly represents a moment of life and death for Israel. Later generations would recall God's deliverance from the tenth plague and the meal that ushered in the Exodus from Egypt as a renewal of God's promise to the people of the covenant. Among the many noteworthy features of the Lord's instructions to Moses is a divine reordering of the calendar: "This month shall stand at the head of your calendar; / you shall reckon it the first month of the year." This would be Nisan, the first of months in which the Passover meal would commemorate the great work of God for Israel.

In a certain sense, Paul's first letter to the Corinthians recalls the very dynamic present with Moses in the book of Exodus concerning divine instruction and its institutional transmission. "I received (*parelabon*) from the Lord what I also handed on to you." The verb that Paul uses for "handed on" is *paredoka*, which can also mean "passed on," even "passed over or delivered to." I am not suggesting that Paul had this in mind, but there is a kind of "passover" going on when he "*paredoka*" (or handed on) to the Corinthians the tradition of the Lord's Supper. Furthermore, the connection of the Passover in Egypt is further established by a meal commemorated through memory. "For as often as you eat this bread and drink the cup, you proclaim the death of the Lord until he comes." This is the *anamnesis*, the remembrance of the saving event of Christ, his Passover, when he was handed over for us.

Jesus' final meal with his disciples is both a Passover and a Passing-on in John's gospel; it is a transmission of how to treat one another. As is well known, John does not include the institution of the Eucharist on the night before Jesus' passion as the Synoptics do. For a variety of reasons, the eucharistic theology of the Fourth Gospel would extend into the symbolic reaches of the whole gospel (such as the "Bread of Life Discourse") and not be limited to the night the Lord was handed over. Nevertheless, there is a *paredoka* going on between Jesus and his disciples. The act of love is replicated by a footwashing, which in first-century Palestine was the province of a slave or servant to offer guests upon entering a household. The tradition of footwashing was probably ubiquitous in many cultures and was recorded in the Hebrew Scriptures prominently in the book of Genesis and elsewhere. Christ was taking on the role of the servant at the meal, then, and demonstrates this behavior *sui generis*, having received no instruction: the Lord's service emerges directly from him, and he passes it, like his farewell Passover with the disciples in the Synoptics, with the instruction for *anamnesis*. "If I, therefore, the master and teacher, have washed your feet, you ought to wash one another's feet." Humility and hospitality, then, are "institutionalized" as ritual actions, as virtues to be observed in the Christian community. Modeling divine hospitality and humility, all take on the role of a servant in service to one another in a kind of passing over from the selfishness of this world to the light of God's grace. Humility and hospitality are integrally related to the celebration of the Passover of the Lord and are virtues upon which the Johannine community, the community of the Beloved Disciple, built its eucharistic theology of table fellowship.

Connecting the Bible and the Liturgy

It is significant that the Church has chosen chapter 13 of John's gospel for Holy Thursday, which has as a fulcrum the footwashing scene. The emphasis on the Servant Christ who handed himself over to death for the sake of many is replicated symbolically by the church's own reenactment of the footwashing at the Liturgy of the Lord's Supper after the homily. In addition, the readings, the presidential prayers, and **Preface** for the day speak poignantly of the way that Jesus' great act of love was institutionalized in the Eucharist.

Consider the **Collect**, which not only draws an emphasis on Christ's being handed over but on delivering *himself* unto death. *"Morti se traditurus"* is a reflexive action, translated by *The Roman Missal* as "when he was about to hand himself over"; the implication here is that Jesus freely gave himself in love (the lavish footwashing scene in John shows this divine hospitality) and "entrusted to the Church a sacrifice new for all eternity, the banquet of his love." But there is more. We know that this is a night of being handed over as well, "for he knew who would betray him; for this reason, he said, 'Not all of you are clean.'" So we are dealing with Christ's freely giving himself but also a human agency acting to betray him. The Roman Canon picks up the double meaning of the verb *tradere* by simply leaving it ambiguous: "Celebrating the most sacred day (*quo Dominius noster Iesus Christus pro nobis est traditus*) on which our Lord Jesus Christ was handed over for our sake." I think Canon I accurately captures the Johannine Jesus: the one who was betrayed but who also freely handed over himself.

For our sake: that is the other, necessary half of Christ's eucharistic offering of love, the self-surrender in service unto death. We are drawn into this Eucharist by the God who has called us to participate in this most sacred Supper "that we may draw from so great a mystery the fullness of charity and of life" (**Collect**). The eucharistic meal then is a purifying one, granting the assembly *plenitudinem caritatis* in this work of redemption. As the **Prayer over the Offerings** makes clear, our very active participation in the Eucharist becomes a memorial of the sacrifice itself and *"opus nostrae redemptionis exercetur"* (the work of our redemption is accomplished). That liberation occurs in the sacrifice of Christ's blood on the cross, an *anamnesis* repeated and institutionalized in the Eucharist. If Jesus named the betrayer as not clean, we hope to find our sins washed away in Christ's blood. As the **Preface: The Sacrifice and the Sacrament of Christ** says, "As we eat his flesh that was sacrificed for us, we are made strong, and as we drink his Blood that was poured out for us, we are washed clean."

Strategy for Preaching

The homily for Holy Thursday may emerge from a number of different fonts, flowing from the same source: divine service, freely given. The institution of the Eucharist, the call to serve in priestly ministry, the community of the beloved all stream from the initiative of Christ's hospitality and mandate to keep his memory in love. The challenge for the preacher will be to center the homily on *one* homiletic core and to develop an idiom that speaks to contemporary culture about a mystery that appears so difficult to comprehend. Jesus' service to his disciples appears clear enough in John's gospel and so is his commandment to do likewise; but do table service and footwashing speak to a fast-food culture with very little sense of hospitality and driven by individualism?

A core homiletic idea will allow the congregation to explore their experience of hospitality and encourage them to serve the community in grateful response. These expressions of welcome and selfless giving mediate God's own surrender of himself for our sake. By naming this grace, the preacher anticipates Jesus' own gospel injunction to serve.

Here is an organizational structure naming some tactics to engage the assembly along the lines of hospitality that might open a window into an understanding of Christ's own self-sacrifice.

I. Who opened a door for us in our life's journey? Was it a parent or a teacher or a friend? Where would we be today without that gesture of love?

 A. A telling example of service that opened a door for countless poor is Dorothy Day and the Catholic Worker. There are Catholic Workers in cities all over that extend the eucharistic table Jesus began this night. The altar of sacrifice becomes our table of service for the poor as we hand ourselves over to them and all those in need in service.

II. Christ was handed over as the Paschal Lamb for our Passover from sin and death to new life. Exodus illustrates the lamb that saved the people; our exodus from sin comes from the Paschal Lamb.

   A. Christ offered himself for our sins and at the Last Supper anticipated the free offering of his life (cf. *The Catechism of the Catholic Church*, 606–11).

III. There is no service without a surrender of power: that is true humility and hospitality. As we partake of the memorial of this sacrifice, we remember Christ as he remembered us. "The work of our redemption is accomplished."

   A. We are mindful of our mission to love, having been loved ourselves and remembered. Name the particular instances in which grace will unfold in my life in the future. Whose feet will I wash in grateful service?

Friday of the Passion of the Lord
(Years ABC)

Readings from the Ambo

Isa 52:13–53:12; Ps 31:2, 6, 12-13, 15-16, 17, 25;
Heb 4:12-16; 5:7-9; John 18:1–19:42

The selection from Second Isaiah is the fourth and longest of the Servant Songs, and arguably the most powerful; it is a fitting icon for Good Friday of the Lord's Passion. The Song is a description of vicarious suffering: "[I]t was our infirmities that he bore, / our sufferings that he endured." The reading places itself at the center of the community as a highly relational text, offering the Suffering Servant as one who purifies the people from their sins. In the experience of the exile, Second Isaiah is well in the tradition of attributing mediated sacrifice of the one for the sake of the many. Indeed, the scapegoat was part of Israel's cultic ritual, and the prophets Jeremiah and Ezekiel also endured pain for the sake of the community's redemption. Moreover, the Suffering Servant is not only an individual but the community of Israel itself, the suffering people in Israel who endure sorrow and loss for the sake of the future revealed by prophetic oracle.

The passage in this First Reading is framed by a haunting presence that opens and closes the Servant Song: "my servant shall prosper" the passage begins; and "I will give him his portion among the great," near its closing. This is the language of the Lord guaranteeing his presence to his Beloved, even in the midst of anguish. Moreover, the last portion of the passage in particular offers hope by way of fruitfulness and new life for the many: "If he gives his life as an offering for sin, / he shall see his descendants in a long life, / and the will of the LORD shall be accomplished through him . . . / through his suffering, my servant shall justify many, / and their guilt he shall bear." The promise from God is that his chosen people remain close to him and find expiation through exile.

The imagery alone would guarantee this fourth Servant Song a place on Good Friday, with its language associated with a servant of God being "raised high" and a man "of suffering," "pierced," "like a lamb led to the slaughter," he "opened not his mouth." The Passion narratives will find their own narrative interpretation of this fourth Servant Song in the Person of Jesus, of course, as does the letter to the Hebrews, which is a kind of theological, christological gloss on the work of Christ the Servant and his priestly sacrifice for the sake of many. Some might claim that the passage here is a bit tough to absorb, but when juxtaposed with Second Isaiah's Servant, the letter to the Hebrews unfolds its riches for the Christian community. The author wraps the mystery of the incarnation (one who is able "to sympathize with our weakness") around a cultic expression of priestly atonement: "In the days when Christ was in the flesh, / he offered prayers and supplications with loud cries and tears / to the one who was able to save him from death." In so doing, Hebrews helps us to understand how Christ's suffering became redemptive, a purifying offering because "Son though he was, he learned obedience from what he suffered; / and when he was made perfect, / he became the source of eternal salvation for all who obey him." The writer of this very rich text's last observation allows the community to participate in the offering of Christ through their own obedience.

The first two readings provide a crucial antechamber for our passage into John's passion narrative, with its rejection of the Servant, his being led to the slaughter like a lamb, but also his glorification. The high Christology present in the text contrasts to varying degrees with the Synoptic texts proclaimed on Passion Sunday: John's account of the passion repeatedly alludes to a Jesus aware of his fate, as when the Lord says to Peter, "Shall I not drink the cup that the Father gave me?" That Christ is brought to slaughter and pierced at precisely the moment of the day of preparation for the Passover links Jesus to the Lamb brought to sacrifice for the sake of liberation for the community. The numerous allusions to the Hebrew Scriptures during John's passion narrative also remind us of the fulfillment of a plot greater than the one that is transpiring before us, with God as the author and the one who will vindicate his Son and raise him to glory, even as "he shall be raised high and greatly exalted."

Connecting the Bible and the Liturgy

The striking entrance of the celebrant and his assistants with a full prostration at the beginning of the liturgy suggests that this is one day that the church is without words, all the more to underline the letter to the Hebrews in which Jesus himself "offered prayers and supplications with loud cries and tears." The silence that troubles this day acknowledges the Lamb that is dumb before the slaughter. The opening prayer breaks the silence with a plea from the whole church that this assembly of the presanctified enters the protection of God's mercy to "sanctify" his servants, "for whom Christ your Son, by the shedding of his Blood, established the Paschal Mystery." The use of the word *famulos* (servants) aligns the congregation with the role of Christ himself as Suffering Servant, who was obedient unto death. As servants of God, we find our "source of eternal salvation" precisely as servants—"for all who obey him," as the letter to the Hebrews suggests. Moreover, as servants, we are helpless before God, urgently begging his mercy.

The unusual ritual that accompanies this day highlights the work of Christ's passion like no other, and the readings climax to the moment when the Suffering Servant is offered up on the cross. The crucified Christ has an exalted place in the Fourth Gospel as a disclosure of God's glory. And the Solemn Intercessions place a special emphasis on the mediation of the cross for the sake of all human kind, from the church itself to those of every nation and religion, from the faithful to the unbeliever. Each of the prayers that follow the orations have specific allusions proper to the intention, but the first one "For the Holy Church" seems to set the tone for the rest of these supplications when it says, "Almighty ever-living God, who in Christ revealed your glory to all the nations, watch over the works of your mercy." The reach of Christ's intercession is as unfathomable as God's mercy and so we can only adore the one in gratitude who pleads for us by the wood of the cross, the instrument of our salvation and redemption.

Strategy for Preaching

The advantages of preaching on Good Friday are many, since the assembly will be comprised of the devout members of the congregation seeking to understand the mystery of the Lord's passion and death in a deep and meaningful way. The liturgy itself is a kind of homily, with the cross as its center, and so the preaching forms something of a companion piece to a mysterious disclosure, giving voice to the profound articulation of the Word voicing its "loud cries and tears." Along these lines, a theological explanation of the sacrifice of the cross is certainly in order, but it would be useful if it occurred in a way that allowed the listening assembly to feel and experience the event in an immediate, rather than abstract, way. After all, the sacrifice of Christ on this day is a purifying event, and so the closer the homily approaches a catharsis for the congregation, the more the preaching approximates the liturgical action of which it is a part.

I think that one creative way of approaching a homily on Good Friday by way of an indirect theological expression is through a monologue, in this instance an eyewitness report of the events surrounding the passion. The monologue is something along the lines of a dramatic retelling of an event from one person's perspective. A monologue on Good Friday would pull out a character from the passion narrative in John's gospel and relate the events from the perspective of that character. What would the garden in the Kidron valley and the events of the betrayal look like from the point of view of one of the participants, say Malchus, the high priest's slave? Or how about the gatekeeper who had an encounter with Peter in the courtyard? Mary, the mother of Jesus, or the Beloved Disciple at the foot of the cross? We already have a popular gospel song suggesting witness: "Where you there when they crucified my Lord?"

Here are some of the advantages of the monologue homily:

1. A subjective point of view allows the hearer to participate in a very affective way the events of the gospel, from which he or she might be otherwise separated by a cultural distance. This separation might be particularly true when we consider the events of the cross.

2. Holy week should offer a variety of modes of preaching, and the monologue homily for Good Friday allows for an intimate, vivid expression of an interior witness that is particularly suitable to the Johannine Gospel.

3. There is a chance to problematize the way we view and judge characters. If we are quick to assign blame to Peter or even

Judas, granting them a "hearing" fills the picture out a bit more on this day when God's compassion is boundless.

4. This style of homily could also lead the congregation to further meditation on the passion of the Lord, particularly imagistic prayer of the kind Ignatius Loyola encourages his retreatants to engage in the *Spiritual Exercises*.

Easter Sunday
of the Resurrection of the Lord

The Easter Vigil in the Holy Night
(Years ABC)

Readings from the Ambo

Gen 1:1–2:2 (First Reading); Ps 104:1-2, 5-6, 10, 12, 13-14, 24, 35

Genesis's first (Priestly writer's) account of creation is a story of origins, a fitting initiation to the Liturgy of the Word for the Easter Vigil. The Liturgy of the Word begins with a familiar text, underneath which is a brave and simple faith: *"Bereshit bara Elohim et hashamayim ve'et ha'arets"* (In the beginning, when God created the heavens and the earth). The root of the first word of the Hebrew Bible, *bereshit*, is from *"rosh,"* meaning head or chief, underlining this story of origins. In contrast to the second (Yahwist writer's) reckoning of creation, this passage reveals a lofty and mysterious maker of the cosmos whose *ruah* or spirit hovers over the waters and permeates the corners of all created things, breathing into the nostrils of humankind the breath of life. The story climaxes with the creation of human beings, made in the image of God. This *"imago Dei"* becomes a key theological term that will underlie Christian anthropology for centuries and continue into the present day. With the proclamation of this reading at the celebration of the passion, death, and resurrection of the Lord, the recognition of the human subject as *"imago Dei,"* crystallizes the gift of our redemption purchased for us in Christ, now restored.

Gen 22:1-18; Ps 16:5, 8, 9-10, 11

The story of Abraham and the *Akedah* or Binding of Isaac is a heart-wrenching moment in salvation history, which the patristic fathers would seize as an allegorical representation of God's surrender of his own Son unto death. Needless to say, the violence of a text in which God asks the first patriarch of Israel to sacrifice a child can only strike the hearer as barbaric. Yet, as some have argued, this may be a story that rails against human sacrifice, since God prohibits Abraham's actions and finds a ram in his stead. Still, the violence is hard to ignore. Benjamin Britten's *War Requiem* (1962) renders the ferocity of the sacrifice of Isaac palpable when he retells the story: Abraham ignores the angel's intervention and slays his son anyway. The story as Britten refashions it locates the violence to kill in the heart of the human subject, stretching back to antiquity. That iconoclastic reading notwithstanding, the raw emotion present in the text as we have it here points us to an emblematic example of unflinching obedience to God's command, even at the expense of one's dearest love. It is that white-knuckled emotion that is meant to wash over us, singling Abraham out as the father of our faith.

Exod 14:15–15:1; Exod 15:1-6, 17-18

The selection from the book of Exodus catches the chosen people at a climactic moment on their journey from Egypt to the Promised Land, when a definitive boundary has been crossed and their ruthless pursuer has been eradicated. With the crossing of the Red Sea, as with many key moments in the Hebrew Scriptures, the patristic authors would find a christianized allegorical reading. Origen, for instance, would discover a profound symbolic connection between the crossing of the Red Sea and Christian baptism, which allegorizes Pharaoh as the power of Satan drowned in the waters of new life in Christ. Therefore the response of the people of Israel and the newly baptized is the same: "I will sing to the Lord, for he is gloriously triumphant." This text, then, gathers the community of Israel and the Christian faithful on the side of the same sea, all of us waiting to cross into the Promised Land of our redemption. In addition to an allegorical interpretation informing Christian baptism, this passage has been a hermeneutical blueprint for those kept in bondage awaiting freedom from the 1960s civil rights movement to apartheid in South Africa.

Isa 54:5-14; Ps 30:2, 4, 5-6, 11-12, 13

In the last of the Zion oracles, Second Isaiah speaks to the exiles of a God who will never give up on the chosen people: the promise will endure forever. Beginning in verse 1, Isaiah uses a series of spousal images that vividly bring to light God's covenantal love. At the same time, the immanent presence of the Lord contrasts strikingly with the transcendent God of the universe: "the One who has become your husband is your Maker; / his name is the LORD of hosts." Like some powerful images in the Bible, these metaphors can be somewhat troubling and patriarchal for contemporary hearers. Are we to take the Lord calling back Israel during the exile as "a wife married in youth and then cast off" or in a "brief moment . . ." "abandoned" and "in an outburst of wrath" faced a God who hid his face? To understand the "enduring love" expressed by the biblical author we may have to suspend modern sensibility for a moment and lean into the historical presence of the text that desires to convey a God of mercy and pity. Interestingly, there is another side to this God, infinitely more complex than we imagine. The portrait of the Lord given by Second Isaiah is of a repentant God, who likens these days of exile to the time when he renewed a covenant with Noah, which became an eternal promise. The passage's overriding intention asks us to see a God of unconditional love, remembering with some sentiment, "a covenant of peace."

Isa 55:1-11; Isa 12:2-3, 4, 5-6

One way of understanding this passage is to see the text precisely as a kind of rejoinder or companion piece to the previous reading. Having testified to a steadfast covenant in which justice and peace will be established in foundations and battlements of precious stones, God now prepares a banquet for his people. This festive meal is extended to everyone without cost, a fitting celebration from the God who loves unconditionally. Yet alongside this promise of water to the thirsty and grain for the hungry, there is also the plea for conversion, to heed God and eat well, to "Seek the LORD while he may be found, / call him while he is near." Once again, we face a God who is both merciful and powerful. These two seemingly irreconcilable characteristics converge in God's *dabar*, the word that, like "seed to the one who sows / and bread to the one who eats," achieves its proper end and does not return to God "void." God's power is accomplished in the very act of intending goodness, which is mercy and abundance—watering the earth and making it both fertile and fruitful. From a Christian perspective, the baptismal imagery and invitation to conversion and renunciation is clear enough: all are invited to renew themselves in God's saving waters and at the table of God's endless mercy. The Lord's banquet gathers the lost, even as God's memory of the covenant assured to David identifies his descendants as precious. In the response that follows, taken from First Isaiah, that promise is reified: "You will draw water joyfully from the springs of salvation."

Bar 3:9-15; 3:2–4:4; Ps 19:8, 9, 10, 11

Speaking to Israel in a time of captivity, Baruch presents God's wisdom and commandments as the anchor of salvation. Although Israel has rejected "the fountain of wisdom," Baruch offers a return to prudence as a pathway back to the Lord. "Turn, O Jacob, and receive her; / walk by her light toward splendor." The underlying virtue embedded in Baruch's admonition to Israel is hope, since when we know where prudence, strength, and understanding abide, then we will also know "where are length of days, and life, / where light of the eyes, and peace." The advice Baruch has for Israel is echoed in the psalm response: "Lord, you have the words of everlasting life." The word of God and the precepts of the law are the building blocks for faithful and virtuous living in the land of exile. In a sense, Baruch has to rearticulate a whole tradition to a people who have lost everything, including their sense of direction, as it were. Which way is home? He speaks to Israel of a wisdom tradition in order to refound a people in the midst of exile and darkness. It is the Lord God who has found these precious people and gives them direction. In Baruch's hands, wisdom becomes the arbitrator of life, a handmaid of the Most High, the law that can be returned to over and over again: "She is the book of the precepts of God, / the law that endures forever." This rebuilding for Israel will be a pathway lit by the splendor of wisdom, a light that will never go out, even in the midst of the diaspora.

Ezek 36:16-17a, 18-28; Ps 42:3, 5; 43:3, 4

Ezekiel's utterance is both a rebuke and a promise. The Lord recalls the reality of Israel's transgressions and the penalty they paid—scattering and dispersion among the nations. Most of all, it is for the sake of God's holy name, which has been profaned in exile, that the Lord has relented and will redeem his people by sprinkling clean water upon them to cleanse them from their impurities and idols. A central image that focuses on this redemption is a promise of transformation: "I will give you a new heart and place a new spirit within you, / taking from your bodies your stony hearts / and giving you natural hearts." The spirit of the Lord will also inhabit this new Israel, even as that same spirit will give life to the "dry bones" in the valley the prophet encounters and records in chapter 37:1-14. God guarantees new life to those in exile, since those who have been lost will be gathered. Like Second Isaiah, the water imagery is a baptismal mystic bath when seen from a Christian perspective. When the catechumen dies to sin in baptism it is then that that new life begins in Christ: that is the coming of the spirit that animates the hearts of those who have traded their stony hearts for ones made of flesh. Christians have been gathered in from sin, that place of reckless and unruly exile, and have been brought under God's re-creative vision.

Rom 6:3-11; Ps 118:1-2, 16-17, 22-23

Paul finds himself in the company of Isaiah and Ezekiel as he also promises newness of life, once we are dead to the power of sin and alive in Christ Jesus. In a certain sense, Paul's theological discourse on baptism and its connection to the death and resurrection of Christ forms something of a commentary for all those who have listened to Isaiah and "come to the waters" and have found "new life." This newness of life has been purchased by Christ's own death and resurrection, freeing us from being "in slavery to sin." Paul makes it abundantly lucid that all those who are baptized participate in Christ's work, since they are "dead to sin / and living for God in Christ Jesus." The liturgical context of this reading of the epistle from Paul shifts the tone of the vigil rather dramatically, since after the last reading from Ezekiel the presider will intone the *Gloria in excelsis Deo* and then acknowledge that the Lord has made holy "this most sacred night with the glory of the Lord's Resurrection." Paul's words to the Romans, then, are blooming with the reality of new life brought by Christ and the place baptism holds for Christians since "We were indeed buried with him through baptism into death, / so that, just as Christ was raised from the dead / by the glory of the Father, / we too might live in newness of life."

Matt 28:1-10 (Year A)

The action in Matthew's version of the resurrection is a bit jumbled: Mary Magdalene comes to the tomb, then the angel appears after an earthquake rolls back the stone, and sits on it. Having dazzled the soldiers, the angel announces that "He is not here, for he has been raised just as he said." Well, how could Jesus have been raised (and now moving around Galilee) if the angel just rolled the stone back?

Unlike most of the readings heard this night, the listening assembly will have a variety of pictorial versions of the resurrection in their mind, all of them an amalgamation of paintings, gospel readings, and popular representations. Matthew is not really interested in the physical details or even the sequences of the resurrection event; rather the biblical author attends to the eschatological significance of Jesus breaking out of dead time into God's time and focuses on the glorified Lord who calls out to his disciples, "Do not be afraid." The earthquake is not an excuse to roll back the stone for a little piece of action as much as it is a sign of the kingdom breaking into our world, which is the moment of the resurrection. God's raising up of Jesus the crucified also becomes the source of faith and proclamation for the disciples who are "fearful yet overjoyed." For those who are about to be baptized, the reality of the resurrection is God's triumph over sin and death, which is the baptism into which they will now be submerged and rise to life in Christ Jesus.

Connecting the Bible and the Liturgy

The opportunities to make connections with the Scriptures and the liturgy for the Easter Vigil are almost too many to innumerate, to say nothing of doing so in such a short space. But from the perspective of unique opportunities, the *Exultet*, that ecstatic announcement like no other, certainly presents a panorama of salvation history filled with emotion that will find its echo in the sweep of the scriptural readings. Indeed, the bringing of the light of Easter to the earth echoes with excitement of Prometheus unbound as the fire radiates, "ablaze with light from her eternal King." The Genesis text will bring to our horizon the Creator who first created that light that now finds its benediction as Easter fire. Indeed, the coming of the light is also the brightness brought to the exiles, led out of Egypt and given the good news of hope by Isaiah and Ezekiel. When it comes to the **Blessing of the Baptismal Water**, this text rehearses the primal waters fashioned by the Creator from the beginning and now made new in Christ. The freedom from bondage, "set free from slavery to Pharaoh," expressed in Exodus now celebrates the gift of living water offered in gratuitous largesse from the God who invites all to "come to the waters" that have no price.

Additionally, there is a wonderful opportunity to connect the Scriptures with the liturgy at the Easter Vigil in the **Prayers after the Readings**. The global reach of the readings to all people is highlighted in the prayer after Genesis 22:1-18, for instance, when the presider begs God to pour out "the grace of adoption throughout the whole world . . . [and] through the Paschal Mystery make your servant Abraham father of nations." The prayer makes the obedience of Abraham so astonishingly vivid in the Scriptures that there ensues an immediate invitation to the liturgical assembly to do likewise in their own (sometimes painful) call to do God's will: "Grant, we pray, that your peoples may enter worthily into the grace to which you call them." Similarly, after the reading concerning Israel's passage through the Red Sea, the parallel with the congregation is once again established between the two worlds: "grant, we pray, that the whole world may become children of Abraham and inherit the dignity of Israel's birthright." In fact, the prayer makes it clear that the Lord has not ceased from doing such wonders, since this is a God, *"cuius antiqua miracula etiam nostris temporibus coruscare sentimus"* (whose ancient wonders remain undimmed in splendor even in our day). Needless to say, asking God that in *Abraehae filos et in Israeliticam dignitatem totius mundi transeat plenitudo* in the current political climate is a bold claim, but the connection between the people of Israel and the Christian community ought not to be overlooked, or its interfaith relations go underappreciated—especially during the Easter Vigil. With the catechumens crossing the Red Sea into baptism and the Christian community renewing their baptism by renouncing the slavery to the pharaoh of Satan, the liturgical assembly and the people of Israel are deeply united, and, in this very recognition, God's promise of liberation becomes clear from age to age, even as Abraham has become the father of faith and of many nations.

Strategy for Preaching

The lavish richness and the deep breadth of the readings and the liturgy for the Easter Vigil present the preacher with a formidable task: how to capture the incredible panoply of texts, scriptural and liturgical, which encompass this night in a homily that is less than ten minutes in length. We have just watched salvation history being retold before our eyes. That makes the Easter Vigil a unique preaching experience. Indeed, the homilist should not make the mistake of thinking that preaching for the vigil is identical with that which will be proclaimed at the liturgy during Easter Day. The character of the Easter Vigil will mark a homily that understands the sweep of salvation history, the gift of baptism, and the place of the resurrection in the life of the Christian community.

I will suggest three practical tactics for preaching on this night of nights, all of which may be expanded or diminished as needed.

The arc of the homily can first be sketched by attending to all of the readings and identifying *one* characteristic in each of them during a session of *lectio divina*. I am recommending one characteristic so that these features might be resources when the homily is shaped: First Reading: Gift; Second Reading: Obedience; Third Reading: Liberation; Fourth Reading: Covenant; Fifth Reading: Rebirth; Sixth Reading: Hope; Seventh Reading: Redemption; Eighth Reading: New Life; Ninth Reading: Faith.

1. After the characteristics are identified, use the orations following the readings to enter into a prayerful dialogue with how you understand the text. What do you want to ask these texts based on the liturgy that responds to each of the scriptural selections?

2. After this process, see what homiletic core emerges. This core might look like the following: This is the night when God has brought us out of the darkness of sin and death and liberated us in the waters of redemption. Given the multiple combinations of readings and liturgical texts, there are any number of core homiletic sentences that might surface in the course of a prayerful encounter before the homily is preached.

3. After the core homiletic idea is established, introduce the variety of dialogue partners to start organizing the homily. There are the scriptural texts that will broaden the core homiletic idea. In the case of the core I just recommended, the readings from the vigil such as Exodus, Isaiah, Ezekiel, Paul, and Matthew all help to establish credibility to the focus or core homi-

letic sentence. Lastly, the liturgy for the vigil provides further text to establish a dialogue such as the *Exultet*, the Baptismal Liturgy, the **Preface I of Easter**, and the proper presidential prayers for the Eucharistic Liturgy.

Based on this strategy, a possible outline for the homily could be organized in this fashion:

I. Introduction (leading into the homiletic core sentence)

II. This is the night when God has brought us out of the darkness of sin and liberated us in the waters of redemption.

    A. Exodus 14:15–15:1

    B. Prayer following this reading

    C. *Exultet*

    D. Blessing of Baptismal Water

III. But we tend to live in exile, away from God, unaware of the covenant that has endured forever.

    A. Ezekiel 36:16-17a, 18-28

    B. Isaiah 54:5-14; 55:1-11

    C. Prayer following the reading

    D. Preface

IV. So it will take faith to live out of the experience of the resurrection.

    A. Matthew 28:1-10

    B. Romans 6:3-11

    C. Baptismal promises

    D. A story (short) illustrating a discovery of new life. This may be a secular story or a religious one illustrating making alive what once was dead.

V. Conclusion (closing off the core idea). We are united this night with the children of Abraham as we are freed from our bondage, even as the earth shakes us loose into God's kingdom of his Christ.

Easter Sunday
of the Resurrection of the Lord
At the Mass during the Day (Years ABC)

Readings from the Ambo

Acts 10:34a, 37-43; Ps 118:1-2,16-17, 22-23;
Col 3:1-4 or 1 Cor 5:6b-8; John 20:1-9

The First Reading from Acts is a fitting summary leading up to the moment of Jesus' resurrection. Peter's address to the centurion Cornelius and his household recapitulates the life, ministry, death, and resurrection of the Lord for the Gentiles. The rising of Christ from the dead is a message that is meant for all. As Peter begins his speech (not included in the selection from Acts here), "In truth, I see that God shows no partiality" (10:34b NAB), or more graphically in the Greek text, *"prosopolomptes,"* meaning to lift up someone's face, showing favorites. As Paul would say in 1 Corinthians, this message of the resurrection is the good news that allows us to celebrate the feast of the paschal lamb with a little yeast that "leavens all the dough." Therefore Jesus himself showed no partiality but "went about doing good and healing all those oppressed by the devil, for God was with him." After Peter's speech, Acts 10 will conclude with the Holy Spirit falling upon all who heard the Word in the house of Cornelius. The Spirit falls without partiality as well but comes to those who hear the Word.

While the Good News is meant for all, Jew and Gentile alike, there are certain demands placed on the receivers of the Word. Like Peter, Christians proclaim and witness to the life, death, and resurrection of Jesus. Like Cornelius and his household, the invitation is to hear and believe. Hearing the Word opens those present to the eschatological moment of the coming of the Holy Spirit; that is as true for those who hear Peter's preaching as it is for the assembly of the baptized gathered for Eucharist on this first day of the week on Easter morning in the twenty-first century.

In a very different context than Acts, Paul writes to the Colossians in prison encouraging them to be hearers of the Good News of the resurrection of the Lord. Throughout the letter to the Colossians, Paul stresses the authority granted to Christ through the power of the resurrection, which has rescued them from death and pagan practices and "*metestesen*" or transferred us into the kingdom of his beloved Son. Paul, himself in chains, is conscious of being transported by "what is above, not of what is on earth," longing for Christ to appear with him in glory. So the source of Paul's encouragement is abiding in Christ, which is accomplished in baptism because the Christian's "life is hidden with Christ in God."

The selection from John's gospel brings about closure in so many ways. Having run to the tomb where Jesus once lay, the Beloved Disciple "saw and believed." The story of the resurrection is something like the last piece of a puzzle that has gone unsolved until the final ecstatic moment. In John's gospel, Jesus has performed signs from the wedding at Cana to the cleansing of the temple, until he himself became the definitive sign of God's glory on the cross. Now, at last, the disciples who were closest to Jesus put the missing and jagged piece into its place to complete the picture. The astonishment of the resurrection now begins a new age and a new *kairos* of creation: the first day of the week. The site of the empty tomb yields to an acknowledgement of profound understanding of the Scriptures and Jesus' teaching concerning his place in salvation history. In Luke, two other disciples will have a similar moment of faith, but its revelation comes not from the empty tomb, but from Jesus himself in the Scriptures, the breaking of the bread, and the prayers.

Connecting the Bible with the Liturgy

With the dramatic events in John's gospel close at hand, a poignant phrase in the **Collect** to recall is this: "O God, who on this day, through your Only Begotten Son, have conquered death and unlocked for us the path of eternity." As described by the author of John's gospel, the tomb is locked, and then Mary Magdala came there and "saw the stone removed from the tomb." She at once proclaimed to the disciples, as the **Sequence** says, "The tomb of Christ who is living, the glory of Jesus' resurrection." Moreover, the writer is at pains to describe a race on the path to see if what Mary said was true, as Peter and "the other disciple" ran and made their way to Jesus' empty tomb. They arrive, breathless, to a new discovery of life and resurrection. Therefore God has literally helped us to beat a pathway to the gates of eternity, or *"aeternitatis nobis aditum."* The image of the disciples running at the proclamation of Mary Magdalene is also the remarkable beginning of the transmission of this Good News of eternal life: the Word has begotten the Word, which leads quite literally to the *resurgens* of new life. Additionally, Paul's situation in writing to the Colossians is a memorable connection here as well. As we pray in gratitude to God who has "unlocked" the gates of eternity, so too does Paul urge the Colossians to seek the Christ who is above, now glorified at the right hand of God. It is Christ who has trod that pathway to eternity and made it clear for all those who have died in him; they now have a life that is hidden or *kekruptai* in God.

Depending on whether or not the presider chooses to ask the congregation to renew their baptismal promises after the homily, the **Collect** provides a fitting prelude to these prayers when it prays that as we keep the Solemnity of the Lord's Resurrection we may, "through the renewal brought by your spirit rise up to the light of life." With the baptismal renewal, a catechetical moment for the assembly awaits them, as the assembly recognizes the presence of the risen Christ's spirit in their own renewal; it is an invitation to remind the assembly that "we have been buried with Christ in Baptism, so that we may walk with him in newness of life."

Finally, if the Roman Canon (**EP I**) is used, there are the proper forms of the *communicantes* that harken back to the readings and provide yet another catechetical moment. As it begins, "Celebrating the most sacred night (day) of the Resurrection of our Lord Jesus Christ in the flesh." This doctrinal moment concerning the resurrection should not be passed through lightly, since the resurrection of the body is a seminal article of faith and, appropriately enough, is part of the gospel narrative and its clues. When Peter sees the empty tomb, the burial clothes are in separate places, an important indication that Jesus' rising was not based on a hysterical vision or some kind of a spiritual rising, but a corporeal one. The very bodily resurrection of Jesus will be taken up again in next week's gospel as John recounts Thomas's encounter with the risen Lord and his wounds.

Strategy for Preaching

Who would disbelieve the sight of the risen Lord? As I hinted earlier, the popular imagination has cultivated any number of episodes concerning the resurrection that are not entirely biblical in their origin and representation. This first day of the week when it is still dark, Mary Magdalene, Peter, and "the other disciple" Jesus loved face a far more existential encounter than a vision of the Lord; they face the empty tomb and must interpret its consequences. We know that in John's gospel, Jesus will make himself known as a risen body in a variety of ways after this initial moment—appearing to Mary Magdalene in the garden, revealing himself to the disciples in the locked room and by the Sea of Tiberius. But this Easter Sunday faces the Christian assembly with deep questions of faith, baptismal renewal, and the search for Christ amid the darkness of despair. The homiletic core idea is literally a matter of life and death. I would suggest that the question for this Easter morning for the Sunday assembly might be shaped around this: how do I understand the empty tomb as a call to believe God's promise for eternal life?

A good preaching plan for developing this question is to help the congregation to come to the same conclusion as the Beloved Disciple. "He saw and believed," should be the goal toward which the homiletic arc is moving. To this end, the preacher might consider a kind of "retelling" of Jesus' life and ministry, death, and resurrection along the lines that Peter proclaims in the house of Cornelius. According to John's gospel, the site of the empty tomb triggered in the Beloved Disciple an insight, *pisteuein*, "he believed." If we are to take the Beloved Disciple as the first witness of the resurrection, we might consider his witness value to the works or signs of Jesus as a way into understanding and believing. That strategy does not mean a repetition of the whole gospel, but helping the hearer to unlock the mystery of God's gift of eternal life.

To consider one such sign early in John's gospel: the cleansing of the temple (2:13-25). That important episode in the life of Jesus and the disciples precisely because verse 22 makes a specific reference to the activity at the temple and the recollection the disciples have after Jesus rises from the dead. "Destroy this temple and in three days I will raise it up. . . . Therefore, when he was raised from the dead, his disciples remembered that he had said this, and they came to believe the Scripture and the word Jesus had spoken" (2:19b; 22). The preacher might begin by asking the assembly to ponder what it would be like if the very building in which they were worshiping might vanish. What would they have? The Johannine community faced the destruction of the temple and Jesus himself seems to peel off the layers of external temple practices early in John's gospel, seemingly to replace it with himself as the new temple that is raised up. When all is taken away from us—even the security of institutional religion—and we stare only at an empty tomb in the dawn of the morning, do we see the Lord before us?

A courageous story of faith is the episode immediately following this passage (John 10-18) in which Mary meets Jesus in person. She was with him to the end—right up to the cross and came to the (empty) tomb to care for him. That is the faith that begins with love. The homily could build on this premise and use other contemporary stories of the strong relationship between love and faith. It is probably not an accident that the Beloved Disciple reached the tomb first because of this love and was also the first to believe in the resurrection as its first witness. Stories that show love as the gateway to faith and trust will underline the devotion of the Beloved Disciple to love and believe: standing at the foot of the cross and racing to the tomb has born the fruit of testimony—the gospel itself.

In the end, the buildings we come to adorn with our Easter lilies and spring flowers are wonderful places, but nothing substitutes for the temple of the risen Lord. Like the disciples we come to the Lord running with all we have and find ourselves witnessing to his rising from the dead. The Eucharist allows us once again to recognize him in the garden that the church has invited us all to dwell in on this fragrant Easter morning.

EASTER TIME

Second Sunday of Easter

Readings from the Ambo

Acts 2:42-47; Ps 118:2-4, 13-15, 22-24; 1 Pet 1:3-9; John 20:19-31

The outpouring of God's lavish grace in Christ Jesus' resurrection has its immediate effect in the life of the community. In the book of Acts, this communal fidelity is expressed in adherence to the teaching or *didache* of the apostles, the breaking of bread, and the prayers. Moreover, these early disciples in the early church share everything in common and distribute possessions "and divide them among all according to each one's need." Taken together, the practice of holding fast to the Word, breaking bread, and reciting the prayers all fit under the pluralistically colorful umbrella of *koinonia*; the common life and its practice will form the spine of the early Christian community.

It is worth considering the attention the book of Acts pays to community and its demands for equity and harmony. It would be an understatement to say that we have heard this communal language before in Luke's gospel, especially in Jesus' demands for true discipleship (Luke 14:25-35), and parabolic language of God's future when the last shall be first, and the first shall be last, as in the story of the Rich Man and Lazarus (Luke 16:19-31). The resurrection of Jesus and the outpouring of his Spirit (Acts 2:1-13), has reversed the event immediately leading up to his passion and death. Where there was confusion, timidity, and perfidy before, the postresurrection Christian community in Acts is marked by proclamation, unity, and sharing of goods. The point is that the resurrection of Christ and its aftermath engaged a behavior change in the disciples and in those who would hear the word of God preached to them. The Word bets a multitude of followers as consequence of the resurrection. "And every day the Lord added to their number those who were being saved."

The gospel for this Sunday makes it clear how much the Good News of the resurrection depends on hearing and believing. The disciples are literally locked into their fear, imprisoned in a room of their own choice because they have not believed in Mary's proclamation of the risen Lord. So Jesus makes himself visible. In the process of his appearance in the fearful and sequestered room, the Lord dispels their anxiety and gives them the Holy Spirit; it is that same Spirit that, in Acts, enables Peter to boldly testify to the Lord's resurrection. Jesus' passing on of his Holy Spirit is an outcome of the resurrection in which God's generosity extends to the forgiveness of sins.

Thomas's role in the room at a later time is less as a doubter—they all doubted before the Lord appeared to them—as much as a witness dramatically testifying to Jesus' risen body—wounds and all. It is as if John wants the hearer to explore the dynamics of a faith that can fully recognize and embrace this risen Jesus, even the wounds of the crucified. Thomas is facing no dream, no fantasy, no illusion; this is "my Lord and my God," a reality that only faith makes present after it has shoved doubt out the door. It is faith that has brought Thomas to the edge of this experience, provoked by the wounded presence of Jesus himself. All the more so, Jesus reminds him, of those who do not see and yet believe. Along these lines, the first letter of Peter affirms those who have been given a "new birth" and "a living hope / through the resurrection of Jesus." As the author tells us, "Although you have not seen him you love him; / even though you do not see him now yet believe in him." Faith and hope make the endurance of suffering possible, and like Thomas in the gospel the Christian community will all have to explore Christ's wounds. Yet 1 Peter holds out the promise of the *parousia*: when Christ will be revealed to believers in a *kairos* moment, that time that embraces both the risen Lord now and the future Christ yet to be revealed to us.

Connecting the Bible and the Liturgy

The outpouring of the Spirit after the resurrection has brought the early church into the experience of the mystical Body of Christ, the activity of which includes the "breaking of bread and the prayers." This divine unification occurs obviously enough in the celebration of the Eucharistic Liturgy, the source and summit of the church's prayer. The Eucharist is the church's activity that witnesses to the risen Lord, and its very celebration witnesses to the Spirit of the Lord active and present in the lives of the church's members. Consider the Communion or "Second Epiclesis" of **Eucharistic Prayer III**, in which the Holy Spirit is invoked a second time in order to ask that the Holy Spirit fill the people of God with unity and peace: "Look, we pray, upon the oblation of your Church and, recognizing the sacrificial Victim by whose death you willed to reconcile us to yourself, grant that we, who are nourished by the Body and Blood of your Son and filled with his Holy Spirit, may become one body, one spirit in Christ." In effect, the falling of the Holy Spirit on the eucharistic assembly radiates a similar action in Acts: as the sacrifice and rising of Christ unfold before us, we are nourished by his Body and Blood and filled with the Spirit *"unum corpus et unus spiritus inveniamur in Christo."* This pneumatological emphasis is meant to transform the worshipers into those who will be called Body themselves, literally holding all things in common—indeed their very lives—as part of the eucharistic sacrifice of the church.

This Second Sunday of Easter is also "Divine Mercy Sunday," which celebrates God's largesse to the whole world in light of the risen Lord. That same Spirit that labors to make all one in Christ Jesus has mercifully drawn all to the waters of rebirth at Easter. The opening prayer, then, celebrates the God of "everlasting mercy" who renews the church from age to age and "who in the very recurrence of the paschal feast kindle[s] the faith of the people you have made your own." The petition to this merciful God extends mostly for the grace of faith to understand the mystery that has been celebrated, "in what font they have been washed, by whose Spirit they have been reborn, by whose Blood they have been redeemed." Clearly, this is a petition *"ut digna mones intellegentia comprehendant,"* or "that all may grasp and rightly understand" for a mystagogical *"intellegentia"* of the Easter mysteries, for an exploration of the "teaching of the apostles," the breaking of bread, and the prayers.

Strategy for Preaching

The Second Sunday of Easter invites the whole church into a mystagogical reflection, which, as the name implies, centers on a pondering of the mysteries we have just encountered in Easter. If the Easter solemnity is too great to be held by a twenty-four-hour day and needs an octave for a celebration, then mystagogical preaching extends the encounter with the risen Lord, especially as the church meets him in baptism, in a prayerful and meditative way. In a metaphorical sense, we are asked to probe the wounds of Christ and to discover by reflection the afterglow of the resurrection, that is to say, his divine mercy. More concretely, the core homiletic idea for this Sunday might focus on the effects of the resurrection in the lives of believers, pondering the mystery of Christian baptism that has drawn us into the death of Christ so that we might rise in his likeness. There is an essential component that should not be missed in the homiletic at hand: to access the neophytes as natural symbols for their fellow congregants as those who have gone to the baptismal font in which they have been washed.

The preacher should take sober instruction from the book of Acts and recognize that this Sunday accentuates the gifts of the Spirit that have made the Body whole. Ironically, it is all too common that after the Rite of Christian Initiation has been celebrated at the Easter Vigil, the neophytes are more or less left to scramble on their own and not fully incorporated into the Body of the parish. These Sundays after Easter offer an opportunity for mystagogical preaching that could draw the congregation together by contemplating the mysteries and include those newly baptized and confirmed into the Christian assembly itself.

The **Collect** is a rich collection of associations that could structure the homily with some support from the readings. An outline for a homily might look like this:

I. God is ever merciful by renewing us from age to age.

    A. Biblical evidence in Acts of a rejuvenated community

    B. Witness of those baptized at Easter Vigil (cf. **Prayer over the Offerings**)

II. But we can always ask for more grace to understand the mystery of our own baptism.

    A. Ritual explanation with citations

    B. "To be washed at the font" is to be incorporated into a faith community.

    C. Thomas experienced the Lord's death by probing his wounds and believed.

III. The Eucharist will nourish us as we continue on our journey.

   A. Image of a mother feeding her young is like the church and the Eucharist.

   B. The risen Christ is always with us as we believe into his divine life.

   C. Divine Mercy Sunday shows us a Christ whose rays of light penetrate the whole world with love (quotes from **Collect**).

Third Sunday of Easter

Readings from the Ambo

Acts 2:14, 22-33; Ps 16:1-2, 5, 7-8, 9-11;
1 Pet 1:17-21; Luke 24:13-35

In the First Reading, Peter begins with what will be a series of speeches recorded in the book of Acts directed at the Jewish opposition; these orations will weave the Hebrew Scriptures into God's purposeful plan for the redemption of humankind in *Christ*. Luke's retelling of the death of Jesus at the hands of the Jews and *ekdoton dia cheiros anomon* (delivered up through the hands of the lawless), suggests that this murderous action occurred inside the "set plan and foreknowledge of God." But providentially, God also delivered Jesus out of the realm of death by raising him from the dead. Peter is reminding his hearers that the handing over and murder of Jesus was used by God to accomplish a greater end. Peter's rhetorical aim is to use the sacred writings to prove God's knowledge and plan for redemption that the Jews missed. So David becomes the spokesperson for the Jewish tradition since he anticipated his descendent on the thrown, the messianic king not waiting to come at an eschatological future moment, but in God's present moment, the coming of the kingdom in the resurrection of Christ from the dead. David "was a prophet and knew that God had sworn an oath to him / that he would set one of his descendants upon his throne, / he foresaw and spoke of the resurrection of the Christ, / that neither was he abandoned to the netherworld / nor did his flesh see corruption." The promise is fulfilled in our midst: "God raised this Jesus; / of this we are all witnesses."

First Peter makes this messianic reality present as well when the author speaks of God's plan in Christ fulfilled in human time; he "was known before the foundation of the world / but revealed in the final time for you, / who through him believe in God / who raised him from the dead and gave him glory." Now that God has sanctified human history, this "final time" has initiated us into resurrection time, the moment when we are ransomed from evil and from the legacy of a dead and sinful ancestry.

Much of Peter's hortatory declarations in Acts focus on the hearers' failure to recognize the presence of God's promise. Appropriately enough, the accompanying gospel draws out the reality of human blindness. The famous passage in Luke that deals with the appearance of the risen Lord to the two disciples on the way to Emmaus centers on one of the most familiar literary devices in world literature: "their eyes were prevented from recognizing him." Here we are plunged, in a certain sense, into a kind of comic world akin to Odysseus's being disguised so that even his friends and family don't know who he is when he returns to Ithaca to claim his wife and household. Unlike the disciples on the way to Emmaus, however, the hearers of this gospel story are very well aware who Jesus is and wait for that final dénouement. The act of hearing (and seeing) becomes a window into privileged knowledge, allowing us a recognition from which the two disciples have been prevented. The little plot then turns precisely on the how and the when of recognizing the risen Lord. After Jesus explains the Scriptures through the lens of his passion and death and breaking the bread, "their eyes were opened and they recognized him, / but he vanished from their sight." In contrast to the comedic reunion of the Odysseus hero with his family, Jesus disappears. So this last dramatic twist yields not to closure (reunification) but to proclamation: "the Lord has truly been raised and has appeared to Simon!" This announcement of the risen Lord is also the legacy of Peter in Acts, who, like Jesus himself, now preaches the passion, death, and resurrection as a sign of God's working wonders and the fulfillment of the divine promise.

Connecting the Bible and the Liturgy

A form of the Latin verb *exultare* is used in both the **Collect** (*exsultet*) and the **Prayer over the Gifts** (*exsultantis*, as a present participle) to signify the state of the assembly and the whole church during this Easter season. We ought not to miss the connection of this particular verb with the ecstatic proclamation of the priest or deacon on the Easter Vigil only a few weeks earlier: "Exult, let them exult, the host of heaven, exult, let Angel ministers of God exult, let the trumpet of salvation sound aloud our mighty King's triumph." The resurrection has yielded a matchless state of rejoicing akin to the disciples on the way to Emmaus who finally recognized Jesus in the Scriptures and in the breaking of the bread: "Were not our hearts burning within us while he spoke to us on the way and opened the Scriptures to us?" The **Collect** recollects this state of rejoicing in the risen Lord as the return to youthful vigor, owed to a God who has restored the joy of our youth. At the same time, this "renewed youthfulness of spirit" looks ahead to a future time when "we may look forward in confident hope to the rejoicing of the day of resurrection." Therefore, the resurrection of Christ straddles both present and future time, the now and not yet of God's in-breaking of the kingdom. Clearly, the **Prayer over the Gifts** echoes this present/future tension as well, when it reminds the congregation that the gifts of the present will blossom into future treasure: "As you have given her cause for such great gladness, grant also that the gifts we bring may bear fruit in perpetual happiness."

Peter's preaching reveals a confident state of exultation as well, the result of postresurrection time and the pouring of the Holy Spirit upon the disciples in the upper room. His speech to the Jews reminds them of the newness of the event and the "renewed joyfulness of spirit" that now pervades the church. There is much to exult in the resurrection because of God's promise, but that plan will not be brought to complete fulfillment until the end time. At that final eschatological moment, of which Jesus' resurrection is the sign, God's people ask that they "may attain in their flesh the incorruptible glory of the resurrection" (**Prayer after Communion**). Fulfillment and renewal capture Peter's proclamation, as does the happenings at Emmaus. All are *"renovata animae iuventute"*—literally in "renovated spirit of youth"—as they are witnesses to the risen Lord. And indeed, the disciples recounting "how he was made known to them in the breaking of the bread" suggests that this mystery has once again been repeated as a future sign of the resurrection. As we partake of the Lord's Body and Blood, so too the faithful pray to attain in "their flesh" the *"incorruptibilem glorificandae carnis resurrectionem,"* the incorruptible glory of the resurrection.

Strategy for Preaching

If we take our clues for preaching from the Scriptures and *The Roman Missal*, then the homily for the Third Sunday of Easter will be characterized by a joyful, exultant invitation to the assembly to consider "the restored glory of our adoption." With the story of the Road to Emmaus in mind, the major block toward rejoicing in "the day of resurrection" will be the failure to recognize the presence of the risen Lord. To this end, the preacher follows Jesus' lead by taking the congregation on a journey to see his presence in the Scriptures and the breaking of bread.

How? I think we need to deal with the condition of the disciples as they first encounter this stranger on the road to Emmaus and remember that they are dejected, disappointed, and disillusioned about "all the things that had occurred." With the announcement of the empty tomb, they await an interpretation and so does the congregation. If Jesus says that the disciples he encounters were "slow of heart to believe all that the prophets spoke," then the homily should cast itself along the lines of a retelling of God's plan and fulfillment. This requires, as we might guess, some knowledge of the Hebrew Scriptures, particularly of Moses and the prophets. I am thinking of how the preacher might effectively use Moses as a kind of image of the deliverer, together with the Servant Songs in Isaiah, passages from Jeremiah, Ezekiel, and some of the Minor Prophets. Some, or some combination of these prophetic figures, begin to stitch together a grand narrative or a miniature portrait of salvation history. This strategy, of course, is not only part of Jesus' explication in Luke but also present with Peter's address to the Jews in Acts, where he preaches the Christ who was "delivered up by the set plan and foreknowledge of God." The preacher should seize a self-understanding as one who weaves a tapestry of salvation history leading up to Christ's victory over death.

The gospel also points us to the crucial link between the presence of the risen Lord and the breaking of bread, a eucharistic moment that no preacher should miss. A homiletic core idea might face the congregation directly with the mystery of the Eucharist as the site for the baptized to "renew by eternal mysteries" their own ongoing conversion in the context of Jesus, newly raised up. There is a lot of recognition to be made available here to be sure. Consider an example that would name the demon of dejection and lack of zeal, and then name the grace that could be intuited with the eyes of faith in the Eucharistic Lord. The road to Emmaus is the pathway to insight, to faith, and to love; it should bring the baptized assembly into a mystagogical threshold where they are able to reflect in gratitude on the gift of the Eucharist as a disclosure *par excellence* of Christ to his church. That divine revelation in the eucharistic mystery ought to be explained as the graced reality of Christ's sacramental person in the Scriptures, the assembly of the baptized, the presider, and the elements themselves. In the end, the homily should target for a congregation who have their eyes opened, and move into mission with "their hearts burning" within them.

Fourth Sunday of Easter

Readings from the Ambo

Acts 2:14a, 36-41; Ps 23:1-3a, 3b-4, 5, 6;
1 Pet 2:20b-25; John 10:1-10

As he is represented in Acts, Peter was clearly bold and productive, especially when it came to preaching about the risen Lord. In a sense, there is an echo of John the Baptist in Peter's call for repentance and baptism. The difference now in postresurrection time, of course, is that all are baptized for the forgiveness of sins, *"epi to onomati Iesou Christou"*—in the name of Jesus Christ. With this baptism remains the promise of the gift of the Spirit, made possible by Christ's passion, death, and resurrection.

Peter's rhetorical strategy is worth noting. First, he gets his listeners to admit their need, by confronting his congregation with reality of Christ crucified and raised up. Upon hearing this, they were "cut to the heart." Some translate *"katenugesan"* as they were "stabbed" or "pricked" or "pierced" to the heart. In any case, we can be sure that Peter's words were the catalyst for *metanoia,* since those who heard him asked a question about their own conversion: "What are we to do, my brothers?" In a way, this process of conversion brought about by preaching follows closely St. Thomas Aquinas's well-known maxim of *agere sequitur ad esse in actu*: a change in being has led to a move toward action. That movement, according to Peter, is nothing less than repentance and baptism. Lastly, he tells his hearers that they should save themselves "from this corrupt generation." It appears that this last rejoinder was the most difficult to follow, for the implication of "those who accepted this message were baptized" is that there were some who could not accept this challenge and were not baptized. At the same time, though, the number of converts were impressive, "about three thousand persons were added that day."

I think it is important that we see the process of Peter's rhetorical style, since he *parekalei* (or pleads or exhorts) his assembly. Additionally, though, Acts specifically says that Peter spoke *diemarturato* (literally, through witness). The result of the Pentecost event and the outpouring of the Spirit brought about a profound conversion and change in the apostles themselves—the very thing Peter is asking of his listeners. Peter is himself the result of the Spirit's gift and was able to speak *diemarturato*. Peter's speeches in Acts show us his courage (a reversal of the Peter in Luke's gospel who betrayed Jesus), but also the gift of witness and testimony, which is manifested in clear and well-reasoned calls for conversion that cut to the heart.

In contrast to Peter's speech in Acts, 1 Peter is a sublime meditation on how the sheep have returned to the shepherd. Beginning the first verse of chapter 2, the passage in the Second Reading is part of a plea for Christians to "long for pure spiritual milk" in order to achieve salvation. The author gives them models and metaphors throughout—be like "living stones" being built into a "spiritual house" (5); they are to consider themselves a "chosen race, a royal priesthood, a holy nation, a people of his own," since they were called "out of darkness into his wonderful light" (9). But the crown of the chapter remains a reflection on long-suffering with Jesus as the model for this endurance. In some sense, this meditation is an extension of the Servant Song of Isaiah (52:1-12), in which the Christian community has now appropriated the Servant of the Lord depicted in the Hebrew Scriptures as the one who brings about atonement in God's new order. It is notable that the shepherd is used as the Servant who gathers the sheep to himself.

That metaphor of the shepherd becomes the guiding image for Jesus in the gospel. Jesus' understanding of the role of the shepherd tells us something about how the Lord conceives of his relationship with his disciples. His followers have an intimate bond with the master, and the shepherd will be very zealous to guard his flock from those who attempt to steal them away. Interestingly, the passage is also a response to the Pharisees who play a major role in the episode of the man born blind, where Jesus confronts these Jewish leaders concerning their own blindness. Now he speaks metaphorically about another kind of blindness—those who deceive the sheep. Jesus shifts the axis on this encounter, however, by deploying another sense to talk about these kinds of relationships: hearing. The sheep are keenly aware of the voice of the shepherd and, so it seems, are less capable of being deceived or being blinded. These strange frauds may try to call out to the sheep, but they will not follow. Interpreting his own history, Jesus says "I am the gate for the sheep. / All who came before me are thieves and robbers, / but the sheep did not listen to them."

Connecting the Bible and the Liturgy

The **Collect** makes an important connection with the dominant imagery used in the readings for this Fourth Sunday of Easter: "Almighty ever-living God, lead us to share in the joys of heaven, so that the humble flock may reach where the brave Shepherd has gone before." The prayer suggests a gathering that will occur when the "humble flock" reaches where the "brave Shepherd has gone before." This is a kind of cosmic collecting of the sheep at the end time (perhaps recalling the judgment that casts sheep on the left and goats on the right in Matt 25:31-46). The Shepherd is there as both a model and one to follow.

At the same time, the **Alternative Opening Prayer** in the *Sacramentary* makes a much more pastoral link with John 10:1-10, by associating the voice of the Shepherd as an ongoing experience of Christian life: "Attune our minds to the sound of his voice, lead our steps in the path he has shown, that we may know the strength of his outstretched arm and enjoy the light of your presence forever." This (former) alternative to the opening prayer allows for an ongoing movement of the people of God here on earth but clearly motions the faithful toward the promise of eternal life as well. I should point out that the *Sacramentary* makes no attempt to make explicit that the congregation is to be associated with sheep; it is as if the Shepherd functions to guide people without the (perhaps derogatory) associations of being referred to as sheep. In fact, the **Opening Prayer** in the *Sacramentary* itself asks God to "give us new strength from the courage of Christ our shepherd," but says nothing of the role that the congregation plays as a "humble flock." The Latin is *"humilitas gregis,"* which probably does mean humble flock but can also mean a humble gathering of the generic sort of people with common interests, such as a eucharistic assembly gathered for worship. It is probably the latter the *Sacramentary* has in mind when it closes the **Collect** with a petition to "lead us to join the saints in heaven." In the end, the earlier translation is attempting to make contemporary an agrarian image that may not mean much to a contemporary culture; it chooses rather to see this apocalyptic gathering more as a reunion with the blessed than as a collection of sheep, a humble flock. That said, the new *Roman Missal* is simply picking up on a common metaphor used not only by Jesus but in ecclesiastical artwork, popular representations of Jesus dating from antiquity and, of course, the testimony of both the Hebrew and Christian Scriptures. Many of these images, unfortunately, have been romanticized and sentimentalized over the years. But in the last analysis, while the contemporary hearer may be able to translate the shepherd/sheep image, the real task will be to own it; that will be left to the task of preaching.

Strategy for Preaching

The core homiletic idea this Sunday might focus itself on how precisely to capture a crucial biblical image and make it contemporary; this process would allow the community to unpack the biblical realities and implications of being in relation with the Shepherd and consider its consequences. I take it that making the Shepherd image new was very much in the minds of those who translated the *Sacramentary*; the preacher will face the same issue: does the "Shepherd" and the "flock" theme speak directly to the hearts and minds of the hearer? And if not, what are ways to make these important images resonate with the congregation? After all, Jesus was using figurative language deployed to seize the religious imagination of his followers. What can the preachers who follow in his steps do to unearth a similar metaphoric tactic, where the Servant leader has sacrificed himself for those in his care?

First Peter may offer some clues to understanding Jesus' own role as Shepherd. The author of that epistle sees the shepherd as one who sacrifices his life for the flock and is the "guardian" of souls. At this point, the preacher might raise a salient issue: what does it take to lay down one's life for another? I suggest that this might be the opening line of the homily. In other words, what we are really asking the congregation is not so much about translating a metaphor but the more basic questions concerning the origins of altruism. Why does a soldier throw himself on a grenade for his troop? Why does a mother risk her health to attend to a child with a contagious disease? Why does a teacher work long hours will little pay for her students? These are contemporary shepherds. They are also gateways, in exactly the way Jesus describes his own role, into "pasture," or "to settle in eternal pastures the sheep you have redeemed" (**Prayer after Communion**), places of refreshment and sustenance. These shepherds are not only gates; they are windows into the great Gate himself, the Good Shepherd, who laid down his life for his sheep.

The invitation here, it seems to me, is to be both sheep and shepherd, which can be shored up as a homiletic core idea. On the one hand, the congregation is invited to see the great gift of the Shepherd given over for the salvation of many. At the same time, the congregation is also challenged to see its own role as shepherd guiding fellow members of the Christian community. Finally, we ought not to forget that Jesus has meant his figurative discourse in John 10:1-10 not only as a reassurance to the community who hears his voice but as a confrontation to the religious leadership who misleads the sheep. The use of the voice as the authentic indicator of Jesus' presence serves as a reminder that the people of God must be aware of false signals and empty promises from the powers who continually bait them away from their relationship with Christ. The preacher might consider viewing Elia Kazan's *A Face in the Crowd* (1957) or Sidney Lumet's *Network* (1976), both of which tackle false shepherds in the media.

Fifth Sunday of Easter

Readings from the Ambo
Acts 6:1-7; Ps 33:1-2, 4-5, 18-19; 1 Pet 2:4-9; John 14:1-12

Diversity has its complications, even in the early church. Although the portrait from Acts of the disciples in action is rather far from the utopic blueprint mapped out in chapter 2 after the descent of the Holy Spirit, the process of handling disruption and disagreement still reveals the legacy and work of the Spirit, an altogether important feature in the book of Acts as a whole. The dispute here seems to involve the proper handling of ministries, particularly in regard to the potential neglect of widows, the *almanah*, a venerable state in biblical literature that can be traced to early antiquity. In fact, ministry to widows in the emerging church appears precisely at this time due, at least in part, to the conflict depicted in Acts around the Hebrew Christians and their Greek counterparts. This portion of Acts, then, addresses a crucial feature of how the early church will care for the *anawim*, the poor ones identified as widows, orphans, and strangers in the Hebrew Scriptures; they are the ones the Lukan Jesus calls "blessed."

We might consider the way in which the conflict begins and how it is resolved. The riff is cultural and social, with a long legacy of religious affiliation stemming from ancient Hebrew and Greek origins to complicate the issue. We do not really see how the particulars of this conflict are resolved, except that there is a problem at the table, since the widows "were being neglected in the daily distribution." But we are given some insight into how such conflict is reconciled. "So the Twelve called together the community of the disciples together and said, / 'It is not right for us to neglect the word of God to serve at table.'" I think the author of Luke-Acts renders a vital insight into

129

administration that is guided by the Spirit: consensus occurs when the community is gathered for consultation. Others have followed the lead in this collegial process. In his Rule for monks, St. Benedict will advise the abbot to ask the whole community for counsel, including the youngest member as well as the guest. The impulse for monastic life would come from the spirit of collaboration and common ownership present in Acts, as well as its way of governance. The decision to appoint "seven reputable men" is neither arbitrary nor autocratic, but driven by a proposal that was "acceptable to the whole community." This implication at the end of this section—that the "word of God continued to spread"—is that good order allows for the Word to move among the people, so that "the disciples in Jerusalem increased greatly."

Given the seminal reality and importance of diversity that faced the early Christian community, 1 Peter deploys a powerful metaphor in order to create a locus for equanimity of vision and action: "Come to him, a living stone, rejected by human beings / but chosen and precious in the sight of God." The author strikes at the foundation that most often troubles a community of believers: the site of its worship. With the temple playing such a vital role in the history of Israel, the author subverts this physical and temporal reality (the temple was already destroyed, of course, by 70 AD, making this image in 1 Peter even more applicable) with one that is spiritual and invisible. There is an interesting wordplay going on with the use of the stone: it is first laid as an *akrogoniaios* (chief corner) by God in Zion but then rejected by builders, only to become the cornerstone by which those who rejected him fall; they become the *hoi proskoptousin*, the ones who stumble. Fittingly, the author invites all to come to this *lithon zonta*, or a "living stone" in order to participate in another kind of site for worship, where all who believe will become a "royal priesthood, / a holy nation, a people of his own."

Jesus himself is no stranger to metaphorical restructuring, as he applies an architectural image to speak of the Father's house. These are the "dwelling places" (the Greek is simply "rooms" or *monai*), which Jesus refers to as a home to which he himself will attend. This is a comforting and domestic image and will receive commentary over later centuries by the likes of St. Teresa of Jesus who speaks of yet another kind of building, an *"El Castillo Interior,"* an "Interior Castle," a kind of subdivision of prayer on the journey to God. More to the point, however, Jesus begins to speak in chapter 14 of his departure from earthly existence but insists on carrying on a relationship with his disciples after he is gone. This is a very reassuring passage because of the promise of a relationship not only with Christ but with the Father who sent him and, as we will see in the second portion of this text, with the Spirit who is to come.

Connecting the Bible and the Liturgy

We know that a key characteristic in the Johannine text is to disclose Jesus' Sonship with the Father and, in turn, our relationship with him. Christ's disclosure here is one of several such revelations in the Gospel of John, of course, but Jesus' explicit use of an *"ego eimi"* statement (exclusive with the Fourth Gospel) underlines the trinitarian truth of his origins and his connection with those he loves. "I am the way and the truth and the life. / No one comes to the Father except through me." The access we have to the Father, then, is achieved by Christ himself and his work of redemption. "Whoever believes in me will do the works that I do, and will do greater ones than these, because I am going to the Father." Indeed, the **Collect** prays that this ongoing work of the paschal mystery continues its effect on us, explicitly those who have been baptized. "Almighty ever-living God, constantly accomplish the Paschal Mystery within us, that those you were pleased to make new in Holy Baptism may, under your protective care, bear much fruit and come to the joys of life eternal."

It is worth mentioning at this point that the **Collect** implies a work that is in process. The Latin verb that is used in this instance to describe this ongoing work is *perficere*, which means to bring to a proper end or to complete or "constantly accomplish." It can mean to bring to perfection, which is something of a consequence not only of the sacrament itself but of being made new (*renovare*) in its saving waters. So the prayer here is that almighty God will bring to perfection or accomplish the paschal mystery begun in baptism so that those newly born will "bear much fruit" or *"multos fructus afferent."* This image of bearing fruit is itself one that suggests a process of *perfectum*, with God tending his own in baptism with "protective care."

The paschal mystery that is constantly being accomplished or perfected within the baptized is echoed in Jesus' testimony to the

Father before his disciples. When he says that "I am in the Father and the Father is in me," he is acknowledging the Father acting to bring the paschal mystery to its fulfillment to those who are "through him, in him and with him in the unity of the Holy Spirit." Hence, the **Prayer over the Offerings** proclaims the God "who by the wonderful exchange effected in this sacrifice have made us partakers of the one supreme Godhead." With God accomplishing in us the work begun in baptism, then, in the words of 1 Peter, we become "a chosen race, a royal priesthood, a holy nation, a people of his own."

Strategy for Preaching

There are a number of useful images to occupy the homiletic process, some of them quite countercultural. Beginning with 1 Peter, the reading is really a dismantling of the way in which we think that our social identity—both individual and corporate—is established. The author's intention cuts to the heart of a culture and a people that build, need to institutionalize a fixed order, and rigidly nationalize its borders. If we are to take the author of this important text at his word, then the only cornerstone is an interior one, consecrated by God in Christ. That is where the Christian faithful builds its dwelling, the "mansions," which Jesus himself redesigns not as human palaces and showplaces, but of eternal resting places with him. If we intend to preach to the baptized assembly about a paschal mystery "constantly accomplished" within us, then the homily will necessarily concern itself with the congregation's cooperation with God's work to make the faithful "bear much fruit."

The homiletic core idea might challenge the assembly on their ability to live out their baptismal commitment. If the baptized are to allow the paschal mystery to unfold within them, how are they cooperating with God's grace to see this process to its proper end, that is, to "come to the joys of life eternal"? I think that the preacher should acknowledge the reality of discipleship as a site of potential confusion, witnessed by Jesus' encounter with Philip, who asks to see the Father. "Have I been with you for so long a time and you still do not know me?" The same question could be asked of all those who have been baptized, since we are all in the process of understanding Jesus' work within us and how that is disclosing the Father through the work of the Holy Spirit. It stands to reason that the neophytes who have been recently baptized at the Easter Vigil ought to be brought into this discourse; they should be encouraged, together with the congregation who have long lived out a witness to their baptism.

A caution prevails: do not let the intense theological language of the gospel become translated into an abstract homily. Examples or stories where we miss the presence of the Lord, but are then brought to recognition, will prevail upon the congregation as a common experience. The trajectory of the homily should head toward this: how can we best allow God to continue to call us out of darkness into his wonderful light; that means conversion into "a people of his own"? Open your favorite news source in either a paper or cyberspace, take a walk in the city, or read a blog; there is always a miracle a day within our grasp.

Sixth Sunday of Easter

Readings from the Ambo

Acts 8:5-8, 14-17; Ps 66:1-3, 4-5, 6-7, 16, 20;
1 Pet 3:15-18; John 14:15-21

Philip's missionary activity described in the First Reading from Acts places him in Samaria, and there he "proclaimed the Christ to them." When looked at in the context of the book of Acts as a whole, Philip's missionary activity in Samaria occurs shortly after the death of the deacon Stephen and before Paul's conversion on the way to Damascus. From Samaria Philip will head south and encounter another prospect altogether different than these members of the Abrahamic religion who reckon their religious practices prior to the Babylonian exile: an Ethiopian eunuch, whom Philip converts and baptizes. Finally, Philip preaches to all the towns in that region until he comes to Caesarea. This little episode in the life of the evangelistic life of Philip and the early church may seem somewhat inconsequential to contemporary ears, but the procession of conversions from Samaria to Caesarea discloses the power of the Spirit to effect transformations among non-Jews. It is probably not an accident that Philip's activity leads directly into the episode in Acts dealing with the conversion of Paul himself, the Apostle to the Gentiles. The power of the Spirit does not discriminate and gathers all together in unity and peace.

Apparently, Philip gained a lot of attention in Samaria by means of what he said and the *semeia* (signs) he accomplished there. The Samaritans literally lived an edgy life, with their own temple on Mt. Gerizim, the rival to Jerusalem, and their own cultic practices. They may have been especially vulnerable to magical practices of the kind practiced by Simon (a section eliminated in the Lectionary reading but that fills out Philip's intense missionary activity in Samaria more broadly). Indeed, the collective exorcism described by the narrator when Philip enters Samaria was quite dramatic: "For unclean spirits, crying out in a loud voice, / came out of many possessed people, / and many paralyzed or crippled people were cured." It seems clear that the Spirit's presence has moved rapidly to undo the occult and other undesirable practices that would be incompatible to the Gospel way. When Peter and John arrive on the scene, their prayer intercedes and the Spirit is received.

In the gospel text, Jesus himself intercedes for the Spirit when he announces his departure to the disciples. Christ fulfills a necessary part of his promise by asking the Father to send the Advocate (*parakletos*) "to be with you always." The Son asking the Father for the Spirit in chapter 14 of John's gospel anticipates Jesus' death and resurrection, but liturgically the church awaits the Ascension and the Pentecost event that follows closely thereafter. Finally, Jesus seems to suggest that the coming of the Spirit will help his followers keep his commandments of love. As 1 Peter explains, keeping the love commandments is a process that will "sanctify Christ as Lord" in the hearts of believers. "For it is better to suffer for doing good, / if that be the will of God, than for doing evil." For this, we need the Advocate to help us in our weakness.

Connecting the Bible and the Liturgy

When the **Prayer after Communion** asks God "to pour into our hearts the strength of this saving food," we might well ask: strength for what? Why would our hearts need strength? Jesus holds the key to this question. We are to keep the love commandments, so the Eucharist serves as a food for the Christian community to abide in the charity of Christ, even if it means suffering "for doing good, if that be the will of God, than for doing evil." That means loving as he loved us and praying for the Spirit to intercede for us. The Eucharist keeps us faithful to the love commandments so that "what we relive in remembrance we may always hold to in what we do." This last phrase is a somewhat awkward translation of "*quod recordatione percurrimus semper in opere teneamus.*" I think the point is that the *anamnesis* of the liturgy, the very remembrance of the Lord's Supper, will give us the strength to accomplish the love that this sacrament signifies.

Keeping the commandments of the Lord requires zeal, which often defuses in the years after conversion. Therefore the work of the Spirit becomes crucial precisely as Advocate to help the church in its commitment to the love commandments. The faithful celebration of the Eucharist is a reminder that this Spirit is always with us because, as 1 Peter says, Christ was "put to death in the flesh, he was brought to life in the Spirit." The celebration of the Eucharistic Liturgy itself is an act of change for the congregation, a moment of conversion to a greater zeal to love. The **Prayer over the Offerings** says that "May our prayers rise up to you, O Lord, together with the sacrificial offerings, so that, purified by your graciousness, we may be conformed to the mysteries of your mighty love." As we remember the death and resurrection of the Lord in the Eucharist, we are purified by God's "graciousness," which conforms us to the mysteries of the Lord's own love. These are powerful reminders to the baptized that the work of "putting on Christ" is accomplished not once but over and over again as we "sanctify Christ as Lord" in our hearts.

Strategy for Preaching

It dawns on very few people that love could possibly be a commandment. Yet Jesus' teaching is very clear: "whoever has my commandments and observes them is the one who loves me." In a very real sense, this injunction could not be more appropriate to the baptized assembly who have put on Christ as a garment and strive day after day to live out their commitment. The zeal for the love commandments will yield an outpouring of the Spirit, the discovery of the love of the Father, and the revelation of the Son.

One way to approach a core homiletic idea is to begin with an examination of how romantic love is constructed in our culture and then go on to contrast the difficult baptismal task of loving our neighbor. This window into romantic love might unveil a variety of popular culture trends from music (rock, blues, or country) to contemporary television and cinema. One thing seems absolutely clear: the "selling of love," no matter what the story, is an affair of the heart; the merchants of love rely on an unreflective consumer to purchase the emotional, feel-good quality that "being in love" promises.

But Jesus makes this love a commandment, an indication that love cannot be as easy as we think—or rather, feel. It takes an act of will to love. By God's grace in the Spirit the heart will cooperate with our wills. Jesus' mandate is that our love for him will emerge to the extent we are able to love one another, and that may mean not particularly liking one another either. The Holy Spirit will help us along the way.

At this point, it seems to me that it would be very useful to consider teasing out the meaning of *parakletos*—Helper, Advocate, Consoler—all of these identities of the Holy Spirit come to the aid of those who actively will to love for the sake of Christ. Facing the congregation with the gaping holes of lackluster love in their lives will put flesh on this challenge; it will require some imaginative visualization of the assembly to get them to see their own wounded wills. John and his sister Helen have not spoken for ten years because when their mother was dying, John was not as present to this difficult situation as he might have been; Bill still blames his father for walking out on his family five years ago and can barely tolerate a conversation with his parent; Cindy betrayed a confidence and now her closest friend, Marcia, will not forgive her. These are broken love commandments, but they can be healed. For this homily to be effective, the examples should be concrete and real enough to imagine. They are named for the community for what they truly are: failures to love one another and Christ. Having named the demon, the preacher can go on to name grace—the healing of the Spirit that moves us toward our relationship with Christ and the Father, even as we will to love. We are encouraged by the sharing of the Eucharist with one another, broken people made whole in the Lord, as we beg that God will "pour into our hearts the strength of this saving food." A resource for preaching might be Blessed Mother Teresa's posthumous autobiography, *Come Be My Light* (2009), in which she accounts for decades of dryness and the courage to love even in the darkness.

The Ascension of the Lord

Readings from the Ambo

Acts 1:1-11; Ps 47:2-3, 6-7, 8-9; Eph 1:17-23; Matt 28:16-20

Luke's address to Theophilus, who was probably a catechumen at the time of the present writing in Acts, begins with a recapitulation of the gospel concerning Jesus Christ and then transitions to his ascension into heaven. This last sequence gives us a close-up and protracted view of the last moments of the Lord's life on earth before "a cloud took him from their sight." Jesus' departure leaves his disciples with a poignant sense of loss and unanswered questions. When will the promise of the Holy Spirit be fulfilled? Will Jesus restore the kingdom of Israel and at what time? When will Jesus come again? We are left with a dominant image of the somewhat dumbfounded disciples "looking intently at the sky as he was going." But we are given a sign of hope in the form of two men who witness to a larger reality. These two individuals are highly reminiscent of the episode of the resurrection in Luke 24:4 when the disciples were puzzling over the empty tomb when *"duo epestesan autais en estheti astraptouse"* (two men dressed in shining clothes stood before them). I read these two men as both interpreters and signs of hope attesting to the same reality: that Christ has been raised up and transcended sin and death. So they face the shocked disciples with what appears to be common sense questions about the reality of faith: "Why do you seek the living one among the dead" (Luke 24:5) and now its companion text: "why are you standing there looking at the sky? / This Jesus who has been taken up from you into heaven / will return in the same way as you have seen him going into heaven."

On the Solemnity of the Ascension, the beginning of the book of Acts places the contemporary Christian community inside a promise from both Jesus himself and the men who testified to his resurrection and ascension. From Luke's perspective, the witness to the ascension positions the disciples to await the coming of the Spirit in chapter 2. Like those early disciples, the Christian community awaits the return of the Lord, having been promised that the Holy Spirit will come with a baptism greater than John the Baptist. Meanwhile, the congregation celebrates the joy of Christ's return to the Father with the Responsorial Psalm, "God reigns over the nations, God sits upon his holy thrown." The eucharistic assembly waits in anticipation for the coming of the Spirit, all the while longing for Christ's return. Still we remember God's triumph this day over sin and death in a rule that has already begun.

Not surprisingly, Paul's letter to the Ephesians expresses supreme confidence over Christ's victory. The passage in the Second Reading exemplifies an exultation characteristic of the assembly's response to Christ's victory; it is a reveling over "the surpassing greatness of his power / for us who believe." Christ has been granted authority by God "as head over all things to the church, / which is his body, / the fullness of the one who fills all things in every way."

Matthew concludes his gospel even as Luke begins Acts. Jesus gives his final instructions to the disciples, while proclaiming his authority over heaven and earth. In contrast to Luke's picture of Jesus' departure from earthly existence, however, Matthew's Jesus commissions his disciples into mission and the steadfast command to "make disciples of all nations, / baptizing them in the name of the Father, / and of the Son, and of the Holy Spirit." Despite the doubts, he tells the disciples that he is with them "always, until the end of the age." That divine presence will become clearer in Acts with the coming of the Holy Spirit, mentioned close to eighty times in that book.

Connecting the Bible and the Liturgy

The **Collect** for the Vigil Mass is a direct reflection from Luke's account of the ascension in Acts: "O God, whose Son today ascended to the heavens as the Apostles looked on, grant, we pray, that, in accordance with his promise, we may be worthy for him to live with us always on earth, and we with him in heaven." The prayer places the congregation alongside the bewildered disciples who "are standing there looking at the sky," but it also expresses the hope that "we may be worthy for him to live with us always on earth." That is the promise of the two men who gave the disciples the assurance that "This Jesus who has been taken up from you into heaven will return in the same way as you have seen him going into heaven." **Preface I of the Ascension of the Lord** expands the horizon of those who view Jesus' journey to the Father when it also includes the members of the heavenly host: "for the Lord Jesus, the King of glory, conqueror of sin and death, ascended to the highest heavens, as the Angels gazed in wonder." The liturgy wishes to express the state of ecstatic joy that encompasses not only earth but also heaven; it is a call for the Eucharistic Liturgy to reflect, as always, a divine reality, drawing in humanity and angels in common joy. Therefore, *"profusis paschalibus gaudiis,"* which *The Roman Missal* nicely translates as "overcome with paschal joy," all the earth praises God, "every land, every people exults in your praise and even the heavenly Powers, with the angelic hosts, sing together the unending hymn of your glory."

The presidential prayers for this solemnity help to fill in what has been occluded for contemporary Christians in the Lectionary readings. From a doctrinal stand point, we know that after the ascension Jesus was seated at the right hand of the Father and intercedes for the world. The **Prayer over the Offerings** expresses this dogmatic reality and is the logical outcome of the **Collect** itself: "O God, whose Only Begotten son, our High Priest is seated ever-living at your right hand to intercede for us, grant that we may approach with confidence the throne of grace and there obtain your mercy." Similarly, **Preface I of the Ascension of the Lord** underlines the doctrinal belief in the intercessory power of the ascended Lord when it says that "Mediator between God and man, judge of the world and Lord of hosts, he ascended, not to distance himself from our lowly state but that we, his members, might be confident of following where he, our head and Founder, has gone before." Moreover, the **Preface** suggests that where Jesus has gone, the disciples will follow likewise. From the perspective of the church living and active in the world, then, Jesus has taken up our earthly reality into himself, leaving us not alone, but striving for heaven with his help to move on toward mission, "baptizing in the name of the Father and of the Son and of the Holy Spirit." The **Prayer after Communion** petitions God that "the gifts we have received from your altar, Lord, kindle in our hearts a longing for the heavenly homeland and cause us to press forward, following in the Savior's footsteps, to the place where for our sake he entered before us." Thus the eucharistic meal becomes yet again the manifestation and source of divine strength.

Strategy for Preaching

The good news about the Solemnity of the Ascension is that this occasion allows for some very important doctrinal input that is very germane to Catholic catechetical teaching. The more difficult news is that this doctrine of the ascension of Christ to the right hand of the Father is quite abstract and tough to visualize. Some years ago, a young man in a catechism class I was observing asked the following question: "So what is Jesus doing right now after he ascended into heaven?" Young people can be very pragmatic but often ask what others are thinking and doing—even Jesus! We might take our preaching clues from Luke's address to Theophilus in which the author accounts a brief retelling of the work of God in Christ leading up to the promise of the coming of the Holy Spirit at Pentecost. So the homiletic core idea for this solemnity might center on the work of Christ, the intercessory power owed to him as Redeemer and the promise of the Holy Spirit who is to come.

As we enlist the help from *The Catechism of the Catholic Church* (article 6: "he ascended into heaven and is seated at the right hand of the Father," 659–67) we will want to keep the following questions in mind in order embody the homiletic core idea: What exactly did Jesus come to do and to what has he returned? What are the consequences of the ascension, particularly the coming of the Spirit? How is Christ's work continuing to flourish here on earth?

In order to make these very visual, I suggest three panels to sketch out as part of a triptych that might lead the congregation through these doctrinal questions:

1. The cross: the place of reconciliation and the work that is accomplished
2. The resurrection and ascension: the triumph over sin and death and the promise of the Spirit
3. The place Jesus has at the right hand of the Father: the intercessory power of Christ who now has returned victorious

If the listening assembly is allowed to picture these visualizations sequentially, then I think the process of the homily would do its work in forming the congregation by the Word.

Seventh Sunday of Easter

Readings from the Ambo

Acts 1:12-14; Ps 27:1, 4, 7-8; 1 Pet 4:13-16; John 17:1-11a

As befits the Sunday poised between the Ascension and Pentecost (in some dioceses in the United States the Ascension of the Lord occurs on a Thursday), the Seventh Sunday of Easter is a transitional feast, with appropriate texts to support the church's vigil for the great Solemnity of Pentecost. To this end, the First Reading asks the pragmatic question: what did the disciples of the Lord do after his return to the Father? This selection from Acts sets them—and the worshiping assembly—in place to receive the Spirit.

When it comes to the aftermath of the ascension, we are given answers to some of our lingering wonderments, and these questions begin to crystallize around the church's origins. What did the disciples do, and where did they go? They prayed together, having gathered to the Upper Room from Mount Olivet, the place from which the Messiah was to enter Jerusalem, according to Zechariah (14:4). The Mount of Olives, of course, is the site in Luke's gospel of Jesus' anguished prayer to accept God's divine will (Luke 22:39-46) and betrayal (vv. 47-53). It would seem that we might conclude something about the movement from Mount Olivet to the Upper Room: the former has been transformed from a place of expectation of a conquering messiah to an arena of vigil for the promised Spirit. Indeed, the disciples now return to day-to-day living, *"proskarterountes homothumadon,"* or devoting themselves to prayer with a single mind together. It is notable that the cast of characters includes all those who were chosen in Luke 6:14-16, with one notable exception, Judas Iscariot. The eleven will choose his replacement, Matthias, by the end of chapter 1. This last piece of information, dealing with the symbolic reconstitution of the original group of disciples called by Jesus, suggests that it was possible to rekindle a kind of sanctified regrouping in the earliest days of the church, a change that meant adding one disciple to the original Twelve by virtue of his witness to the resurrection together with the rest. The historical Jesus has returned to the Father, but the charism that lingers invigorates his followers.

First Peter 4:13-16 has a quality of vigil about it, undoubtedly meant as an encouragement to its original hearers to bear suffering for the sake of Christ. In a sense, the author is lending a mystical quality to the everyday work of being a Christian. And this participation in the suffering of Christ is not only a matter of holding out until the end, but characterized by its opening word in this translation: *Chairete* (rejoice) "to the extent that you share in the sufferings of Christ." The last portion of the gospel is particularly applicable to this participation in Christ's suffering and suggests in theological, trinitarian grounding. As Jesus addresses the Father, he says, "I pray for them. / I do not pray for the world but for the ones you have given me, / because they are yours, and everything of mine is yours / and everything of yours is mine, / and I have been glorified in them." Jesus' glorification of the Father in his own suffering will allow for those who have been given him to be also raised up into glory. The author of 1 Peter echoes this promise when he says that "whoever is made to suffer as a Christian should not be ashamed / but glorify God because of the name." The work of Christ's suffering is ongoing in his members. The collective members of the disciples participate in Christ's work, just as in Acts we see his disciples carrying on his leadership by reestablishing the Twelve by grace.

Connecting the Bible and the Liturgy

The biblical selections for the Seventh Sunday of Easter make it clear that in the days after the ascension, Christ was made manifest in the reorganization of the apostles and disciples who awaited the coming of the Spirit. They lived by his promise and the practical realities of keeping vigil as they "devoted themselves with one accord to prayer." The **Collect** positions the contemporary church as the bringer of supplications where all of us, as it were, are gathered in a room together awaiting the Spirit. "Graciously hear our supplications,

O Lord," the **Collect** reminds us. As we await the Spirit, we also ask that we may experience "*manere nobiscum*," or what *The Roman Missal* translates as "his abiding presence." The prayer of the church today is a mirror of those poised between Mount Olivet and the place of Pentecost.

The **Collect** also contains an affirmation of belief, as well as "supplications." We "believe that the Savior of the human race is with you in your glory." This very act of faith locates us at the center of the work of Christ, offering himself to the Father in glory, because as Jesus says in the gospel when addressing the Father, "the words you gave to me I have given to them, and they accepted them and truly understood that I came from you, and they have believed that you sent me." From a liturgical point of view, this Seventh Sunday of Easter grants us the possibility for further reflection on the ascension of the Lord, since now we are contemplating his glory. Jesus himself testifies to this reality when he says in the gospel, "And now I will no longer be in the world, but they are in the world, while I am coming to you." Therefore the church asks to participate not only in the sufferings of Christ but also to be taken up with him into *caelestem gloriam*, the glory of heaven. Consequently, the **Prayer of the Offerings** prays with "acts of devotedness" of the kind we might associate with those who wait in fervent hope and with devoted prayer, along with "Mary the mother of Jesus, and his brothers." The church is humble yet confident that the celebration of the Eucharist is the site in which "through these sacred mysteries there will be accomplished in the body of the whole Church what has already come to pass in Christ her Head."

Strategy for Preaching

The First Reading is a reminder to the contemporary church of the realities of everyday church life: filled with longing, anticipation, and waiting for the Spirit. In the days of the emerging church, as in our own, we are devoted "with one accord to prayer." So from the liturgical perspective of the church at the edge of Pentecost, we ought to examine how single-minded we are in our prayer. Related to this consideration is another question: how does this spirituality find itself in harmony with our brothers and sisters? We are all gathered to bring our "supplications" to the altar, which gathers the whole human race into the person of Christ Jesus, the Savior.

A core homiletic idea might concentrate on provoking the congregation to think about the way it is keeping vigil for the Pentecost event, bearing in mind the watchfulness of heart and community of spirit that informs Christian prayer. This homiletic core can be accomplished by specific references to the liturgy, Scripture, and secular history.

Generally speaking, average churchgoers are not really social activists, but the model of such community-minded gatherings literally captures the Spirit of the days before Pentecost. The preacher might begin (for example, using **Eucharistic Prayer III**) with a look at how the Spirit is invoked twice during the liturgy during the epiclesis: it is a single-minded and communal petition to God to "graciously make holy these gifts we have brought to you for consecration." And then again on the assembly, the presider asks that "we, who are nourished by the Body and Blood of your Son and filled with his Holy Spirit, may become one body, one spirit in Christ." Is the hearer aware of these moments of sanctification? The desire for the Spirit to come down on the gifts we offer and on those gathered illustrates the point that the Spirit itself gives us the momentum to be watchful and communal as we celebrate the Eucharist and as we wait for the Spirit. Anticipating the Spirit's action during the liturgy is a foretaste of what is to come with Pentecost, a visualization of the great occasion to come by witnessing the sacrament in graced action. This vigil fills out the action presented to us in Acts, which should be teased out in order to understand the implications of the witness of discipleship to prayer and waiting for the Lord to come in the Spirit.

A practical illustration for today's homily, then, might be something like the civil rights movement in which many gathered to invoke the Spirit of justice for racial equality during the 1960s. It is true that all those gathered in Atlanta, or Washington, or Montgomery and throughout the country to support equal rights for African-Americans did not all share the same faith, but they were guided by a single purpose: God's justice of fairness and equal rights under the law. They awaited the Spirit of justice. In a similar way, every parish and every person in that parish allows the Spirit of God to penetrate his or her deepest self: this is the humanity that Christ is drawing to himself while he awaits the cross and God's glory. Indeed the very call to become one with Christ cannot be separated from the love command to love and to pray, then, with one accord. With the heart of the Savior, then, the church longs for the Spirit of reconciliation and peace to be brought into unity. It is a prayer for a communal epiclesis that extends beyond the walls of the Eucharistic Liturgy and carries into the world. It is also an invitation to understand the work of the Spirit and the imperative link that exists for the disciple who prays for the indwelling of Christ's presence.

Pentecost Sunday
Mass during the Day

Readings from the Ambo

Acts 2:1-11; 1 Cor 12:3b-7, 12-13; John 20:19-23

Pentecost was originally a celebration of the harvest, but the exuberant event in Acts is occasioned by the fulfillment of Jesus' promise of the Spirit and the birth of the church. The scene in the First Reading presents a notable contrast with the coming of the Holy Spirit in John 20:22, when Jesus bestows the Spirit personally on his disciples on the evening of the first day of the week, the day of the resurrection. Luke makes the dramatic coming of the Spirit a more protracted experience as the disciples are gathered in one place and in prayerful vigil. In contrast to Luke's understanding of the Spirit's encounter with the disciples, John makes the Spirit a direct consequence of the encounter with the risen Jesus. Another point of divergence: the disciples in Luke are keeping vigil and watch for the Spirit while the disciples in John are hiding because of fear. Their timidity only underlines the transformative effect the risen Lord has on them as the one who brings peace, reconciliation when he "breathed on them and said to them, / 'Receive the Holy Spirit.' The Johannine passage most obviously becomes the expression of the life of the Trinity. As the Father has sent Jesus into the world, so also does that same Lord breathe the Spirit on his disciples, sending them forth into mission.

There are a plurality of interpretations available to us here, but I read the Pentecost moment in Acts with at least three characteristics in mind. First, the "strong driving wind" that manifests the Spirit is an echo of God's presence in the Hebrew Scriptures, notably the first creation account in Genesis when "a mighty wind swept over the waters" (1:2 NAB). The parallel between the two texts suggests that the

147

scene in Acts is meant to be viewed as an instance of a new creation, the church. Secondly, the descent of the Spirit on the disciples harkens back to the beginning of Luke's gospel with the announcement of the birth of John the Baptist and the annunciation of the birth of Jesus to Mary: both events are marked by the Spirit's role in breaking silence and articulating the newness of speech. Indeed, Mary's encounter with the Spirit in Luke 1:26ff. becomes a kind of bookend with Pentecost at the beginning of Acts, since it is that same mighty wind that has been made manifest in both occasions. What God has brought into existence with the Word has been brought to its fruition. Thirdly, with the disciples' activity after Pentecost, Luke is able to show the consequences of the Spirit's action in the world, a global infusion that reverses the tower of Babel in Genesis 11:1-9. We have moved from the communities of the earth being scattered to their reunification by the Spirit in their very diversity. The nations who might well be at odds with each other hear in their own tongues of "the mighty acts of God."

Those same nations are symbolic representatives of all who experience divisiveness, the kind of fragmentation about which Paul was quite familiar in his relationship to the Corinthians. He advises them of the reality of the Spirit's unifying principle in articulating the very basis of faith in the Lord: "No one can say, 'Jesus is Lord,' except by the Holy Spirit." At the same time, Paul encourages diversity under this unity, defining the community's relationship with one another through his famous analogy of the body: "As a body is one though it has many parts, / and all the parts of the body, though many are one body, / so also Christ." Paul is underlining what will become a creedal principle of "one baptism," the fountain in which "we were all given to drink of one Spirit."

Connecting the Bible and the Liturgy

With numerous texts for Pentecost Sunday now in *The Roman Missal*, including the presidential prayers for the Vigil Mass in an extended as well as simple form, together with the texts for the Mass for the Day, there is an abundant opportunity to find parallels between Scripture and the Mass for the Day on this splendid solemnity. In this regard, what comes to mind immediately is the series of prayers that follow the readings (proposed as options for the Lectionary) for the Vigil Mass in its extended form. At the beginning of the liturgy, the presider reminds the people of the vigil that the congregation shares "after the example of the Apostles and disciples, who with Mary, the Mother of Jesus, persevered in prayer, awaiting the Spirit promised by the Lord": this clearly prepares the assembly for the First Reading from Acts: 2:1-11 to be active participants in the coming of the Spirit. Moreover, the address calls to mind the importance of Scripture in recalling in sacred memory the works of the Lord: "Let us meditate on how many great deeds God in times past did for his people and let us pray that the Holy Spirit whom the Father sent as the first fruits of those who believe, may bring to perfection his work in the world."

The character of this vigil as well as the Mass of the Day might be referred to as sanctification. Jesus' risen presence on the evening of the first day of the week to his disciples dispelled the toxic anxiety of fear and mistrust; the Spirit came to the disciples and bestowed on them gifts of understanding and unity. The prayer of the whole church at Pentecost is for the Spirit to again labor with sanctifying power: "O God, who by the mystery of today's great feast sanctify your whole Church in every people and nation, pour out, we pray, the gifts of the Holy Spirit across the face of the earth." It is interesting to note that the **Collect** is not asking for a purification of the church alone but in the world, because "by the mystery of today's great feast [you] sanctify your whole Church in every people and nation . . . across the face of the earth." The **Collect** cannot but recall the gathering of nations that occurs in Acts and therefore begs for the same grace "when the Gospel was first proclaimed." The implication, of course, is that this is the same Spirit at work yesterday and today, the same Spirit into which all were baptized and which has animated all creation from the beginning. The **Preface: The Mystery of Pentecost** echoes this biblical reality of the coming of the Spirit when it acknowledges that the coming of the Spirit brings the "Paschal mystery to completion . . . this same Spirit, as the Church came to birth, opened to all peoples the knowledge of God and brought together the many languages of the earth in profession of one faith."

Strategy for Preaching

We know that Pentecost Sunday is a supremely important and significant solemnity in the liturgical year, but unlike Christmas and

Easter, there is no corresponding secular celebration. There is an opportunity here to draw the congregation into a room where they will all be together in one place with a single heart, undistracted by holiday concerns, and sing the **Sequence**, *Veni Sancte Spiritus*. It would be hard to imagine secular culture co-opting Pentecost. Nevertheless, the preacher will need to be even more inventive than usual to make Pentecost Sunday new and impress upon the congregation the realities of this solemnity's significance for the church and the whole world. The risk is that the day and the homily become somewhat clichéd, a condition that could not be more inappropriate for the coming of the Spirit. I will suggest three steps that the preacher might consider in preparing for the homily, which could be tailored to the needs of particular assemblies as needed.

1. Having spent fifty days after the resurrection awaiting the coming of the Spirit, the preacher will benefit, as always, from some degree of interior discernment. Where is the Spirit working in my life and in the lives to whom I minister? Is there a sense that there is "to each individual the manifestation of the Spirit [which] is given for some benefit?"

2. With the associations of new birth with this solemnity, how will the parish be born anew? It is always crucial that the preacher exegete the assembly, but we can take their collective identity for granted and not really understand the changes that have affected peoples' lives. Is the community suffering economically? What does it mean for the Spirit to come and bring unity amid the diversity of this particular parish?

3. What are the challenges for the future mission of the parish, and is this opportunity in line with the larger church? The prayer for unity certainly encompasses the way in which parishes of varying sorts understand themselves in the context of the diocese and the world church. To this end, it seems to me that Pentecost is an invitation to recognize the presence of immigrants in the United States, particularly those who are poor and fleeing from violence. The USCCB has called the Hispanic presence in the United States a "blessing." Does the parish community receive the gifts of the Spirit in such a way so as to welcome the stranger?

It is well to consider the dominant image in the book of Acts that the biblical author uses to convey the coming of the Spirit to the disciples: tongues of fire. If God were to write on the preacher's heart or on the life and mission of the parish, what would that new and vigorous text look like? In other words, what would the core homiletic idea look like?

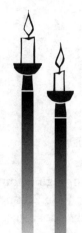

ORDINARY TIME

Second Sunday in Ordinary Time

Readings from the Ambo

Isa 49:3, 5-6; Ps 40:2, 4, 7-8, 8-9, 10; 1 Cor 1:1-3

"The LORD said to me: You are my servant, / Israel, through whom I show my glory." These haunting words from chapter 49 of Second Isaiah remind us that this passage contains some of the most magnificent poetry in the Hebrew Scriptures. The selection taken for the First Reading is a portion of one of the four Servant Songs, of which this is the second. We know that the early Christian community appropriated these songs to signify the suffering Christ, but the first line clues us in to the corporate context of this passage that specifically identifies Israel as the servant. Here is Isaiah summoning Israel to a communal vocation to service and also an acknowledgement of God's plan, "from the womb," forming a nation comprised of a gathering of Jacob and Israel, all of them "made glorious in the sight of the LORD." A parallel vocational call occurs in Jeremiah 1:5, which echoes the same understanding of God as the author of human existence even before the consciousness of history.

There is a notable twist to this vocational call since, by the end of the passage, the call to service is marked not by servitude but a covenantal relationship to become "a light to the nations." From a liturgical perspective, the Christian community finds its own communal vocation on this Sunday after the Lord's baptism, not with a great feast, but the call to service; this is a vocation that is part of the Ordinary Time of the faithful, underlining the enduring covenant God has made and the call of the beloved to live inside that divine promise. The Responsorial Psalm and the Second Reading function as direct responses to God's call to service. If the Servant has been called through the prophet, then the congregation answers in union with that invitation, "Here I am, Lord. I come to do your will." That is a refrain coming from the prophet Isaiah and the psalmist and a people who waited and discovered "a new song" and are able to announce God's "justice in the vast assembly." The psalmist's response articulates the birth of proclamation, even as Paul announces his own call "to be an apostle of Christ Jesus by the will of God."

John the Baptist remains a monumental expression of such service and embodies the prophet who puts the psalmist words into action by uttering what would become the golden thread of John's gospel, the sign of God's glory illuminating every page: "Behold the Lamb of God, who takes away the sin of the world." In the Book of Signs, Jesus embodies the first of all these wonders, attested to by John. The Baptist's vocation to announce "from the womb" the glory of the Lord as "a light to the nations" speaks to us of the challenge of recognizing the Lamb where ever he goes, acknowledging God among us as baptized Christians in the vast assembly.

Connecting the Bible and the Liturgy

Second Isaiah makes it clear that Israel is a chosen servant, so selected because that nation will be the vessel through which the Lord will show forth his "glory." The link between the chosen people and those gathered today in worship and thanksgiving runs like a glorious, sacred river throughout the landscape of the liturgy. That "royal priesthood" has been gathered by Christ, the High Priest, and this crucial theological insight is certainly available in **Preface I of the Sundays in Ordinary Time**: "For through his Paschal Mystery, he accomplished the marvelous deed, by which he has freed us from the yoke of sin and death, summoning us to the glory of being now called a chosen race, a royal priesthood, a holy nation, a people for your own possession." Christ, then, is the mediator, the Servant of the servants of God, who makes possible our call to an eternal covenant, not of servitude, but a "light to the nations," so that God's "salvation may reach to the ends of the earth." And so the same **Preface** also emphasizes the vocational call of the Christian community to announce the gospel, having received the gift, or "to proclaim everywhere your mighty works, for you have called us out of darkness into your own wonderful light."

The Christian call to understand the paschal mystery as a call to love and service becomes galvanized in the eucharistic transformation

of the assembly. Like Paul, the congregation witnesses its own sanctification in Christ and the universal call "to be holy, with all those
everywhere who call upon the name of our Lord Jesus Christ, their
Lord and ours." The purification by the Body and Blood of the Lord
is recollected in the **Prayer after Communion**: "Pour on us, O Lord,
the Spirit of your love, and in your kindness make those you have
nourished by this one heavenly Bread one in mind and heart." Surely,
the ability to recognize one another as members of the Body has
begun in already in Christian baptism, and John the Baptist himself
sets the tone for this acknowledgement: first when he leaps in his
mother's womb sensing the presence of the Lord, and then again on
the Jordan in today's gospel when he says, "Behold, the Lamb of God,
who takes away the sin of the world." In a certain sense, John is the
example *par excellence* of the prophet who has restored the tribes
of Jacob and become a "light to the nations" so that God's salvation
might reach the ends of the earth. The liturgical assembly identifies
with this proclamation most strongly when it assents to the words of
the Lamb of God: "Behold the Lamb of God, behold him who takes
away the sins of the world. Blessed are those called to the supper of
the Lamb." Blessed, yes, because we have been called to recognize
the Word made visible in the breaking of the Bread, and then sent
out to mission to announce the Gospel to all nations.

Strategy for Preaching

John the Baptist is truly a link between the Hebrew Scriptures
and the Gospel. On the one hand, he is closely identified with Isaiah, witnessing to God's mercy and restoration through repentance
and conversion. At the same time John is the first person in John's
gospel to name grace in the flesh. He sees Jesus coming toward
him and testifies to his presence when the Spirit came down and
remained upon him "that he is the Son of God." The homiletic core
idea today allows the congregation to recognize Christ's presence
in their own baptism and in all creation; it is the essential call to
unity after sharing the "one heavenly Bread" that has made us "one
in mind and heart."

The homily risks becoming rather predictable if the preacher
simply focuses on the expected ways that God's presence is made
known (e.g., sunrise, flower gardens, and children). But in fact, the

Scriptures surprise us by focusing on the ways that the Holy is *discovered*. I will suggest an outline for a homily that moves through the three readings in succession and offers the congregation an opportunity to reflect on how they might discover "the Lamb of God" in everyday life.

1. Discover God in ourselves. Isaiah's vocational call is radically personal and asks that we consider our ability to proclaim the Good News, having received the experience of covenantal love.

2. Paul urges the Corinthians to be mindful of unity, something we are not always quick to accomplish. Note the **Collect**'s emphasis on asking God to endow us with "peace on our times." Recall the sanctification of the waters of baptism and the purification received by the Blood of the Lord.

3. Ordinary Time invites us then to find God in the mystery of the Spirit, who freely descends on the beloved, that is, you and me. No longer servants, we come to God's table as members of the same family in Christ.

Third Sunday in Ordinary Time

Readings from the Ambo

Isa 8:23–9:3; Ps 27:1, 4, 13-14; 1 Cor 1:10-13, 17; Matt 4:12-23

In the First Reading Isaiah is recalling a conquest and a triumph. The defeated people of Zebulun and Naphtali in the Assyrian province of Galilee were conquered in 733–32 BC. The oracle announces that "Anguish has taken wing, dispelled is darkness." The power of the Lord has disclosed a luminous presence and great rejoicing, likened to the day of Midian, an event that is recalled because Israel was victorious with God's help (cf. Judges 7:15-25). Overall, the passage's controlling image is darkness and light, but the selection we have here in the Lectionary begs for a rejoinder, or an answer to the question "How?" Now Isaiah 9:6ff. answers this question by the promise of a divine birth, a "Wonder-Counselor, God-Hero." The Christian community has famously incorporated this "Prince of Peace" into its understanding of Jesus as the Messianic King. The last time the liturgical assembly heard this passage from Isaiah proclaimed it was on the Nativity of the Lord (at the Mass during the Night). On that occasion, the "How?" was answered by including the reference to the Divine Child. But in our selection for the Third Sunday in Ordinary Time, the hearers are waiting to find an answer to how the darkness will be dispelled. There is a kind of tension that exists, because the Isaiah reading will pose a question that the gospel will address.

The answer to that question is in the Gospel of Matthew, which specifically references the Isaiah text. Matthew intends to link Isaiah's promise about the coming of the light to a defeated people to the person and mission of Christ. In a sense, Matthew provides the congregation with a theophany in the context of ministry: this is the Wonderful Counselor in action, with his movement into the

Galilee region and the call of the first disciples. Interestingly enough, Matthew makes it clear that this Light comes with the demands of preaching: "Repent, for the kingdom of heaven is at hand." So Isaiah's oracle concerning God's promise is fulfilled not only in the messianic birth but also in the proclamation of the kingdom of heaven. All are to be gathered around the Word. In his first letter to the Corinthians, Paul would also sense the crucial importance of coming to the Word in baptism, when he expresses the unity of purpose that comes from being washed "in the name of our Lord." In all three readings, we can sense an assemblage around Jesus, a gathering focused on a fulfillment of what God has promised.

Connecting the Bible and the Liturgy

When the Responsorial Psalm sings that "the Lord is my light and my salvation," the psalmist signals the hope and confidence that all Christians place in God. Consider, then, the reversal of fortunes taking place in these Lectionary readings: the degraded land of Zebulun and Naphtali, once in darkness, have now seen a great light; John is arrested but Jesus steps up to bring God's illuminated grace to his new disciples in Galilee; Paul gathers the dispersed Corinthians into a single, holy purpose. All of these rebirths are folded into a collective **Prayer after Communion**: "Grant, we pray, almighty God, that receiving the grace by which you bring us to new life, we may always glory in your gift." In the end, the call to worship is the call to seek an abundance of life and to live it to the fullest expression of our God-given humanity, making God present by our expression of being alive. I take it that this necessary interface that the baptized assembly has with grace continues to unfold within the relationship we have with the Trinity so that we can pray, as the **Collect** does, that God might "direct our actions according to your good pleasure."

The grace that brings us and our actions to new or a revitalized life comes from the Eucharistic Liturgy, the site of a people who have been rejuvenated, recognizing that "the yoke that burdened them, the pole on their shoulder, and the rod of their taskmaster" has been vanquished. Our participation in the paschal mystery has granted us the newness of discipleship, as if we were being called on the shores of the Sea of Galilee for the first time. We gather in unity because we have been called by name, and come together in baptism through no other than the name of Christ Jesus our Lord, in whose Body and Blood we share. Even as Paul reminds the Corinthians of that singular baptism, the **Collect** prays that God may "direct our action accorded to your good pleasure, that in the name of your beloved Son we may abound in good works." It is in the name of Jesus that disciples are chosen, sanctified, and sent forth.

Strategy for Preaching

All three readings suggest reasons for the Christian community to be revivified, or brought to "new life," as the **Prayer after Communion** puts it. The preaching for this Third Sunday in Ordinary Time, then, is far from ordinary but maintains a call to awaken intimate discipleship with the Lord. That enlightenment comes from recognizing the works of the Lord accomplished in salvation history and expressed definitively in Christ, who even now offers all of us a sharing of the grace of discipleship.

One of the chief reasons people give up on organized religion results from plain apathy. It is true that scandals in the church have contributed to a good deal of disaffection on the part of the faithful, but I would bet that in many cases these horrors perpetrated on the part of some members of the institution are simply the straw that broke the camel's back. Some might say, "What is the point of it all?" "So what?" In fact, while there may be danger in the ongoing relativism occurring in our culture, there is another "r" word equally as troublesome: relevance. If preaching does not deal very directly with the substantial questions in the lives of men and women, then our homilies are not emerging from God's Word, which is offering the people of God a light in the darkness. Indeed, both the Liturgy of the Word and sacrament promise that we will be revitalized or that when we come to the altar of God, this same Lord will renew "the joy of our youth," in the words of the psalmist and a traditional prayer for the **Introit**. Preaching must always deepen discipleship or else the congregation will be lost, if not in complete night, then like Dante, in a "darkened wood."

Can our preaching foster a *new hearing* for the baptized assembly; can we hear our names uttered on the lips of the Savior? The core idea for this homily might be this: How can I help my congregation to explore their own discipleship more deeply in order that they may "abound in good works"? The initial foray into the homiletic text could explore regions of darkness and the loss of hope that these situations engender. Personal stories might be brought into the picture as well. But the fulcrum for the homily will turn on engaging the assembly in its ability to understand their own "so what?" question. What difference does religion make in my life? This might enable the assembly to count their blessings and to begin to see God's grace work in their lives, which, in turn, begs for both thanksgiving and the abundance of good works. If the point of the homily is to deepen the faith of the baptized, then a keen understanding of the activity of grace and its movement toward discipleship preaches well for this Sunday.

Fourth Sunday in Ordinary Time

Readings from the Ambo

Zeph 2:3; 3:12-13; Ps 146:6-7, 8-9, 9-10;
1 Cor 1:26-31; Matt 5:1-12a

The selection from the prophet Zephaniah sheds a bright spotlight on several oracular judgments the Lord has made against Judah and the nations that occur in the rest of that book. While these peoples await God's justice, a significant motif surfaces early in Zephaniah beginning at 1:7 (NAB): "Silence in the presence of the Lord GOD! / for near is the day of the LORD, / Yes, the LORD has prepared a slaughter feast, / he has consecrated his guests." The promise, then, is swift and steadfast for those invited to this feast, who are the humble and the just, the "remnant of Israel."

In a way, the passage here has a lot in common with last week's First Reading from Isaiah (8:23–9:3), which also extends hope to those walking in darkness for now they have "seen a great light." In the end, God's justice will prevail because "the yoke that burdened them, / the pole on their shoulder, / And the rod of their taskmaster" has been obliterated, "smashed, as on the day of Midian." The Day of the Lord will triumph. Both Isaiah and Zephaniah are concerned with power reversals, a situation in which human control (mostly idolatry and other false worship) is overturned by God's righteous power.

Jesus also looks forward to the Day of the Lord in proclaiming the Beatitudes, an apocalyptic litany of God's righteousness that will extend God's invitation to the remnant outside of Roman imperial power. This stunning series of blessings on the poor in spirit, those who mourn, the meek, those who hunger for righteousness, the merciful, the clean of heart, the peacemakers, and the persecuted present the hearer with the crashing in of God's righteousness, the moment of the kingdom, the Day of the Lord; this is the *now* of God's justice. The Beatitudes introduce the so-called Sermon on the Mount, part of a discourse (the first of the five great discourses in Matthew) that will extend from 5:1 to 7:29. As Jesus reinterprets the law, he is offering a blueprint for discipleship in the kingdom. In a sense, the Day of the Lord runs all through the Beatitudes because they seek to undermine traditional power structures: God's favor is with the lowly, the humble, and the meek, not with empire or the religious establishment. The Beatitudes form a new way of thinking and, as such, help establish the spine of Catholic social teaching and Christian ethics.

Paul wants the Corinthians to take a moral inventory of their own discipleship as well, especially from the point of view of power. Paul deploys some remarkable rhetorical flourishes to unseat conventional thinking: "God chose the foolish of the world to shame the wise." We can note here that even traditional religious virtues such as wisdom count as nothing in God's realm of justice. This passage will become the undercurrent of Paul's theology of the cross, the ultimate symbol of shame and powerlessness, but, paradoxically, also the great sign of victory and redemption.

Connecting the Bible and the Liturgy

The readings for this Sunday speak very powerfully about awakening our hearts to the needs of others, especially the poor and those who are disenfranchised in our society and throughout the world. Undoubtedly, the **Collect**'s emphasis on the double commandment to love God and neighbor highlights the ethical bind the Christian assembly faces when it emerges from worship to the wider culture: "Grant us, Lord God, that we may honor you with all our mind, and love everyone in truth of heart." Our offerings "of service" (**Prayer over the Offerings**), then, is not only about what we bring to the altar but what we bring to God's poor. Moreover, the emphasis that Zephaniah places on the Day of the Lord brings to mind the eschatological sense of the Eucharist, the bread and wine of righteousness in which all share in the bounty of God's justice and mercy.

Along these lines, an interesting connection to make between the readings and the liturgy is the **Eucharistic Prayer for Use in Masses for Various Needs**, which highlights bringing the assembly into a consciousness of the poor. Coincidentally, the USCCB has named the second week in January as National Migration Week and this Sunday's readings may occur sometime after that week, but there is no reason why our concerns for immigrants should not be recalled some time later—and more often! *The Roman Missal* advises the use of this eucharistic prayer for such occasions, and the readings would also suggest its use as well. "Open our eyes to the needs of our brothers and sisters; inspire in us words and actions to comfort those who labor and are burdened. Make us serve them truly, after the example of Christ and at his command." Indeed, this eucharistic prayer forms a wonderful partnership with the Beatitudes and with Paul's teaching in the epistle for this Sunday as well, extending those blessings into the immediate world of eucharistic worship. The call to serve and allow righteousness to bloom is also extended to the universal church: "And may your Church stand as a living witness to truth and freedom, to peace and justice, that all people may be raised up to a new hope." Further still, the congregation is encouraged to attend to the Day of the Lord, not only present in our midst by God's presence and blessing among us but also unfolding in God's future, when all justice will be reveal in a heartbeat: "Grant also to us, when our earthly pilgrimage is done, that we may come to an eternal dwelling place and live with you forever." This eucharistic prayer is a poignant and faithful reminder that the Beatitudes are both now and then.

Strategy for Preaching

Preachers will know that with this Fourth Sunday in the Year A Cycle, there will be subsequent selections from the Sermon on the Mount that run into the Ninth Sunday in Ordinary Time. One thing to consider is a preaching plan that might extend throughout all of these weeks and which will treat the first discourse of Matthew's gospel as a whole. In this regard, the Beatitudes form a lens or reference point from which to view Jesus' teaching, since Jesus' reversals of our expectations present in Matthew 5:1-12a ask us to live in a new reality, God's righteousness.

There has been a great deal written about the Beatitudes, some of which has been referenced in a highly useful section in *The Catechism of the Catholic Church*, "Our Vocation to Beatitude" (1716ff.).

Here and elsewhere, the church underlines the charity of Christ in his utterance that begins the Sermon on the Mount and the call to discipleship that makes all of us a partner with the promise of the Beatitudes. The core idea for preaching for this Sunday, then, might be to awaken in the congregation the very urgency for God's righteousness as we await the kingdom of heaven, which is both present to us and yet to come. If the preacher is also the presider, the **Eucharistic Prayer for Use in Masses for Various Needs IV** will be helpful in expanding the necessity of having our eyes opened to the needs of others. Needless to say, the church has a rich history of social teaching that could be mined extensively, asking the liturgical assembly to consider their own use of power and how they confront its abuse. The Beatitudes will be falling on the ears of a working-class or poor congregation in the inner city much easier than a wealthy parish in the suburbs comprised of CEOs. The challenge for the preacher is to comfort the former, while challenging the latter. Preachers who also administer to large parishes with enormous financial needs and assessments (who count on all those CEOs and wealthy executives), will find it difficult to preach power reversals in their assembly. Never mind that Paul inverts our expectations of wisdom and power. In such instances, the preacher might ask the congregation to imagine a reversal of their own fortunes, something not outside the realm of possibility in tough economic times. Destinies change in an instant. That personal apocalypse, even in a dreamscape, places the emphasis on God's power to which all of us bend as lowly and humble creatures.

Fifth Sunday in Ordinary Time

Readings from the Ambo

Isa 58:7-8; Ps 112:4-5, 6-7, 8-9; 1 Cor 2:1-5; Matt 5:13-16

The First Reading is taken from a section of (Third) Isaiah 56:1–66:24, a collection of writings dating from about 535–20 BC, or some years after the exile in Babylon. If the apocalyptic restoration has not yet come to pass as promised in Second Isaiah, then this third section of the book deals with the consequences of that collapsed eschatology; these are oracles concerning the ethical and overall religious behavior of the community of Israel, particularly the call to righteousness, worship, and the care for the poor. Isaiah announces that in this postexilic period, true renewal will come to pass from corporate conversion and accountability: "Share your bread with the hungry, / shelter the oppressed and the homeless; / clothe the naked when you see them, / and do not turn your back on your own." These are the good deeds of justice and mercy that will yield another kind of restoration, a rejuvenated Jerusalem that is truly vindicated, when "ancient ruins shall be rebuilt" (v. 12, NAB). The promise continues: "then light shall rise for you in the darkness, / and the gloom shall become for you like midday."

Jesus seeks the same accountability from his disciples as he continues his discourse in Matthew 5, the Sermon on the Mount, with a word of challenge and encouragement. The disciples who hear this teaching represent all the Christian faithful and so, from our contemporary horizon, Christ affirms the baptism that makes the members of his Body "salt of the earth." Some will remember the use of "baptismal salt" for catechumens, an ancient practice often associated in antiquity with purification and exorcisms. Its symbolic use to ward off evil suggests its preservative function. But even salt goes flat, as Jesus reminds us. So unless we live with the Beatitudes as guides, performing good deeds for God's poor, our baptismal light will be extinguished, our salt lose its taste. "It is no longer good for anything / but to be thrown out and trampled underfoot."

What is true for disciples is also the same for the church. Living out the church's mission as a "light of the world" will undoubtedly mean, as Paul tells the Corinthians, resolving to know nothing "except Jesus Christ, and him crucified." That cross, lifted high, has become the great light of God's righteousness, moving the church forward, "where it gives light to all in the house."

Connecting the Bible and the Liturgy

The Christian community senses the necessity of joining our worship with our action. We take our clue from Isaiah's call to justice and righteousness in which "true fasting" means sharing bread with the hungry. This is the call to perform good deeds based on our encounter with worship, a light to shine forth in the darkness. From a Christian perspective, the worship that begins at the ambo and the altar must extend to be bread for the world. Our worship must match our mission. As the **Prayer after Communion** reminds us, "O God, who have willed that we be partakers in the one Bread and the one Chalice, grant us, we pray, so to live that, made one in Christ, we may joyfully bear fruit for the salvation of the world." The implication here is that as the church, we go forth as the "light" precisely for "the salvation of the world." We might consider at this point the language of the **Dismissal** used at the **Concluding Rite** in *The Roman Missal*. All four options call for a departure that includes a commissioning in peace and proclamation. Two of these are quite specific in this regard for the baptized to take on the role of "light of the world." "Go and announce the gospel of the Lord." And again, "Go in peace, glorifying the Lord by your life."

At the same time, the liturgy makes it clear that we live not only by good deeds but by grace. God's own initiation into the lives of the baptized enkindles the spark of divinity that makes Christian witness possible. And so the **Prayer over the Offerings** asks the Lord "to sustain us in our frailty." Jesus' teaching suggests that yes, salt can go flat. According to Isaiah, who is it but God alone who refreshes the soul? As the Responsorial Psalm reminds us, "the Lord rebuilds Jerusalem; the dispersed of Israel he gathers." The **Collect** highlights God's role in keeping our lamps alight when it prays, acknowledging our dependency: "Keep your family safe, O Lord, with unfailing care, that, relying solely on the hope of heavenly grace, they may be defended always by your protection."

Strategy for Preaching

I have a close friendship with a couple who received a surprising Christmas "wish list" from their eight-year-old twin daughters. At the top of Clare and Eva's request was "to give something to poor people." So saying, the little girls each received a hundred dollar bill for Christmas, and then their parents helped them to decide how to parcel out their gift to various needs in rural Indiana.

People become more righteous when they hear witnesses like Clare and Eva pictured in a homily. There are hundreds of thousands of stories out there that continue to edify. In order for these accounts to be effective to congregational hearing, the stories ought to have at least three "esses." They should be *specific, succinct,* and *special.* Specific language helps the assembly to paint a picture; if there are people, name them. What are some other details that can make the scene more vivid? The example also should be succinct and strive for economy of language. Lastly, what is so special about this illustration that it fits the preacher's point? If stories and illustrations are not strategic, then they should be discarded. Specific language that is concrete and to the point and performs a special function in the homily will help to draw the congregation into a memorable—and pointed—example. These rhetorical aspects of illustration shed light on our language so that what might be flat and abstract suddenly becomes luminous to the congregation. My underlying point here is that the homily itself should be a "light for the world"; if it is not, how can the assembly expect to "Go and announce the gospel of the Lord"?

So I suggest that the core homiletic idea might be to help the congregation to probe more deeply into their own sense of Christian mission and the call to serve through the witness of baptism. As I have indicated, stories are especially useful in illuminating witness of how others are living out their baptismal commitment and practicing moral development. Finally, does the Eucharist, the Great Feast for the baptized, encourage Christian witness and allow our worship to shine forth? A resource to consider and ponder for this homily is Dorothy Day's *The Long Loneliness* (1952).

Sixth Sunday in Ordinary Time

Readings from the Ambo

Sir 15:15-20; Ps 119:1-2, 4-5, 17-18; 1 Cor 2:6-10; Matt 5:17-37

The book of Sirach (or Ecclesiasticus) belongs to the collection of deuterocanonical writings, and its author, Ben Sira, was writing around the year 180 BC. Evidently, Ben Sira was a highly educated man, and his work evinces the prayerful experience with the Torah, together with a penetrating familiarity with the hellenization of his culture; he has a unique ability to reinscribe Hebraic thought in the midst of Greek social and religious hegemony. The unspoken question throughout the book of Sirach is this: Where is the spiritual heart of a particular community? Ben Sira provokes this question by making the following of God's commandments a matter of "life and death, good and evil"; these are the mandates for rightful living, the moral underpinnings of daily life, the choices that face the human person day after day in any age. Ultimately, happiness resides in making righteous decisions and our guide is God's law, the commandments that forever mentor the just.

God's law, though, must not be a matter of external performance but interiorized behavior. Therefore, Jesus knows well that the *law* was made not to be "abolished" but fulfilled and lived in accordance with absolute obedience to God's will. So, for example, when Christ preaches the fifth commandment, it cannot only be about not murdering, but *thoughts* of harm and anger to our brother and sister that matter in the kingdom of heaven and the law of the Beatitudes. Jesus' Sermon on the Mount, like Ben Sira's writings before it, encourages the hearer to get to the heart of the matter; that is, the center of the self: where is true meaning, ultimate justice, real happiness?

Paul calls this interior probing an exploration of "God's wisdom," a hidden mystery Christ came to reveal. Paul's hearers were undoubtedly waiting to learn of a "wisdom" more in line with the Mediterranean culture with which they were most familiar. But for Paul, it is the Sprit that transcends all things, that "scrutinizes everything, even the depths of God."

Connecting the Bible and the Liturgy

There is a graced parallel between the Word of life and the Bread of salvation on this Sixth Sunday in Ordinary Time. Ben Sira and Jesus offer us pathways to life by following God's commands more closely, more deeply. These commandments are the precepts for which we long, if we are to find true righteousness in the human community, true fellowship with God and our fellow creatures on this planet. In a similar way, the eucharistic table calls the community to go forth together to be satisfied by God's bountiful justice. Word and sacrament offer an existential call to true refreshment. So the **Prayer after Communion** says, "Having fed upon these heavenly delights, we pray, O Lord, that we may always long for that food by which we truly live." Christ's commandment to "do this in memory of me" marshals his disciples not only at the table of Eucharist but also means for them to live in the presence of gratitude and inside God's wisdom, so that there is no division between worship and daily living. That table is our heart.

True wisdom acknowledges that God's presence abides everywhere, that the Spirit *erauna*, or "probes," everything. This is the work of the Spirit abiding with us. What is our worship if we do not sense that the Lord is present to all creation at all times and in all ways? God dwells in the hearts of the hearers of the Good News. Therefore the **Collect** reminds us, "O God, who teach us that you abide in hearts that are just and true, grant that we may be so fashioned by your grace as to become a dwelling pleasing to you."

Strategy for Preaching

Over a half century ago, Gaston Bachelard published *La Poétique de l'Espace* (*The Poetics of Space*, 1958), a philosophical exploration of how we live in the psychological territory of domestic space. Houses are symbolic regions of the self, and how we conceive of them in our psychic life speaks the truth of who we are. Put more colloquially, what do we have lurking in our basement? What are the memories hidden in our attic?

I mention Bachelard's fascinating work because it is worth spending some time thinking about houses this weekend, a particularly important metaphor deployed in the New Testament at various times, which will help to concretize the readings for the Sixth Sunday in Ordinary Time. Using the controlling image of a house provides the architecture for a concrete way of exploring how we make sense of the commandments. Preaching on wisdom or the Torah can become a meditation on abstract principles or worse, the devolution into some kind of a harangue on the congregation's moral failings. Preaching is always more effective if the assembly begins to yearn and desire to be faithful rather than be told, like little children, what to do. In the end, the preacher is called to allow the Spirit to interrogate the congregation in freedom, to search out the goodwill present through God's grace.

So the core homiletic idea for this Sunday might be closer to a *space* to invite the congregation to enter, rather than linguistic principle to ponder. We can begin by asking the assembly a question that I have suggested runs underneath the book of Sirach and beneath Jesus' preaching: On what kind of foundation have I built my house? I take it that this searching sentence is the work of the Spirit built around all three readings, including the **Collect**, which asks that we "become a dwelling pleasing" in God's sight. Here is my recommendation for an outline:

I. Introduction: The recent economic crisis was driven by many things, not least of which was the collapse of the housing market.

    A. Lives are changed in an instant, mortgages disappear, and banks fail.

II. How solid is our foundation? (Visualize for hearer.)

    A. Ben Sira asks his community of Israel living in a Hellenistic world to remember the commandments and the call to holiness.

    B. Jesus does not want to replace the commandments, just get us to interiorize them.

    C. Paul's guide: the Spirit

D. Central image to close: we can stand outside a house and just look at the appearance, but we really know what it is like when we walk through the door and examine its contents. Examples for this illustration might be found in magazines or shows like *House Hunters International*. Spirit gathers all the material together.

III. **Collect** reminds us that we are "fashioned by grace."

   A. God is our master builder and the stones of our foundation are the commandments.

   B. Building blocks can be named, following the commandments; stones of Moses' tablet are cornerstones, built on charity for love of God and neighbor.

   C. What kind of rooms are there in our house; what do we have hidden in the attic?

IV. At the center of the house is the table where all are invited.

   A. Open the door and the Spirit will come in on our lives, even as the Spirit comes upon the Eucharist.

   B. We take that Spirit home to our dwellings.

Seventh Sunday in Ordinary Time

Readings from the Ambo

Lev 19:1-2, 17-18; Ps 103:1-2, 3-4, 8, 10;
1 Cor 3:16-23; Matt 5:38-48

In a certain way, the book of Leviticus forms the axis of faith on which the entire Pentateuch turns and finds its center of gravity. Leviticus, as the name suggests, is not only a book for a priestly tribe about ritual performance; it is a witness to the Torah, a meditation on the life-giving and community saving aspects of the *law*. Although much of the book might be regarded as highly antiquated and technical in nature, the selection for the First Reading demonstrates the text's universal importance.

"Be holy, for I, the LORD, your God, am holy." This utterance is a foundational principle for the law and would underlie later Christian theology crucial to constructing an anthropology of the human person. The *imago Dei* is clearly at the core of God's creation of humanity in Genesis 1:27: "God created man in his image, / in the divine image he created him; / male and female he created them" (NAB). The recognition of the dignity of all human beings created in the *imago Dei* and the call to be holy as God is holy forms the normative ethical behavior for the Judeo-Christian community; it is obviously the backbone to the central commandment in the Torah and the teaching of Jesus: "You shall love your neighbor as yourself." We are hardwired to be happy only when we love, since God himself can do nothing but act in goodness and love, and we are fashioned in that image. As the Responsorial Psalm recalls, "The Lord is kind and merciful." It is out of the model of God's own charity that we justify our intentions and actions in the world.

When the Second Vatican Council emphasized the "universal call to holiness," this teaching was looking back to our very identity as *imago Dei* and, of course, Jesus' mission to deepen our awareness of that call to holiness. How far will we go to love our neighbor? That is the provocative subtext that Jesus provides in his continuation of the masterful Sermon on the Mount. The gospel mandates that this love has no limits and that we are continually placed in new situations that ask us to surrender to the power of love: to give the cloak, when asked for just a tunic; to go two miles, if asked to go one; not just to tolerate the enemy but to pray for him as well.

Paul wants the Corinthians to own their identity as *imago Dei* by recognizing that they are "the temple of God, / and that the Spirit of God dwells" in them. The language Paul chooses to emphasize the call to holiness is not unrelated to the various prescriptions in the book of Leviticus but adds a radical twist on the complicated rites of ancient worship. Christians are expected to treasure their own bodies as the true temple of the Lord, acknowledging that this dwelling is the place where the Spirit resides. "Do you not know that you are the temple of God (*naos Theou*), / and that the Spirit of God dwells in you?" Paul seems to be simply making a matter-of-fact statement here: that the Corinthians ought to know that they are temples of God and that God dwells or "*oikei*" in them. The richness of the Greek text does not really come across in the English translation, since this verb *oikeo* (I live or dwell) has a nominative form in the word *oikia*, or house. So Paul is really telling his people that God is "housing himself" with them. The implication with this observation is also matter of fact: if the Lord is with them, abiding in them, how can they act otherwise?

Connecting the Bible and the Liturgy

Jesus' preaching in Matthew asks his hearers to deepen their awareness of an already firmly established call to holiness based on an adherence to the *law* of Moses, the call to holiness and charity for the neighbor. Indeed, Leviticus and Paul are, in a sense, stretching their congregations to go into a deeper awareness of their call to be holy, to understand themselves as *imago Dei*. To this end, the **Collect** in today's liturgy invites the liturgical assembly to remember the fate of the human heart in contemplating the command to love: "Grant, we pray, almighty God, that, always pondering spiritual things, we may carry out in both word and deed that which is pleasing to you." The summons here is to recollect our consecration as baptized Christians and the mission to "carry out in word and deed" what will please God—that is, reflect our lives as *imago Dei*, a condition imprinted definitively on Christians in baptism, who "put on Christ," and become children of God.

How do we deepen the awareness of the baptized of this great gift of living as a temple where God has chosen to dwell? Spending some time with the Rite of Christian Baptism would strike a helpful parallel with the biblical readings in order to explicate the universal call to holiness. Moreover, a useful liturgical text in *The Roman Missal* to ponder from the perspective of today's readings might be **Preface for the Dedication of a Church and Altar**, particularly, "From the mystery of the Temple of God, which is the Church." Although the **Preface** is not used for today's Sunday liturgy, it is still a resource to be deployed in connection with the Lectionary for today's readings, with the emphasis placed on the human person as a consecrated dwelling for the Lord. Indeed, this **Preface** makes an important connection between the "visible house that you have let us build" together with the "family on pilgrimage to you in this place," as well as the personal vocation to become a dwelling for the Spirit: "you wonderfully manifest and accomplish the mystery of your communion with us."

Strategy for Preaching

Somewhat along the lines of last week, preaching today's readings might well become an exercise in abstraction, or worse, moral hammers to clobber the congregation. Such homiletic "tactics" are never good preaching, and this weekend we have perfect examples of Ben Sira, Paul, and Jesus who do otherwise: they invite their hearers to plumb ever deeper into the mystery of the sacred, challenging conventional assumptions. The preacher ought to keep in mind the gentle words of the liturgy that ask that the assembly remain "always pondering spiritual things" (**Collect**). I take this opening prayer at the liturgy as a mandate for the homily to deepen the awareness of the baptized of God's grace at work. So the core homiletic idea here could be taken directly from Paul himself to the Corinthians: "do you not know that you are the temple of God, and that the Spirit of God dwells within you?" This question might well become a kind of refrain deployed throughout the homily, stated directly or indirectly.

What would this homiletic strategy look like? If the preacher has concretized last week's homily as I suggested (only one of many options), with the use of a domestic space in order to aid the congregation's self-understanding of God at work in the rooms of their lives, then today that house becomes consecrated more deliberately as a temple. This architectural shift already begins to hint at Paul's language in the Second Reading, as well as Jesus' penetrating challenge to his hearers in the Sermon on the Mount. How are our houses consecrated? Answer: Baptism. Who dwells in our sacred homestead? Answer: The Spirit of God. Will we set the table for a feast for the Lord and those he calls blessed? Answer: That is up to us.

I think that the homily could go on to suggest that we are quite comfortable as dwellings of the Spirit when we are secure in our churches, prayer spaces, synagogues. But when we leave, do we recognized the worship space in our own hearts and provide a place of radical welcome for God and our neighbor? The preacher has many resources to support this homiletic strategy, including biblical material outside of today's readings (say, for instance, John 2:13-21), the **Prefaces** or Presidential Prayers for the Dedication of a Church and Altar. More basically, the congregational dialogue continually reminds us that God dwells within us with the exchange: "The Lord be with you." "And with your Spirit." And again: "Lord I am not worthy that you should enter under my roof, but only say the word and my soul shall be healed."

In a sense, this week's homily is an opportunity to partner with last week's preaching, extending the invitation to interrogate the call to be a dwelling place of the Lord even more deeply.

Eighth Sunday in Ordinary Time

Readings from the Ambo

Isa 49:14-15; Ps 62:2-3, 6-7, 8-9; 1 Cor 4:1-5; Matt 6:24-34

Although the First Reading is extremely short, it still packs a wallop, a kind of kernel of the divine promise: that despite our feelings of abandonment, God will never forget us. The passage fits snugly into the context of Second Isaiah, something of a promissory note from God concerning Israel's restoration after the exile. More particularly, though, the passage follows closely on the heels of one of the Servant Songs, an oracle majestically disclosing messianic deliverance. As such, this Second Servant Song forms a prelude to our First Reading: God's affirmation never to forsake his chosen people. The servant comes to a mystical insight concerning his vocation "from birth" and tells us that "from my mother's womb he gave me my name."

This Servant Song is closely identified with Israel itself, who we sense has been both formed and reformed. The oracle goes on to say that this servant received a call "from the womb." This maternal imagery reaches its most poignant state in the passage for today. It is as if God has co-opted the role of mother and given birth to a servant with a new awareness of parental care and attachment. Earthly relationships—even foundational, biological ones like mother and father—will pass away, but only God can ask this question and maintain credibility: "Can a mother forget her infant, / be without tenderness for the child of her womb? / Even should she forget, / I will never forget you." Divine memory supplants maternity.

Paul reminds the Corinthians of their vocation as servants and, in that marvelous expression, helps these folks to own their roles as "servants of Christ / and stewards of the mysteries of God" (*uper-etas Christou kai oikonomous musterion theou*). The Greek word for "steward" contains the word for "house" (*oikos*), which may also mean family, nation, people, temple, or sanctuary. Paul sees his own vocation linked to a steward of God's mysteries of love and care for the people who have been entrusted to him. The enduring love that knows no limits outlasts human institutions or the judgment of any "human tribunal." In a sense, Paul is giving us a glimpse of the final judgment that is God's alone, when the just Judge will "bring to light what is hidden in darkness / and will manifest the motive of our hearts." This should comfort those who understand God as very close to the human heart. Paul sees only God's mercy. This apocalyptic moment is disclosed when "everyone will receive praise from God." What could be more comforting?

Jesus clearly operates instinctively out of the model unique to him alone, of the confident Son who will not be forgotten by the Father. In this sense, Christ is an embodiment of Israel as seen in the Servant Songs in Isaiah. His ongoing teaching in the Sermon on the Mount discourse is the occasion for the Lord to put things in their proper context. If God has ordered the world by love (feeding birds in the sky) and beauty (wild flowers growing), how can we be preoccupied by trivialities and interests of self-care? If we enshrine worry so that we become the stewards of the unknown, living from one anxiety to the next, then we have created idols that live far beyond the kingdom of God. Jesus advises us to "seek first the kingdom of God and its righteousness" because this single-minded pursuit will free us from self-absorption and the concerns for our tomorrows. The future is not ours to own but God's. When we seek the kingdom we make way for that future.

Connecting the Bible and the Liturgy

The biblical readings for this Sunday call to mind the reality of our vocation as creatures before the Creator. In Paul's dynamic and foundational vocabulary, we are stewards of God's mysteries; for Jesus, that servanthood means living in gratitude without anxiety for the advent of the kingdom.

Eucharistic Prayer IV is a veritable chorus of praise, a field of generous associations, a cacophony of colorful flowers rising up to the sun in acknowledgment of the debt owed to the Creator of all things visible and invisible. In celebrating the Eucharist, of course, the presider becomes a steward of God's sacred mysteries in the Lord's house among the people of God. As the **Preface for Eucharistic Prayer IV**

reminds the congregation, our Creator dwells in "unapproachable light" (*inaccessibilem lucem inhabitans*). This sublime phrase echoes Paul's observation that only God can judge because he "will bring to light what is hidden in darkness." Since God abides permanently for all eternity in this mysterious light, he alone is able to draw the curtain back at the end time, disclosing the coming kingdom that has now only partially been revealed to us.

Jesus' teaching in the gospel this Sunday holds special sway in the context of **Eucharistic Prayer IV** as well. To the Lord's point concerning God's care for all creation and our openness to the kingdom, **EP IV** raises a voice to the Father saying, "You have fashioned all your works in wisdom and love. You formed man in your own image and entrusted the whole world to his care, so that in serving you alone, the Creator, he might have dominion over all creatures." I think that we should read "dominion" here precisely as stewardship of God's mysteries, as Paul would claim. Humanity's dominion over all creatures does not meant to suggest, in my estimation, power and manipulation, but the role of a steward for all creation. Surely the vocation of a steward of creation suggests the vital importance of caring for the earth; as Pope Benedict XVI said: "human ecology is an imperative." That we have been entrusted with creation and become stewards of God's mysteries in the house of God for the people of God calls for a response on the part of all the baptized assembly; that word spoken back to God can only be gratitude. For despite our sins, God did not forget us, but "time and time again" renewed the promise of an everlasting covenant. Isaiah has given us a testimony of this very vocational invitation from God, as we have seen in the First Reading. That endless divine care has been extended to us in Christ who "destroyed death and restored life." Our call to be servants and stewards finds its origin and fulfillment in the Spirit of Christ Jesus whose gift of vocation breathes on us the utterance that "we might no longer live for ourselves, but for him." Ratification of that call by all the baptized is an affirmation that we are "servants of Christ and stewards of the mysteries of God."

Strategy for Preaching

There is a potential trap that lies in wait for the preacher with the readings this week, particularly the gospel. The tendency might be to pull out one of the phrases of Jesus like "you cannot serve God and mammon," and make the homily about the depravities of culture (as if we could be separate from this human habitat and hover above it) and the importance of living for God. Or the preaching may turn into some kind of self-help advice about not worrying and "just be happy" because God knows what is good for us. All of these efforts are only superficial skating over a series of complex texts. Rather, the readings are getting at something very crucial, as they ask the listening congregation to grapple with (1) the realities of God's gift of creation; (2) our vocation within that graced world; and (3) how we respond in gratitude by our servanthood in Christ Jesus. These three coordinates form the touchstones that form a core homiletic idea and organize its narrative shape.

The preacher might consider using **Eucharistic Prayer IV** as part of the initial foray into the homily, which envisions the assembly responding to the Father for the gifts of creation, and further, for the inestimable treasure of our salvation in Christ. It would be useful here to present the baptized assembly with a challenge: after seeing all that has been laid before us, how are we to respond? Isaiah and the First Reading, together with Paul in the Second Reading, present us with two vocational responses. Isaiah locates his call as a prophet by God's providential activity before this future voice for Israel was born; Paul sees himself as a steward and calls others to be the same. Have we thought about our vocation as creatures who are cared for by God? Jesus describes that condition when he accounts for God's activity in the world and drives the point even further proclaiming that we should "seek first the kingdom of God and his righteousness." The Eucharist becomes the occasion, then, for availing a congregational response of praise and thanksgiving, the fundamental vocalization of our vocation. In the end, we are sent forth to be servants of Christ and stewards of God's mysteries when we go and preach the kingdom by our lives.

Ninth Sunday in Ordinary Time

Readings from the Ambo

Deut 11:18, 26-28, 32; Ps 31:2-3, 3-4, 17, 25;
Rom 3:21-25, 28; Matt 7:21-27

The book of Deuteronomy is occasionally referred to as the "second law" because it repeats a number of mandates found elsewhere in the Pentateuch; this seminal book gives us a profound indication of just how important keeping the law was to the people of the covenant. The overall weight of the book of Deuteronomy remains heavy with a single word: fidelity. The passages selected for the First Reading shows us the extent to which Israel was to carry out their faithfulness to the Lord, with Moses urging them forward in their faithfulness to God's promise. Speaking for God, Moses says, "Take these words of mine into your heart and soul. / Bind them to your wrist as a sign, / and let them be a pendant on your forehead."

The law was to remain that close: taken in and part of the very soul. We should not be naïve to think that following the law was some externalized practice; no, the law was meant to be consumed and become part of the heart. Indeed the Jewish custom of wearing phylacteries on the head and wrists would be a physical manifestation of just how close the law would come to the human person. The people are asked not to just pay lip service to God's commands, but to take this covenant to heart. God commands Israel not to be simply external practitioners, but faithful observers in obedience to God's promise. To internalize the law as a faithful witness is to devour the word of God completely without hesitation, even as the prophets like Ezekiel consumed the *dabar elohim*—the word of the Lord—as a response to their mission to Israel.

The injunction to remain faithful so prevalent in Deuteronomy is clearly emphasized in Paul's letter to the Romans in the Second

Reading. We might remember here that Paul was himself a zealous practitioner of the law, but his "fidelity" made him a slave to his own designs against the early church before his conversion. Now transformed by the risen Christ, Paul would preach justification not by works (perhaps he knew more than anyone how those acts could become acts of bitter zeal) but by faith in Jesus Christ. That manifestation of God's righteousness has been testified by those who have internalized the covenant and remained faithful. In the end, it is the one who has given the covenant in the first place who justifies us in Christ. So our hearts are inscribed by "the righteousness of God through faith in Jesus Christ / for all who believe." We know that Paul's argument for justification through faith in Christ based on God's graciousness is at the heart of his theology in Romans. "They are justified freely by his grace / through the redemption in Christ Jesus, / whom God set forth as expiation / through faith, by his blood."

The message is clear: God's word must go to our hearts and stay there; otherwise, we might be compared to a house built on sand. Jesus encourages his listeners to live deeper than our words by devouring God's word. The word of God must become part of our very heart, mind, and soul. All else is rhetoric, the multiplication of words. So Jesus says, "Not everyone who says to me 'Lord, Lord' / will enter the kingdom of heaven, / but only the one who does the will of my Father in heaven." We must put our souls where our mouths are and build a house not made of flimsy language that disappears in an instant, but with the obedience of our will to God's enduring word. Then we will become like those who can say with the psalmist, "Lord, be my rock of safety."

Connecting the Bible with the Liturgy

The biblical readings for today clearly encourage the congregation to move deeper into the world of honest faith. Relationship with God must take us beyond human language and into a space where *cor ad cor loquitur*—heart speaks to heart. The **Prayer after Communion** highlights the faith commitment of those who have participated at the Eucharistic Liturgy when it says, "Govern by your Spirit, we pray, Lord, those you feed with the Body and Blood of your Son, that, professing you not just in word or speech, but also in works and in faith, we may merit to enter the Kingdom of Heaven." The **Prayer** also recalls Jesus' stern reminder to his hearers that not everyone who says "Lord, Lord" will enter the Kingdom; it is rather the obedience to God, shaped in "works and in truth" that will bring about a deeper relationship with the Father.

As always, then, the Eucharist becomes an occasion for the church to plunge yet more substantially into a conversation with God, "whose providence never fails in its design" (**Collect**). The sharing of the Body and Blood of the Lord takes us beyond words to the Word made flesh, ushering us into the covenant where the law of love is inscribed in our hearts. The breaking of the Body comes to us like grace itself—a free gift of God's righteousness, given in the passion and death of his Son. The table of the Word and sacrament remind us that the common language of the Holy is etched by the Blood of the Redeemer, a feast of the Word where there is no separation, "no distinction." Consuming the Lord's Body and Blood allows the Christian community literally to internalize the Word. The same should be true for how the faithful consume the Word during proclamation: the word of God is devoured and taken in and owned in fullness, not moving rapidly through the ears; the Word goes from the head to the heart and from the heart to the public square to proclaim the Lord's goodness.

Strategy for Preaching

The homily for this Sunday easily lends itself to a conversation about the place of the Eucharist as the "source and summit of Christian life." In this regard, the gospel for today takes us beyond the multiplication of words and into the reality of faith, expressed in the church's thanksgiving to the Father through Christ. A core homiletic idea might consider drawing directly from the **Prayer after Communion**, reminding the listening assembly that we "may merit to enter the Kingdom of Heaven" by ever deepening our relationship with God, especially through the sacraments. I suggest an outline for a homily that pushes the assembly into a fuller dynamic with the preacher by suggesting that the eucharistic nourishing is ultimately one that opens our eyes to the kingdom that is to come—and indeed, unfolds before us at the Lord's table.

Yet there is more. That is a sublime invitation. The Eucharist is not only about being fed at the table of the Lord but is also a grace-filled, saving action that draws us deeper into our relationship with Christ and the Father. At this point, the homily could access a number of patristic or contemporary writings on the Eucharist, including *Sacrosanctum Concilium* of the Second Vatican Council and *The Catechism of the Catholic Church* (esp. 1345–1419). As is well known, the church has placed a special emphasis on "full and active participation" on the part of the faithful gathered to celebrate the liturgy precisely in order to give the baptized assembly a more expressive range with which to engage their prayer. As the work of the whole Christ, head and body, the congregation worships in fullness and in truth, not simply saying "Lord, Lord," but crying out from the depths of our hearts, "Abba, Father," through the intercession of Jesus crucified. We gather with praise and thanksgiving as a memorial of the Christ who, in his passion, death, and resurrection has drawn all things to himself. Our relationship with the Trinity grows ever deeper as we participate in this saving meal.

And there is still more: after we have received what we are to become, we are reminded that with Eucharistic Communion there is, like any relationship, a powerful intention for commitment, "professing you not just in word or in speech but also in works and in truth" (**Prayer after Communion**). Thus, if our relationship with God grows in love and truth, we will live each day by the commandments to love one another and do good works. We await the Lord's return in glory, where human language, like a house of sand, will fall away into the sea and Christ will be all in all.

Tenth Sunday in Ordinary Time

Readings from the Ambo

Hos 6:3-6; Ps 50:1, 8, 12-13, 14-15; Rom 4:18-25; Matt 9:9-13

The First Reading is part of a longer section taken from the book of the prophet Hosea 5:8–7:16. From a literary perspective, it is a monologue from God that allows us a partial glimpse into the Almighty wrestling with a central theme of the book of Hosea: the faithlessness of Israel and Judah. Hosea preaches against Israel's alliance with the Assyrians and Egypt, which was tantamount to idolatry; their liaison with this foreign power would ultimately mean the destruction of the northern kingdom of Israel in 722–21 BC. The lackluster fidelity of Israel and Judah manifests itself in a piety that evaporates "like the dew," even though they cry to the Lord in affliction. The sacrifices and holocausts are shallow shows, compared to living inside God's covenental love. That is why God says that "it is love that I desire, not sacrifice, / and knowledge of God rather than holocausts." We are aware about the possibility of this love of God by virtue of God's interior monologue, which is vulnerable, transparent, and, yes, angry.

Although the sociopolitical reality is plain enough in Hosea, the Christian community is also charged to live an interiority deep within the love of God's covenant as well. Christians also have their dalliances and alliances with foreign powers and empty idols. If the prophets called Judah and Israel to repentance, so now God's word that "slew them" also convicts us and summons us to righteousness, faith, and the conversion that will deepen those realities. That word, though neglected by Ephraim and Judah, was consumed by Abraham, according to Paul, who devoured God's commands and lived by covenant. "He did not doubt God's promise in unbelief; /

rather, he was strengthened by faith and gave glory to God, / and was fully convinced that what he had promised / he was also able to do." Paul's remarkable use of Abraham as a source of righteous faith illuminates a life justified not by good works or the law of Moses, but faith that is *plerophoretheis*—completely persuaded and utterly convinced that God would do what he had promised. Trust in God, then, *"was credited to him as righteousness"* and so also credited to us "who believe in the one who raised Jesus our Lord from the dead."

We might envision the call of Matthew in the gospel today as a little like the call of Abraham: God summons the patriarch to leave behind household gods—both had to leave the comforting world of idolatry (what is this, after all, but that to which we are attached or addicted) and move into a promised covenant. Neither hesitated. Paradoxically, the Pharisees, whose practice of the law reckons them in their minds as "righteous," become less so when compared to Matthew the tax collector. Like Abraham, Matthew, the new disciple of the Lord, musters hope and trust in Jesus and is transformed from hopeless sinner to a sinner made righteous, or what Martin Luther would later call *Simul iustus et peccatur*—that is, all of us.

Connecting the Bible and the Liturgy

The church's **Collect**, as the word implies, is always an invitation to gather our prayer at the onset of the Eucharistic Liturgy and recognize God's own power to bring together the baptized assembly in thanksgiving and praise. Like the readings for today, the **Collect** for the Tenth Sunday in Ordinary Time places special emphasis on the Lord's holy initiative. "O God, from whom all good things come, grant that we, who call on you in our need, may at your prompting discern what is right, and by your guidance do it." Both Abraham (as Paul recollects this ancient leader) and Matthew, the former tax collector, are shining examples of those who were prompted by God and discerned what is right. Christian discernment, so crucial to spirituality since antiquity, is a virtue that allows us to recognize God's Spirit working in our lives and in the world. Discernment after God's prompting by grace requires a lively faith that is fully convinced (*plerophoretheis*) that God will accomplish "what he had promised."

The presider's invitation to the congregation to "Lift up your hearts" at the beginning of the **Preface** is an opportunity to respond to God's promptings and be joined to the congregation of believers since "it is right and just" to give thanks to the Lord our God. Indeed, the Eucharist itself purifies us and our discernment, not by any of our own works, but by Christ's saving work of justification and redemption, in which we steadfastly put our faith.

Strategy for Preaching

With the colorful examples of Abraham and Matthew in today's readings, the preacher has the opportunity to place the listening assembly in the space of collective discernment, a recognition that God's promptings in their lives await the cogitation and process of an active life of faith in the one in whom we live and move and have our being.

Effective Christian preaching relies on the unfolding of God's works for the assembly in a way that reaches the ears of the heart. Paul's use of Abraham as a witness to righteous faith and God's call underlies this important homiletic dynamic in specific ways and suggests the biblical origin of homiletic listening. Faith comes from what is heard, as Paul tells us, so the retelling of God's fidelity in sacred history testifies to a God who will accomplish what he said he would do. We could take as the homiletic core for today a passage from **Preface I of the Sundays in Ordinary Time**, which shows God's historical prompting of his people, especially through the sacraments. "For through his Paschal Mystery, he accomplished the marvelous deed, by which he has freed us from the yoke of sin and death, summoning us to the glory of being now called a chosen race, a royal priesthood, a holy nation, a people for your own possession, to proclaim everywhere your mighty works, for you have called us out of darkness into your own wonderful light." God has called us and continues to do so. Are we going to reject the invitation (think of God's struggle with Israel and Judah in the First Reading), or will we apply our discernment to move from our tax shelters to the world of grace? The congregation's recognition of the grace *already present in their lives* and a faith in the divine promise that never fails in Christ can only deepen a faith in the One who makes all things new—by constantly renewing our lives.

Eleventh Sunday in Ordinary Time

Readings from the Ambo

Exod 19:2-6a; Ps 100:1-2, 3, 5; Rom 5:6-11; Matt 9:36–10:8

The First Reading initiates a crucial section of the book of Exodus (19:1–24:8) in which God establishes an everlasting covenant (*berith olam*) with Israel; this new relationship includes the revelation of the Decalogue (20:1-17) and the Book of the Covenant (20:22–23:19), mediated by Moses and disseminated among the chosen people.

It is important to note the most obvious feature here: that the origins of the covenant emerge from God's own initiative. From a Christian perspective, the definitive expression of the new covenant will also come through God's initial action through the Incarnate Word. Additionally, the covenant is perpetuated through an invitation to remember this divine love, an *anamnesis*, a living communal memory: "You have seen for yourselves how I treated the Egyptians / and how I bore you up on eagle wings / and brought you here to myself." Indeed the very act of remembering God's saving deeds forms a sacred logic for this covenant. Israel is to remember that it is loved, dearer to the Lord, "than all the other people . . . / a kingdom of priests, a holy nation." A people set apart. Once again, it is hard to resist the Christian parallel with the new and eternal covenant established by Christ, who, when celebrating the Passover with his disciples enjoins them to "do this in memory of me"; that *anamnesis* becomes the refrain for the whole church at the eucharistic table.

Paul's interpretation of God's saving covenant in Christ occurs much like the biblical author of Exodus: "Christ, while we were still helpless, / yet died at the appointed time for the ungodly." As Paul argues in Romans in what would become a centerpiece of his theology, "it is God who justifies" because "while we were still sinners Christ died for us." Interestingly, there is something of a foil going on here between "helpless" and "sinners." The Greek word used here for "helpless" is *asthenes*, which is to also say "weak." Therefore, Paul is equating sin with weakness or helplessness so that the only way we can be justified is through Christ's gift of reconciliation. Remembering Christ's saving act is our acknowledgement of the freedom we have been given from our own helplessness or weakness, delivering us from the Egypt of our sins and into the promise of an eternal covenant.

Jesus' summoning and sending of the apostles is rooted in God's own initiative, compassion, and covenantal love. In a certain sense, the beginnings of the passage in Matthew 9:36 can trace its footprints back to the book of Exodus when God called Moses to deliver his people from bondage. God's heart was moved with pity at the misery of the people, the biblical author tells us (Exod 3:7), compassion that will be renewed again and again in the covenant. Similarly, Jesus' own heart, the gospel tells us, "was moved with pity for them / because they were troubled and abandoned, / like sheep without a shepherd." The apostles' ministry is a response, then, "to the lost sheep of the house of Israel." This call is not meant to exclude as much as to evoke the memory of God's covenant for Matthew's Jewish-Christian community. The proclamation that "the kingdom of heaven is at hand" sows the seeds of a covenant not long forgotten, but made present in the "now" of God's great mercy.

Connecting the Bible and the Liturgy

Based on even a cursory exploration of the readings for this Sunday, it is hardly difficult to forge an alliance with the covenantal language of the Bible and the liturgy. After all, the eucharistic celebration, as we know, finds its very core in *anamnesis*, in the memory that, in Paul's words, "God proves his love for us in that while we were still sinners Christ died for us." This saving action is what the community of faith remembers in praise and thanksgiving; it is a memory underlined everywhere in the liturgy and finds a specific parallel in today's Exodus reading in **Preface I of the Sundays in Ordinary Time**: "For through his Paschal Mystery, he accomplished the marvelous deed, by which he has freed us from the yoke of sin and death, summoning us to the glory of being now called a chosen race, a royal priesthood, a holy nation, a people for your own possession."

Along these lines, then, the **Eucharistic Prayers** in *The Roman Missal* offer a thesaurus of covenantal language, and any of these may be brought to the table as an enduring (and often neglected) witness for the homily in order to underline God's covenant of love—not only in the past but now. Indeed, the words of institution are themselves a kind of covenantal pact for the living community present and gathered for worship. "Take this, all of you, and eat of it, for this is my Body, which will be given up for you." Underneath this divine injunction linger God's words to Moses: "If you harken to my voice and keep my covenant, you shall be my special possession, dearer to me than all other people, though all the earth is mine." Similarly, the liturgy enjoins the baptized assembly: "Take this, all of you and drink from it, for this is the chalice of my Blood, the Blood of the new and eternal covenant, which will be poured out for you and for many for the forgiveness of sins. Do this in memory of me." **Eucharistic Prayer III** seems to catch the assembly in the midst of this act of memory: "*Memores igitur, Domine, eiusdem Filii tui salutiferae passionis.*" There is something quite wonderful and mysterious about recollecting this saving memorial of Christ's passion while it is in our very midst, a "holy and living sacrifice." The sacred memory emphasizes not so much a repeat of a past action as much as the recollection of the saving moment *par excellence*. Such language not only recalls God's saving action in Christ but binds the baptized assembly together as witnesses to this received reconciliation. Therefore, the **Prayer after Communion** is a petition for unity, brought about by the full and conscious reception of the eucharistic gift. "As this reception of your Holy Communion, O Lord, foreshadows the union of your faithful in you, so may it bring about unity in your Church." The very language of the prayer calls forth Christ's gifts of peace and reconciliation.

Strategy for Preaching

I can think of at least three focal points that might form three separate core homiletic ideas for this Sunday: saving memory, corporate worship, and divine dependency. Here are these areas sketched below for which the preacher will obviously need to construct separate outlines (which can be broadly intuited by each of these descriptions).

Saving Memory

If there is a single sentence that unites the Scriptures and the liturgy it is this: we remember God's saving work. But since our society generally encourages us to live episodic lives—rather than ones that recollect historical memory—the preacher will find that even using the word "covenant" will be a strain to a contemporary assembly. The rhetorical structure for the homily might begin with a recognition of those who have been deprived of memory (e.g., dementia) and then a reminder to the congregation how vital such a faculty is to us all. The homily could then go on to the remembering of God's promise in Christ, having recalled that it is God who has remembered us in covenant.

Corporate Worship

My experience has been that listening assemblies must be taught to pray in the course of years how to worship as a unified Body. They also must be taught to listen as a congregation during the homily. The liturgy, as the work of the people, devotes itself to common gestures, language, and actions that forge "one Body, one spirit in Christ." The homilist might attend to the formation of the Israelites in Egypt as examples of the community at prayer (with all their struggles) and then of our own passage as a people of the covenant, a holy nation, a people of God's own possession. Reminding the baptized assembly of its function as the Body of Christ moves individuals caught up in private prayers alone at the Eucharist, to think of themselves as part of the whole.

Divine Dependency

Self-reliance, though a key word for Ralph Waldo Emerson and contemporary America, should be checked at the church door and left there. Paul's words to the Romans concerning our helplessness and weakness are incompatible with rugged individualism. That self-reliance is so important to surviving in our contemporary society is hard to reconcile to God's justification of sinners and even more, Jesus' compassion on a crowd that was "troubled and abandoned like sheep without a shepherd." Paradoxically, our very insistence on independence underlines our need for God. How can the preacher effectively demonstrate the need for God's mercy and love in the present age? Weakness is not dependency on God—quite the contrary. It is the lone wolf who starves because it becomes truly helpless—such as we are in our own sin. The generosity of God in Christ begins in the saving passion, death, and resurrection of Christ. All we need to do is to recognize that while we were still helpless sinners Christ died for us. And remember.

Twelfth Sunday in Ordinary Time

Readings from the Ambo

Jer 20:10-13; Ps 69:8-10, 14, 17, 33-35; Rom 5:12-15;
Matt 10:26-33

The First Reading positions the listening church in the dead center of one of the saddest and most difficult moments in Israel's history. The lamentation is hard enough to hear during Lent but surprisingly difficult to hear during Ordinary Time: why this grief on this particular Sunday? Jeremiah has delivered very bad news indeed: a succession of symbols designed to represent the fall of Judah and Jerusalem into the hands of Nebuchadnezzar and propel God's holy people into long exile. Chapter 18 famously describes the potter and the clay, representing God's power to shape the people of Judah. In a connection that is hard to miss, chapter 19 then finds Jeremiah buying an earthenware jug that God asks the prophet to smash. For all this Jeremiah was relentlessly persecuted, imprisoned, and put into shackles by Pashhur, the chief officer in the house of the Lord. He is renamed Pashhur "Terror-all-around."

The passage for this Sunday follows right on the heels of this ghastly oracle and the fate of the prophet. Yet we are meant to see the emphasis on Jeremiah's resilience and faith, despite the persecutions that assail him. In a way, the little passage is something of a masterpiece of psychological insight moving from the claustrophobic desperateness of interior voices plaguing the man of God to the supreme confidence and trust in the Holy One of Israel. Such inner movement from desolation to consolation also characterizes some of the psalms, of course, particularly Psalm 22, in which the poet's initial fear of being "forsaken" is transformed into praise and thanksgiving. We can see a similar movement in the Responsorial Psalm as well, where the author displays great trust despite the shame that covers his face. Therefore, like the psalmist, Jeremiah ends with a faithful act of trust in God in today's reading. "Sing to the LORD, / praise the LORD, / for he has rescued the life of the poor / from the power of the wicked!"

Jesus, himself no stranger to the world of the faithful witness, characterizes Jeremiah's confidence in God when he tells the Twelve: "Fear no one." The bold instruction of the Lord is really the core of prophetic preaching, which finds its origin in the assurance of God's love and, as the Responsorial Psalm puts it, "his own who are in bonds he spurns not." The Twelve can have the zeal to "proclaim on the housetops." As he tells his chosen ones, "all the hairs of your head are counted." There is an echo here of Jeremiah as well, who reckons his own prophetic authority precisely in the love of God who called him and knew him before he took shape in his mother's womb.

Paul's letter to the Romans underlines that steadfast love of God for his faithful as a "gift." Paul himself becomes the steadfast, confident, and steady witness to God's consolation when he expresses his assurance from the rooftops, as it were: "For if by the transgression of the one the many died, / how much more did the grace of God / and the gracious gift of the one man Jesus Christ / overflow for the many."

Connecting the Bible and the Liturgy

If we would ask the Scriptures how it was that Jeremiah, Jesus, and Paul remained fearless and faithful in the face of opposition and cruelty, we would find God at the center. The **Collect** for this Sunday affirms the Lord's own enduring love when it says, "Grant, O Lord, that we may always revere and love your holy name, for you never deprive of your guidance those you set firm on the foundation of your love." What Jesus knew by virtue of being Son and Jeremiah and Paul recognized in faith is this: that it is to God that we have entrusted our cause. Indeed, it is from the foundation of God's love that we are able to apprehend our salvation in Christ because "the gracious gift of the one man Jesus Christ" has been given to us and "overflow for the many."

With Paul's phrase taken from Romans in mind, we might remember that there was some controversy over the revision of the current *Roman Missal* surrounding the words *pro multis* deployed during the words of institution that were formally rendered in English as "for all" but now have become "for many." It is easy to see where, comparatively speaking, "many" appears to be a quantitative reduction of "all." That is a fair assessment. But I read *pro multis* as an echo of the Pauline language in today's Second Reading expressing an *overflow* of God's grace. It is precisely in unaccountable excess that we can account for God's generosity in Christ; it cannot be measured but overflows, rather, "for the many." The grace of God, as Paul understands it, is inestimable and its recipients incalculable. In a word, "the many" might very well indeed be "all" of us. Additionally, we can see the liturgy exquisitely pointing us in the direction of God's gracious gift overflowing for the many in **Eucharistic Prayer III**, when it makes intercession "for the entire people you have gained for your own," as well as **Eucharistic Prayer IV** that prays for "all who seek you with a sincere heart . . . and all the dead, whose faith you alone have known."

That gift of grace is further underlined in the **Prayer after Communion**, asking that "what we celebrate with constant devotion may be our sure pledge of redemption." It is bread offered and wine poured out that renews the people of God because these gifts are signs of God's steadfast love—the Sacred Body and Precious Blood, a sign of God's enduring presence and care *pro multis*.

Strategy for Preaching

The preacher should be aware of some common misconceptions about our relationship with the living God, which the Scriptures point out are fraught with joys and tensions, highs and lows. The homily might deepen the awareness of the congregation concerning the cost of discipleship, the demands of which will expand faith but may involve a trial. These difficulties are clearly represented in the prophet Jeremiah, Jesus, and Paul, all of whom struggled as bridges between God and his people. A core homiletic idea, then, could be a simple question: what does it take to be a prophet?

Having posed this question of prophetic vocation, the homily might then commence with some contemporary illustrations of the prophetic, perhaps tapping into some contemporary social justice issues. As we know from the Scriptures, the prophetic vocation is less about pushing a particular agenda—still less about predicting the future—than it is about witnessing to the present truth and standing at the center of that God-given reality. This witness to the truth discloses both human and divine fidelity.

It might also be useful to sketch out the life of Jeremiah and to show the parallel with Jesus (a long honored tradition) but then to say that such vocations are not out of reach for the rest of us. At this point, the homilist might advert to the rich texts on Catholic social teaching, which calls the Christian community to live day after day as faithful, ethical witnesses to the truth. In the end, the congregation should be uplifted to know that we are all "set firm on the foundation" of God's love.

Thirteenth Sunday in Ordinary Time

Readings from the Ambo

2 Kgs 4:8-11, 14-16a; Ps 89:2-3, 16-17, 18-19;
Rom 6:3-4, 8-11; Matt 10:37-42

The selection given for the First Reading taken from 2 Kings accentuates Elisha the Wonder Worker. We see only a portion of Elisha's miracles in this snip from the Scriptures, of course, and this encounter with the woman of Shunem follows closely on the verses articulating the prophet's experience of his mentor, Elijah, storming through the heavens on a whirlwind. Elisha has become the inheritor of his mentor's prophetic mantle (1 Kgs 19:19), which, like Moses' staff, parts the Jordan. In chapter 4 Elisha involves himself with a family of Shunammites. The woman of the household was childless and her husband old, but she offered the prophet hospitality. For his part, Elisha tells the woman that she will bear a son the following year.

At its most minimal level, the point of this story seems to suggest the mercy of God and the mediation of divine wonders through human agency. The process of regeneration and fertility are obviously operative: first, Elisha becomes a new Elijah and carries on his mission; then a family is blessed by new life. It is hospitality that welcomes not only the prophet but the gifts he bears in God's name. We have only to welcome these extraordinary moments to be beneficiaries of their great fecundity. The story of the Shunammite family and their son does not end here, which, once again, reminds us that sacred narrative itself bears fruit. The child grows but eventually is taken ill and dies. After begging Elisha to come and save the child, Elisha goes and, in a celebrated scene from the Hebrew Scriptures, raises the child from the dead (4:33-37). God's regeneration is capable of defeating death, a metatheme that, from a Christian horizon, will

197

carry us from the cross to the empty tomb. The Responsorial Psalm is an appropriate rejoinder for the Shunammite woman as well as for the Christian community to these events that have sparked new life. "Forever I will sing the goodness of the Lord."

Like the psalmist, Jesus wishes to underline the great compassion and mercy of God as well but also challenges his disciples to extend to others the same graciousness of which they have been beneficiaries. The second portion of the gospel is particularly appropriate with its interface with the First Reading. "Whoever receives you receives me, / and whoever receives me receives the one who sent me. / Whoever receives a prophet because he is a prophet / will receive a prophet's reward." God's hospitality knows no limits, just the fathomless depth of love incarnated in Jesus Christ—a bottomless ocean of mercy. That is why the Lord asks his disciples to leave everything—much like the prophet Elisha was asked to do (1 Kgs19:20-21)—and follow the path God has mysteriously designed.

Our call to follow such a divine road will be set before each one of us in the ordinary circumstances of life made extraordinary. We have only to receive these moments as God's merciful gifts; that is, to be holy in putting on the mantle of Christ in the life of the baptized. We need to be reminded of such a vocation and its essential dignity from time to time, to welcome our baptism each day as if we were receiving a prophet into our home. "Are you unaware," says Paul, "that we who were baptized into Christ Jesus / were baptized into his death? / We were indeed buried with him through baptism into death, / so that, just as Christ was raised from the dead / by the glory of the Father, / we too might live in newness of life." The newness of life, which reaches back to the Hebrew Scriptures, is the life of the baptized and inextricably linked to the renunciation of our own ego and its neurotic desires and self-centered activity. Why? So that our discipleship will bear the fruits of regeneration, the glorious fruits of the Beloved's own sacrifice, a love poured out for all.

Connecting the Bible and the Liturgy

The **Collect** for today immediately grabs our attention as an invitation to see discipleship linked to baptism and ponder its consequences: "O God, who through the grace of adoption chose us to be children of light." That we have been chosen by God—not as an elitist sect or secret society but as adoptive children who are beloved by the Father—recalls the mercy of God whose wonders raise the dead and whose prophets continually pour forth signs that the kingdom is at hand. If Elisha has revealed God by means of transforming what was sterile into new life, then the Christian assembly has reason to rejoice in the life of grace that makes us children in the House of God. We acknowledge in the **Prayer over the Gifts** that God will "graciously accomplish the effects" of the mysteries we celebrate. Therefore the Eucharist endlessly witnesses to Christ's gift of himself to the church and the whole world, a life of divine charity, which never runs dry. Here again, we acknowledge our true host who performs for us the hospitality of a saving meal for the baptized, leading us to perfect love. "May this divine sacrifice we have offered and received fill us with life, O Lord, we pray, so that, bound to you in lasting charity, we may bear fruit that lasts for ever" (**Prayer after Communion**). "Fill us with life," we say, even as Elisha was a sign of hope. This life is a sure sign of God's presence, the awareness of which instills in the believer the power of the resurrection and Christ's work, a gift that is irrevocable. As Paul says in the letter to the Romans, "We know that Christ, raised from the dead, dies no more; death no longer has power over him." Some English translations prefer to use the word "dominion" instead of "power" for the Greek verb *kurieuo* (I have dominion or influence over). "Dominion" probably gets to the heart of Paul's meaning, which is that death no longer has *jurisdiction* over Christ, since he is Lord of the living and the dead. Indeed, the dominion of death has been vanquished, and now the faithful do battle for Christ the true King.

Strategy for Preaching

It will always bear repeating that God's compassion remains ongoing and astonishing in its affects; indeed, the beginning of each Eucharistic Liturgy asks the Lord to give those gathered who have been brought into the light as adopted children, abundant mercy. Like the Shunammite woman, we are asked to receive the signs of fecundity and life into our own dwelling places. The incarnation was itself brought about by the assent to grace by the Virgin Mary, who welcomed the Spirit into her home. The Word becoming flesh and dwelling among us is a singular historical event. But that reception of the Word also occurs in the ongoing world of the gracious incarnate Lord, living and active in our midst, transforming lifelessness into living bread and wine, remaking us as children of light through baptism. A core homiletic idea may focus on this: we are constantly in the presence of God's merciful and fruitful love; we have only to be aware of that grace to be filled with gratitude and zeal and to live more fruitfully—and abundantly—the life of the beloved, an adopted child of God.

A positive tactic to carry out the focus or core homiletic idea would unwrap in the midst of the congregation of listeners "an attitude of gratitude," as the popular cliché goes. With that goal in mind for the homily, let's look at a rough sketch of a strategy of what the preaching for this Sunday might look like.

(First Part) The best way to help others to be grateful is not demanding that this be so—God forbid. Rather the homily might begin by cultivating a spirit of welcome and hospitality, and suggest that the house of God to which all of us are now gathered is made doubly blessed by the people of God who have entered its gates. We are signs to one another. Indeed, the holy is being disclosed all around us, so how will we welcome these prophetic moments breaking into the course of our everyday lives? The whole church responds to God's gift of life in Christ with the Scriptures and ceaseless voice of the psalms in the Liturgy of the Hours, which recollect God's wonders among us. As St. Augustine points out, it is Christ who is praising the Father in thanksgiving in the midst of the psalms, and so we join our voice with that of the Savior. Additionally, the Eucharist allows the baptized to speak a word back to the Father in Christ so that "the deeds by which we serve" will "be worthy of these sacred gifts" (**Prayer over the Gifts**). Thanksgiving is that ongoing word uttered back from the creature to the Creator who has put an end to death and gives eternal life.

(Second Part) As we live inside the eucharistic world of gratitude, Christ abides in us as he praises the Father in our prayer. (In this section, some visual illustrations would be useful of people who impress us by never failing to say "thanks." The preacher can undoubtedly draw on some personal encounters.) The adopted children of God are grateful to be brought into God's house and sing with joy with their brother Jesus about the Father's mercy and love. That experience can only be like a restoration to new life (First Reading); we are awakened by Jesus and the prophetic memory of the church.

(Third Part) Therefore, the baptized are continually involved in building up the Body of Christ in prayer and gratitude as we go forth into the world (gospel) where we work and love, "until we all attain to the unity of faith and knowledge of the Son of God, to mature manhood, to the extent of the full stature of Christ" (Eph 4:13). The congregation should finally be challenged to welcome the prophetic sign of ongoing conversion, loving more perfectly the Christ who dwells in all of God's adopted children.

Fourteenth Sunday in Ordinary Time

Readings from the Ambo

Zech 9:9-10; Ps 145:1-2, 8-9, 10-11, 13-14;
Rom 8:9, 11-13; Matt 11:25-30

The gospel for today gives us a glimpse of the Lord Jesus engaging in a spontaneous act of worship offered to the Father and in the Spirit. Christ's prayer of praise and thanksgiving follows a period of potentially discouraging moments for the Lord. In chapter 10, Jesus summons the Twelve and sends them forth to preach that the kingdom is at hand, "to the lost sheep of the house of Israel" (10:6). Like a wise mentor, the Lord gives the apostles wisdom—which is encouraging, sobering, and empowering, yes—but giving them a healthy dose of reality as well. Travel light, he tells them. And there will be rejection (10:14-15), but the Spirit will speak the power of the kingdom (10:16-23). Therefore a mixture of fearlessness and faith closes chapter 10, and its proof largely follows sequentially in chapter 11, where today's gospel is situated. Jesus finds inconsistency and misunderstanding, especially when it comes to those claiming to look for the one who is to come. John was rejected and now Jesus will soon find himself in a similar position: those he came to save miss the signs—the miracle of the Word in their midst.

Isn't it rather peculiar, then, that Jesus' praise of the Father comes immediately after these disappointments? Perhaps. But Christ is celebrating those who would receive the kingdom in its fullness, not dwelling on those who miss its presence: the pure of heart, as promised earlier in the Beatitudes, for they shall see God. In this regard, the bottom line for discipleship is living by the Beatitudes through receptivity and humility in preparation for the kingdom. The Good News for the downtrodden is that these poor ones are already well disposed to the disclosure of the kingdom from their lowly position. The downtrodden and humble are also disposed to come to Jesus himself—the embodiment of God's kingdom: "Come to me, all you who labor and are burdened, / and I will give you rest. / Take my yoke upon you and learn from me, / for I am meek and humble of heart."

The prophet Zechariah proclaims a similar power reversal in the First Reading. The king will come not in imperial glory but in meekness, "riding on an ass, / on a colt, the foal of an ass." This passage, like much of the book of Zechariah, is loaded with symbols for understanding the restoration of Israel, a reconstruction after the exile. The "daughter Zion" suggests a familial relationship with the chosen people, a covenant that is unbreakable because it is sealed in a blood relationship. Israel had been brought low and defeated, but now God promises communal healing through peace, a dominion that "shall be from sea to sea, / and from the River [Euphrates] to the ends of the earth." In God's kingdom, justice comes not in strength but in humility; not in the white stallion of a champion but the donkey—the beast of burden—of a servant king.

In Paul's language, then, life in Christ means embracing God's humility—the divine humanity—and not becoming "debtors to the flesh / to live according to the flesh." Now we tend to read "the flesh" in a rather limited way, but living according to "*sarx*" does not limit the flesh to sexual experience alone, but draws in the *whole* of human fleshly existence. Living by the flesh, broadly speaking, means being caught up in the human passions to which all humanity is prey, which can include worldly power and prestige. Paul expands on this "flesh" more specifically in the letter to Galatians 5:19, including among vices such as impurity and licentiousness, idolatry, hatreds, rivalry, jealousy, acts of selfishness, and envy. Living by the flesh runs contrary to the Spirit because these attitudes are contrary to the Beatitudes; those teachings reverse the order of things so that we mark our road maps according to the treasures to be found in the kingdom.

Connecting the Bible and the Liturgy

If the Scripture selections for today encourage the congregation to welcome the word of the humble God with the mind of the Beatitudes, the **Collect** immediately sets the tone for the listening assembly to welcome a kingdom not of the mighty but of the lowly.

"O God, who in the abasement of your Son have raised up a fallen world." The opening of the prayer harbors the paradox of Christian teaching: the last shall be first; the first shall be last. The God of glory comes riding an ass. The kingdom will be revealed to the little ones and hidden from the powerful, the cleaver, and the strong.

God incarnate has experienced "abasement." It is interesting to contrast the *Sacramentary*'s translation of this **Collect** with the new *Roman Missal*. The earlier version used the word "obedience" to translate the Latin *humilitate*. In some sense, there is a way in which humility is expressed in obedience to be sure. But the insightful, paradoxical language of the **Collect** is captured better with "abasement." An abased God *"iacentem mundum erexisti"* or "raised up a fallen world." This is the God behind the Beatitudes, one who became poor so that his people might become rich; that is the anomaly of the incarnation. At this point, I am reminded of a similar paradox in the Rule of St. Benedict. In chapter 7 ("On Humility"), the author spells out a "ladder of humility." Paradoxically, one ascends the ladder only by descending in humility. Perfection comes by descending. Along these same lines, **Preface III of the Sundays in Ordinary Time** grabs a nice turn of phrase when it says, "For we know it belongs to your boundless glory, that you came to the aid of mortal beings with your divinity and even fashioned for us a remedy out of mortality itself, that the cause of our downfall might be the means of our salvation, through Christ our Lord." So it is a divine contradiction that restoration, like healing for those in exile, would come in weakness; the crucified God has come not in earthly ambition but in love.

Strategy for Preaching

One of the homiletic tasks this weekend, it seems to me, is to reveal for the hearers the legacy of the Beatitudes in Matthew's gospel, particularly in foregrounding those called "blessed" because they are pure of heart; the Lord promises that they shall see God. To understand the pure of heart it is necessary to understand the uprooting of power relationships that runs through the readings and the liturgy. So the first issue the preacher must confront is personal power and how it has been deployed in his personal life and pastoral ministry.

I do not see that there is any other way to preach these texts than to desire humility of heart in the first instance, which is the example of the preacher. There is really no use waxing eloquently about God's divine condescension if the preacher is not a credible witness who fully embraces a servant King. The listening assembly is also the watchful assembly during the week and throughout the year. Needless to say, the congregation of parishioners would find it a strain to listen to a discourse on seeking God in meekness, while the preacher-pastor is known to control the parish council and school issues. Jesus lays a claim on all of us, saying that salvation has been revealed, that the kingdom has come, not in power or wisdom. So what can a homily do under these circumstances to encourage the witness value of the preacher?

I might suggest an open-ended formation of the homiletic text for this week, which has received input from various members of the parish. In my estimation, almost every homily could benefit from some kind of sharing with the parishioners. A question for such a focus group—perhaps a parish staff, or a composite of various members of the parish forming a small cohort—is to consider how the king and the kingdom have been disclosed to them personally during this past year. The preacher could then weave these interpretations together and describe the very process of forming the homiletic text to members of the congregation as part of the introduction. This process affirms what Jesus declares about the gift of the Spirit and that this wisdom will be revealed to those we often do not expect. So really the strategy for preaching here involves a slight shift of the axis of rhetorical power not for the actual homiletic event itself, but its formation. Once again, I am reminded of a parallel to the Rule of St. Benedict, in which the saint advises the abbot, when taking council, to heed the voice even of the youngest members of the community.

Fifteenth Sunday in Ordinary Time

Readings from the Ambo

Isa 55:10-11; Ps 65:10, 11, 12-13, 14; Rom 8:18-23; Matt 13:1-23

No one could ever read Isaiah 55:10-11 and insist that God remains disengaged with the world. Isaiah understands a new renovation and transformation of Israel to come imminently after great sorrow but that this reality is linked to the irrevocable divine promise of the Word among us. Indeed, the word of God is a force of nature, according to the prophet. That Israel's restoration after the exile would be tied to the natural world makes the return from a wayward, marginalized expanse re-creative: it is as if God has set in motion another kind of genesis, adorned in the heavens another rainbow, one that will see the heavens and the earth parted in the midst of chaos again and where rains fall on the earth "making it fertile and fruitful, / giving seed to the one who sows / and bread to the one who eats." This is Israel's covenant renewed not only as a restoration but as a re-genesis, another way of proclaiming, "In the beginning," *(bereshit)* for a people who have lost everything. Israel's impending rejuvenation after captivity is inseparable from the Creator who first called the chosen people to be his own.

From a distinctly Christian theological perspective, the Word *(Logos)* present from the beginning of creation is still at work to re-create once more. The famous hymn in Paul's letter to the Colossians sings of Christ's restoration of creation: "all things were created through him and for him. / He is before all things, / and in him all things hold together" (1:16-17). The Word comes to the earth in fulfillment of the divine plan in Christ who will re-create all things disfigured by sin, in exile because of humanity's rejection of God, but now reconciled by the incarnate Word. The magnificent passage

206

from Paul's letter to the Romans today reminds us once again that the disfigurement of sin made us "subject to futility," which now awaits a release from its bondage to decay. We know that Christ has liberated us from sin and the bondage to our enslavement Babylon; but we still await completion, even as nature itself longs to come to perfection in its Creator, to be "set free from slavery to corruption / and share in the glorious freedom of the children of God."

The parable of the Sower seems somewhere between an allegory (the thorns of persecution threatening the young church's growth, for example) and a kind of agrarian folktale. We are the seed sown by the sower groaning to be set free, despite our soil, which will range from rocky ground to rich soil at various times in our lives. Matthew's account of Jesus' parable of the Sower makes it clear that there were a range of responses to the Good News in the early church. Despite the divine fate of the Word made flesh, the hearer must be disposed to absorb the mercy of God's grace and cooperate with the plan to achieve the end for which God sent it. The message is hard to miss: "whoever has ears ought to hear."

Connecting the Bible and the Liturgy

The gospel will always make claims on its believers, something like rain sent to water the earth. Jesus' parable of the Sower is a lesson about how to hear the Word in our midst, whatever our condition may be. The **Collect** for this Sunday is the church's collective response to ask God's help in keeping us faithful and attentive believers and hearers. We might note the imagery of light that occurs from the beginning of this prayer; it reminds us that God's word has gone forth from his mouth and shall not return void, but ceaselessly accomplishes his will. Indeed, divine truth, like the Word, is persistent in its intentions and, like light, will seek out the darkness in order to illuminate its shadows: "O God, who shows the light of your truth to those who go astray, so that they may return to the right path." A detour, a wrong turn: these are the twists and turns, the rocky roads and the thorny branches that face the Christian community. But hope for illumination never fails: "give all who for the faith they profess are accounted Christians, the grace to reject whatever is contrary to the name of Christ and to strive after all that does it honor." This is creation groaning—rejecting "whatever is contrary to the name of Christ" and awaiting the glorious freedom of the children of God. So the parable of the Sower remains a vivid portrait of just how easy it is to be choked off by the enemy or to lose the good zeal, which once was present. But the parable is ultimately an extraordinary message of hope, as is the **Collect** itself. As the congregation strives after all that does the name of Christ honor, Jesus promises that the seed that falls on soil disposed to the Word, "bears fruit and yields a hundred or sixty or thirty fold."

The Eucharist, then, unfolds before us as the riches of soil in God's entire garden, since the people of God are all gathered in from exile and longing for restoration. The baptized assembly stand poised to consume the Word and sacrament and then go forth to witness to the Gospel by their lives. The act of faith itself, the listening heart, becomes one with the congregation's common assent to communion. Therefore the **Prayer over the Gifts** asks that the whole church be a place where fruit might bud forth and multiply, even as the offerings brought implore that "when consumed by those who believe may bring even greater holiness." That is the bumper crop of the Word making fruitful the earth.

Strategy for Preaching

Always exegete the listening assembly; I cannot emphasize that homiletic precept enough in preparation for preaching. The preacher honors the listener when this baptized assembly is accounted as a partner hearing the Word, a maxim to remember for any sower of the Word. On the present Sunday, the preacher might anticipate how this familiar parable might be read by the faithful—or misread. There will often be a number of trapdoors that beset the fate of reading, holes that we fall into because our soil is not what it should be or because we are distracted by this or that. The hazard of the gospel today is that the congregation will make the parable of the Sower an exercise in finger-pointing rather than a challenge to deep listening and conversion. In other words, when the parable is read one way, the story might be parsed as a way in which to view different peoples' responses to the Gospel of the Lord. "I am glad that I have heard the Word on good soil, even though my family has been choked by the world. I know I am growing well, since I still come to church every Sunday." That reaction will be especially the case, in all likelihood, to the average churchgoer of all denominations who, like the Elder Son in Luke 15, throws a fit because his younger brother has bailed and taken the family nest egg and run off to Waywardville. To be fair, there are relatives and friends who have dropped out of the church, having listened to many different voices and are (at the moment, anyway) outside the church's garden; so are those who once believed but are discouraged.

But the garden of God's mercy is bigger than any other landscape because it receives water from the Word and will not return void. That is the mystery of God's restoration in Christ. The **Collect** prays for all Christians, not just those who have heard the Word. And indeed, every one of us faces the distress of rocky ground, thorns of conflict—in a word, desolation that leads to disengagement and withering despair. The core homiletic idea for this week, then, might encourage the congregation to listen deeply to God's transforming and irrevocable word and, despite creation's groaning and hardship, the fruits of the Word will be brought about according to the plan of the Sower.

I think that a viable tactic for the homily today is to help the congregation to understand the Word as water in a dry field. How are we dry? Too much talking and not enough listening literally makes our mouth dry. I might suggest three guiding questions that could organize the homily and structure. The challenge for the preacher is to become a good sower, to form a listening assembly organically in the good soil of the liturgical event itself, sending water to a parched field, so that the assembly only has ears for the word of God.

Intro: Specific and quick (no more than eight sentences), illustrating the failure to listen today.

1. When was the last time I reflected on my ability to receive— anything from anybody—a word from a friend or stranger, a gift or a guest?
2. What would I have to do in order to become a better listener, especially in receiving the word of God?
3. Can I visualize the positive fruits of my taking in the Word, cooperating with God's grace? Would I be different? How?

Sixteenth Sunday in Ordinary Time

Readings from the Ambo

Wis 12:13, 16-19; Ps 86:5-6, 9-10, 15-16;
Rom 8:26-27; Matt 13:24-43

If last week's First Reading from the prophet Isaiah focused our attention on the irreversible destiny of God's word, in the selection for this Sunday the Hebrew Scriptures reflect on the unfathomable source of that word. In systematic theological terms, God is the ground of all being, a focus that is acknowledged in the first commandment and the first phrase of the present passage from the book of Wisdom: "There is no god besides you who have the care of all." St. Anselm's so-called ontological argument for the proof of God is "that than which nothing greater can be conceived." The assent to God's supremacy carries with it a relationship born not of power, but of love and justice. God's mastery over all things "makes [him] lenient to all." Here is a contradiction worth pondering: that God's ultimate strength is mercy. From a Christian perspective, of course, the incarnate God suffered and died. But rather than weakness, the cross of Christ discloses the power of love.

It is probably well for us to examine why this relationship between power and love seems so bewildering. Over the centuries, millions upon millions of people have projected onto God a vengeful leveler, but true wisdom knows otherwise. Indeed, we ourselves are taught to imitate God's *kenosis* or abandonment of power, because "those who are just must be kind." We have reason for hope—and for a change of heart. We come to conversion not in fear but in the recognition that the love of God has reached out and embraced all creation, even pursuing us—the unkind, the unjust, the ungrateful—so that we might abandon our selfish egos and recognize the other in our midst, beginning with God himself as the source of all life and being. God teaches us repentance by love.

That is the divine love that astonishes and is certainly linked to the way the kingdom will come as Jesus has disclosed it for us. It is a kingdom quite unexpected. In Jesus' language, the mustard seed, though small, becomes a large bush, and like God's mercy, "the birds of the sky come and dwell in its branches." The imagery of God's mercy can only remind us that we are not facing a God who towers like a cedar of Lebanon, but flourishes when the creatures of the air take refuge in his protection. Moreover, all the birds of the air take shelter in the kingdom God has prepared for them, so we are in no position to judge anyone. Recall that the children of the kingdom grow side by side the children of the evil one until the harvest, at which time, and only then, the Son of Man comes to judge in perfect justice. Until that harvest, we cry out "with inexpressible groanings." Another way to translate *stenagmos alaletos* might be something like "sighs beyond words or language." Those heartfelt aspirations are our deepest longing for the kingdom and come through our weakness, the place where we have no words even to speak of this emptiness. That kingdom is the almost-but-not-yet reality of God's in-breaking. We can hope because the Spirit prays with us and those who are longing for God's righteousness. We are convicted day by day through the Spirit's intercession so that we become children of the kingdom, imitating God's kindness and mercy to all.

Connecting the Bible and the Liturgy

The author of the book of the Wisdom of Solomon, like those who sang Israel's psalms, evinces a very personal relationship with God. We speak of the importance of transparency in all our relationships when it comes to exhibiting emotional intelligence. We might say that there is something like "spiritual intelligence" as well, which courses through the veins of those who allow themselves to be discovered by almighty God. The intimate disclosure of the self to the Holy will undoubtedly involve personal vulnerability in encountering God "who has the care of all." The faithful come to the Eucharist to encounter this loving Creator as a community. The **Collect** encourages the gathered assembly to check their defenses at the church door and to be present to the God who can do all things in the creation he has fashioned. "Show favor, O Lord, to your servants and mercifully increase the gifts of your grace." With the Introductory Rites at the liturgy, the congregation has already begged the Lord for the pardoning of sins and a merciful release from guilt and shame. At this point, the assembly asks the Author of all things to discover a congregation waiting for grace. In addition to acknowledging God's power and presence in community, the congregation directly implores God to increase those gifts already present in the baptized. We might call this petition a desire for the kingdom to break upon us, a fervent plea to become children of that kingdom. So the assembly becomes disposed to see the kingdom coming like a mustard seed transformed into a large bush, which will give them shelter in their praise and thanksgiving, or like a batch of wheat dough, about to be leavened by the word of God proclaimed in the midst of the people of faith. Therefore, those gathered at the liturgy ask that, "made fervent in hope, faith and charity, they may be ever watchful in keeping" God's commands.

The individual in community has a part to play as well in asking God to make that reign come *now*. For as the Spirit prays within us and we see the love of God mercifully poured out to us, we are urged toward conversion as we share this love with others. That change of heart does not come by coercion or accident, but by receiving love itself as a sign of the kingdom. The **Prayer after Communion** says: "Graciously be present to your people, we pray, O Lord, and lead those you have imbued with heavenly mysteries to pass from former ways to newness of life." This *"novitatem vitae"* is for our benefit and conversion, even as we bring our gifts to the altar—the bread and wine that will transform our lives and increase our virtues—that the Lord will accept the sacrifice as he "blessed the gifts of Abel" so that this offering "may benefit the salvation of all" (**Prayer over the Offerings**). We offer this to the merciful God for our good and for the sake of charity because "the Spirit is alive because of righteousness" (Rom 8:10).

Strategy for Preaching

With the Scriptures for today and the presidential prayers univocally reminding the assembly of God's almighty power disclosed in the kingdom of righteousness, the Nicene Creed remains an unfailing touchstone for a homiletic focus. A core homiletic idea, then, might be that God almighty has created us and continues to re-create us in faith, hope, and love as we dwell in the Spirit of the Lord.

If the theological speculations in unpacking the Creed for use in the homily tend to veer toward abstraction, resist these inclinations. The great pastors of the church made difficult theological ideas accessible to their parishioners. The preacher would do well to remember Paul's earthy allusions to creation's screams "with inexpressible groanings" are not to be the experience of the listeners during the homily! That Pauline phrase names the reality of the Christian people, who will grow weary of abstractions that draw no practical implications for their lives. How is the Creed—indeed, belief in the transcendent power and mercy of God all will profess after the homily—relevant to the lives of the hearer? Concrete illustrations and examples will serve to guide the congregation into the creedal response. The homilist might consider this preaching as a twofold process of preaching and then professing; that is an especially good tactic this Sunday because it expresses an opportunity for the gathered assembly to witness to the immediacy of the faith that surrounds them: that the mustard seed is bursting forth in their midst and awaits a community response. Here is a possible outline:

I. Introduction: Human beings have a DNA to seek power and are only converted from its abuse by God's weakness; for example, use children's power games, historical examples, and biblical illustrations.

II. God's use of power is otherwise. When we say, "I believe in God the Father the Almighty," we are professing a humble God. Use examples from the book of Wisdom, Christ's incarnation, Jesus' illustration of the kingdom, the Beatitudes.

III. That power is directed in love and moves us toward conversion and one another in love. Spirit cries out. Not easy to do. Use stories illustrating weakness defeating power.

IV. The church's faith response is not in power but in the vulnerable moments of the Eucharist, where we send forth our groanings to the Father in Christ on the cross.

A. The kingdom manifested almost but not yet: recognize in faith, hope, and love as we profess our faith. We are re-created by the One who created heaven and earth.

Seventeenth Sunday in Ordinary Time

Readings from the Ambo

*1 Kings 3:5, 7-12; Ps 119:57, 72, 76-77, 127-128, 129-130;
Rom 8:28-30; Matt 13:44-52*

I believe that all the readings for this Sunday have a common feature: holy desire. Jesus' mission on earth was to teach the world God's language of the kingdom by making divine love radically present in our own midst in parable and by his own life, death, and resurrection. The gospel today is a *lectio continua* for the liturgical assembly as we hear chapter 13 unfolding before us. The present selection shows us the Lord's own passion for disclosing God's kingdom to the world. In masterful ways that have been observed before by patristic authors, Christ is the man who has sold all he has to buy us, to ransom us, a treasure hidden in a field. Christ is the merchant searching for us, the pearl of great price; he goes and sells all he has. Christ is the one who has cast his net searching for his people, fish of every kind; they are all God's creatures, to whom the kingdom will be revealed. Christ is like the head of a household who brings from his storeroom both the new and the old.

Needless to say, these early allegorical readings have a lot to teach us about God's desire for us. Christ sets the tone by becoming a parable himself of holy longing, desiring our redemption before all else. Who is the object of this transcendent yearning? Everyone; they are fish of very kind—that is the treasure for the kingdom. In the end, the reign of God is impossible to imagine without first attempting (all efforts will remain incomplete) to imagine God's love for us. To this end, the kingdom is available to us only in parable—only in Christ—who is the language, the definitive Word of the kingdom. By surrendering his divinity and emptying himself fully, Christ attained the pearl of great price, the people of God.

214

The language of the kingdom, then, positions us at the center of prayer. If we grasp the way God longs for us, we can respond in thanksgiving and praise. Coming to terms with God's heart is humanly impossible, but this wisdom was something Solomon earnestly desired. In 1 Kings, the Lord appears to Solomon in order to tell him to ask what he desires most. The Lord himself is giving an instruction on prayer. We know from spiritual masters of all faith traditions that our relationship with the Holy is directly linked to our holy desire. Solomon's request for understanding is the search for the pearl of great price. His pursuit of wisdom rather than riches suggests that he wants to explore his desire for God's kingdom and not his own. In the historical context of 1 Kings, Israel is surely endorsing a monarchy that has freed itself from everything but the treasure of wisdom. The narrative in the First Reading makes clear that God has rewarded Solomon because of his humility and his request for wisdom for the sake of good leadership saying, "I am a mere youth, not knowing at all how to act."

To come to understanding and to ask for its fruits to blossom in our midst is a true gift of the Holy Spirit. This desire for wisdom recognizes that "all things work for good for those who love God," as Paul tells the Romans. If we take to heart Paul's admonition to see God's providential hand at work in everything, then we need not be overtly involved in reading into Paul the language of predestination. When Paul says, *"oti ous proegno* [know beforehand] *kai proorisen* [chose beforehand] *summorphous* [having the same form] *tes eikonos tou uiou autou* [of the likeness of his Son]," he is ascribing to God all the attributes of infinite wisdom that Solomon and Israel holds so dear. Rather than adopting the language of predestination, this passage in Paul illustrates that those who are called, justified, and glorified are all those hauled into the kingdom by God's net of mercy. All are configured to work for the good, if they freely chose to cooperate with God's good intention for the fate of humanity. We do so every time we dispose ourselves to that mercy and desire that the kingdom come.

Connecting the Bible and the Liturgy

The **Entrance Antiphon** for this Sunday is taken from the comforting words of Psalm 68:6-7, 36: "God is in his holy place, God who unites those who dwell in his house; he himself gives might and strength to his people." The prayer unites the congregation with those who have made God's abode a priority (think of Solomon the great builder of Israel's temple but also the holder of wisdom). Additionally, the antiphon also sets the stage for the **Collect**, which maintains God's role as host and guardian of his people who have come to worship at his home: "O God, protector of those who hope in you, without whom nothing has firm foundation, nothing is holy."

The liturgy, then, advances the holy dialogue between God and his people now present for worship. If the kingdom is to be truly welcomed humbly in our midst—the way Solomon asked for the gift of wisdom—we must recognize that this reign is only God's to bring and that we are the children of divine mercy. We welcome this gift so that "we may use the good things that pass in such a way as to hold fast even now to those that ever endure." Such a prayer Solomon himself might have uttered. The **Collect** is mindful of the present moment of the liturgy and urges the congregation to seize on the immediacy of the present, the *kairos* moment of the kingdom, which "even now" is coming into our communal horizon.

That is the horizon displaying the glimpse of the kingdom that Jesus sets before us in the gospel. The liturgy encourages the congregation to long for this kingdom, like the pearl of great price, a treasure buried in a field. The Eucharistic Liturgy is itself the desiring assembly hungering for the Body and Blood of the Lord, asking God to send that kingdom into their very midst through the Holy Spirit's gift. This is no future kingdom out of reach but now revealed definitively in Christ so that by the powerful working of God's grace, "These most sacred mysteries may sanctify our present way of life and lead us to eternal happiness" (**Prayer over the Offerings**). In that prayer that we dare to say and uttered by all during the Communion Rite: "Thy Kingdom Come." Here is the desire of the baptized assembly: it is the acclamation inside Christ's prayer to the Father on our behalf, his own holy desire for the kingdom has become one with the church's as he sells all he has in the paschal mystery for our sanctification.

Our response? This can only be one of thanksgiving to the Giver and the One Given. As the **Prayer after Communion** says, "We have consumed, O Lord, this divine Sacrament, the perpetual memorial of the Passion of your Son; grant, we pray, that this gift, which he himself gave us with love beyond all telling, may profit us for salvation." There is a nice touch here in the translation by using the word "profit," since after the merchant Christ has purchased the pearl of great price for God's people, it is only we who are destined to profit by our redemption. Less obvious, but interesting as well, is the use of the Latin verb *tribue* (translated as "grant"), which can mean a variety of things, including "to award" or "to credit." I think we can sense the appropriateness of using this expression in the context of this liturgy: God is giving us credit, but Jesus paid the (pearl of great) price.

Strategy for Preaching

A fundamental question for preachers this Sunday is: How can my liturgical preaching enliven and invigorate in the listening assembly a *desire* for the kingdom? In fact, that question probably underlies all good preaching, but it comes to mind today in a special way. Indeed, as I have suggested before, poor homiletic rhetorical strategy (or the lack thereof) operates out of a system or moral dos and don'ts, intending to place the congregation in the psychological position of children. That power position makes things very easy for the preacher but does nothing for the assembly of the baptized. Additionally, that one-way dynamic lacks the freedom God grants to baptized adults to respond to his gifts and elect to become children of the kingdom, not ethical prisoners of this or that homily. In the end, it is all about desire. And only mature adults know what this longing means.

By way of alluding to Solomon, we might envision in our preparation for this homily God coming into the houses and dreams of the congregation and saying, "Ask something from me and I will give it to you." Preaching that allows the congregation to unpack that divine request uncovers the merciful God who forever desires us to desire the kingdom in its fullness. Preaching makes the listeners aware of this reality at the liturgy by disclosing the power of word and sacrament to enkindle the communal flame of longing for God's reign.

In crafting the homily, I would follow Jesus' lead and proceed by analogy. What I mean by this is that the core homiletic idea could be stated as: "When we ask ourselves what we desire most, we only scratch the surface in realizing how much God wants us." So the homily should get the assembly to image what God's desire for them looks like. Pearl of great price? A treasure hidden in a field? These examples are taken, I am afraid; try something more contemporary. How about God as a great host welcoming guests into his home; you don't even need an invitation!

   I. God has gathered us into his house (**Entrance Antiphon**) and has asked us what we need. We did not have to bring anything, he just served us. God asked me individually what I needed as I sat down for dinner. Here a nice analogy would be food. What is the food that I would ask for at such a gathering? Picture that with all its aromas.

  II. If we have trouble asking what we want most at the table, we are not alone. Some of us do not know how to ask. So Jesus will show us. The gospel reveals people with deep desire. Use a contemporary story for illustration. For example, is there a story about a student who wanted more than anything to be a musician and overcame a lot of obstacles? An athlete but overcame a physical handicap?

 III. Recognizing God's search for us, despite our sins, gives us a glimpse of the kingdom at hand: a "love beyond all telling." Eucharist is the food the baptized desire because it strengthens; God wants to feed us.

Eighteenth Sunday in Ordinary Time

Readings from the Ambo

Isa 55:1-3; Ps 145:8-9, 15-16, 17-18;
Rom 8:35, 37-39; Matt 14:13-21

Chapter 55 of the book of Isaiah is a part of a kind of tidal wave of unfathomable promises to the exilic community. While chapter 40 initiates the discourse we have come to call Second Isaiah, these profound words of comfort crescendo at chapter 51, deploying the language of redemption and free gift. They culminate in chapter 55 as an invitation to the waters, a beckoning to come to a well in a desert place. The words in Isaiah are clearly directed at exiles who long for healing and understanding, words of welcome imaged as "All you who are thirsty, / come to the water!" It probably goes without saying that using water as a symbol of return to a community that dwells in the desert can only be a visceral experience indeed. It is as if God has become an oasis in the wilderness to a people who have lost everything—and that they have. The restoration Second Isaiah promises comes, then, as food for the body as well as the soul. All would "eat well" and "delight in rich fare" and "have life." In Isaiah's terms, this gift is the renewal of "the everlasting covenant, / the benefits assured to David." Israel's exile did not mean that the chosen people would be lost; God's promise is irrevocable. In human terms, exile must have surely felt like the collapse of memory, a place where hearts were hardened and where harps were hung up by the river of Babylon never to be used again.

The Christian community might read this text in a variety of ways, perhaps most significantly as an invitation to receive again the experience of God's unconditional love by recalling the sacrament of baptism. Then again, this passage of Isaiah 55:1-3 would not be unfamiliar to contemporary retreat masters and their retreatants. The text evokes the experience of baptism and God's love that remains steadfast in that sacramental covenant. There are folks who come to retreat who have been away from the church or are lost in confusion and pain—in a word, exiles from themselves and community. Contemporary Americans might find coming to the waters, or returning to the fount of remembrance in baptism, difficult to do because, as the saying goes, "You don't get something for nothing." But in God's reign it is all about the free gift, the grace given to us. So discovering that there is such an experience as an invitation to grace can be life changing.

Another dimension this text raises is God's concern for the marginalized, the hungry, and the thirsty. There are millions in the contemporary world who do not have access to clean drinking water. Divine compassion for those in need and its fusion with the sacramental life of the church finds an iconic status in the gospel for today. Jesus' heart was *"esplagchnisthe,"* translated here as "moved with pity," when he saw the crowds. The Greek word is actually a great deal earthier than the English equivalent. The word literally means "felt in his gut" or "at the depth of his bowels." The implications are, naturally enough, divine compassion. But we must also note that Jesus was feeling the longing of those in need not in just a noetic way, but in the very depths of his own human body. There was nothing abstract about this divine compassion or pity, but a full and complete knowledge of what this hunger for God's presence must really be like from one who knew it firsthand; the Son knows the full love of the Father and what creation longs for. The Son expresses his longing for the Father and knows what it means to yearn for that love. There are those who are yearning for the only food that can satisfy, where God's justice and mercy embrace (Ps 85:11). Nothing is beyond Christ's reach to grant to those who ask and nothing can separate us from "the love of God in Christ Jesus our Lord" (Rom 8:39).

Connecting the Bible and the Liturgy

It is easy to see that God's free gift of overflowing gracious waters are imbued with the sacraments of baptism and Eucharist; the gathered congregation awaits the gifts of the table of the Lord, which endlessly satisfy but which also challenge: "give them some food yourselves." There is no true disciple who does not sense the call to mission after being truly fed; it is a hunger rooted in compassion. To this end, it is worth considering the option of choosing a blessing and sprinkling of waters as a substitute for the customary **Penitential Act** at the beginning of the Eucharistic Liturgy. For obvious reasons, the water rite is a reminder of Christian baptism for the assembly. The Scriptures today call for a substantial link between sacramental language and the biblical spring that lies at the liturgy's source. The water rite at the beginning of the liturgy is an icy awakening to the wonders of baptism that we remember as a community of love.

We know that nonverbal communication speaks volumes, especially to those who are on the margins, cut off from mainstream language. The presider's sprinkling of the congregation is a symbolic gesture that recalls God's bountiful reach; its fall like rain provides the invitation to "come to the waters." Additionally, since this sprinkling remains part of the Penitential Rite, the church reminds the faithful that our true thirst is a longing for sanctification in Christ. "Renew the living spring of your grace within us," the rite says, "and grant that by this water we may be defended from all ills of spirit and body, and so approach you with hearts made clean and worthy to receive your salvation." With the longing for mercy and the waters of life, come the desire for conversion of heart.

Since the First Reading follows very closely on the optional Penitential (water) Rite, or on the memory of the congregation "coming to the waters," the Responsorial Psalm allows the assembly just that: an opportunity to give thanks and praise to God for bringing them out of the exile of sin and death and into the divine and merciful table of redemption. We say or sing, "The hand of the Lord feeds us; he answers all our needs." It would be hard to avoid the inevitable connection between the Scriptures and the liturgy as they create a psychological community between the ancient world of Israel's exiles and the baptized assembled for Christian worship. The faithful are led, then, on a marvelous trajectory toward the revelation of God's gifts, a celebration of gratitude that "nothing can separate us from the love of God in Christ Jesus our Lord." That is not some distant hope. But the Eucharist has made the recognition of God's love an immediate consequence. "We conquer overwhelmingly" as our eyes are opened (as they were at baptism) to the sacramental life of the Eucharist unveiled before us as free gift. The **Prayer after Communion** provides a perfect summary of the congregation's collective prayer of thanksgiving, having been fed with the bread that never perishes, even on a journey in the desert. "Accompany with constant protection, O Lord, those you renew with these heavenly gifts and, in your never-failing care for them, make them worthy of eternal redemption."

Strategy for Preaching

This Sunday the preacher should not miss the opportunity to weave a homiletic text that alludes to all three readings. Even if the optional water rite is not performed, the Scriptures summon the listening congregation to be attentive to what has been offered freely in Christ and how this divine gift unfolds in the sacramental life of the church, which even now is present in the Eucharist. Finally, the gospel places a special emphasis on the mission of the disciples to feed those who are in need, which, broadly speaking, is the call to the entire Christian community to preach the gospel by their lives.

An interesting possibility for a starting point may also be the most obvious, using the symbol of water to craft the homily. That which we need to stay alive is something we take for granted but God's "unceasing kindness" (**Collect**) refreshes us. That said, it is a point of ethics, I think, to consider the world situation today and the availability of healthy drinking water. A way into this appalling situation is to get the congregation to imagine what the gift of water would be like to a desert community like ancient Israel. We are probably unable to know what it is like to be really thirsty when we hear ads for sport drinks that say, "Obey your thirst!" Can we begin to think about those in the world who are truly dying of thirst? Can our compassion reach this far and groan in imitation of our Lord for the crowds? We are able to envision ourselves as needing sanctification and divine goodness; that is thirst also. The great leveler between East and West, rich and poor is that all are hungry for mercy. So the waters we come to are our baptism, we sense our need by the physical hunger of those who still long to be satisfied.

Just how we came to the waters of baptism and, crucially, what we are going to do with this precious gift could be a homiletic core idea for today. Even those who were brought to baptism as an infant might reflect in gratitude on those who brought us. If we came as adults, who were the instruments of this calling? These vessels of divine grace who lead others to the sacraments have responded to Jesus' invitation to feed the crowds. Perhaps some story of a parishioner gleaned during the week would provide an appropriate testimony for the homiletic text at this point. There are a number of elderly witnesses in the parish who have served faithfully for decades, they are living, illustrious testimonials to the call to feed and serve. They have allowed their baptism to take root: they have obeyed their thirst.

Homilists might also contemplate a careful and imaginative use of *The Catechism of the Catholic Church*, as always, not as a list of "shoulds" but in order to expand a dazzling thesaurus of the church's teachings on sacraments, especially the life of the baptized. The patristic authors such as St. Augustine, St. Leo the Great, and St. John Chrysostom also provide a stunning array of analogies and theological explication from which to draw. The interface between the homily and catechesis should be quite natural, and the use of the *Catechism* during this Sunday makes the preaching practical, thoughtful, and instructive. In a word, the preacher's strategy is to place this fountain of the church's sacramental riches before the congregation as something like "returning to the waters." Using the liturgical texts from the Rite of Baptism may also be quite useful in recalling for the assembly this unique gift and the vocation to satisfy those who hunger and thirst in both body and spirit.

Nineteenth Sunday in Ordinary Time

Readings from the Ambo

1 Kings 19:9a, 11-13a; Ps 85:9, 10, 11-12, 13-14;
Rom 9:1-5; Matt 14:22-33

The prophet Elijah and his fate amid one of Israel's most wicked kings (in cahoots with his treacherous wife) provides the people of God with ample reflection concerning God's often turbulent and dangerous call to mission. Indeed, Ahab and Jezebel have become so iconic in their wickedness that their names survive as the centerpiece for the great American novel (*Moby Dick*'s Ahab) and the archetype for the femme fatale in the modern era.

We catch Elijah on the run; the prophet is on a respite from his entanglements with a sad monarchy in the history of Israel in the ninth century BC. Having proven himself as a prophet sent by the true God among the false mouthpieces of Baal (1 Kgs 18:20-40), Elijah has a price on his head thanks to Jezebel who was herself devoted to the worship of Baal. Elijah flees with his servant to Beersheba, a city in the Negev desert, which is in the territory of Judah—beyond the jurisdiction of Jezebel's pursuits. Elijah wanders alone in the desert and sitting under a juniper tree asks the Lord that he might die. Instead, the Lord sends an angel to feed him, and, refreshed and strengthened, he moves on to Mount Horeb, the mountain of God associated with Moses' theophany in the burning bush.

The revelation of God at Horeb presents us with a contrast to Moses' more dramatic encounter on that mountain in the book of Exodus (3:1ff.) and the disciples' vision of Jesus walking on the water in today's gospel. Elijah has faced desolation and discouragement. Paul seems to echo these sentiments in his own journey and tells the Romans that even in speaking the truth in Christ, his conscience joins with the Holy Spirit in witnessing that he has "great sorrow and constant anguish" in his heart. Paul takes on the role of prophet and even offers himself up as a kind of scapegoat for the sake of his Israelite people. Paul is mindful of the cultic language with which the Romans and Israel are intimately familiar. In reading this passage in Romans, one senses that the apostle has come to a reconciliation of his mission to the Gentiles; he will own his past as an Israelite ("cut off from Christ") as well as his future (to "speak the truth in Christ"). Both Paul and Elijah will have to discover God in the quiet acceptance of their own vocation.

I read Elijah's encounter with God in a contemplative whisper as a meeting with solitude incumbent on any prophetic journey. Witness is a lonely road for both Paul and Elijah. The disciples' meeting with what they imagine is the "ghost" of Jesus occurs after the feeding of the five thousand, a wonder that this chosen band seems to have forgotten. Instead of recognizing the divine presence in silence and, yes, even danger (an echo of Elijah), the disciples only affirm Jesus after the fact and in the most dramatic of proofs. As usual, Peter is positioned as the target of a lackluster faith and (literally) sinks. That experience of despair contrasts with Elijah, who, after he is fed by the angel, recognizes the Lord in "a tiny whispering sound." Jesus is acclaimed "Son of God," only after a strong wind is squelched by the Lord on the sea. Interestingly, in the Markan parallel to this episode in today's gospel, there is an authorial observation missing in Matthew. Mark says that the disciples were afraid because they had not understood about the loaves, *"en auton he kardia peporomene"*— their hearts having been hardened. Finally, the thematic thread that runs through this story is suggestive of a faith that is tested under a variety of circumstances, especially danger and fear. That the Lord is worshiped after he works his mastery of nature on the sea is true enough, but what about the miracle of the loaves?

Connecting the Bible and the Liturgy

Today's readings account for a realistic portrait of the human subject inevitably facing the trials and desolation and fears in the search for God and actualizing the call to mission. Paul knows that his pastoral evangelization has made him a living sacrifice (which he will spell out more concretely as something to be embraced by all a few chapters later in Romans 12:1ff.) for his people, with whom he reckons himself inseparable because of their own "adoption" by God as the chosen people. The **Entrance Antiphon** begs God to remember that divine presence: "Look to your covenant, O Lord, and forget not the life of your poor ones forever." We might say that this little antiphon of the church is Elijah's prayer as well, even if he has no strength to lift up his hands to God and sinks in despair under a juniper tree.

It seems to me that the relationship between the Scriptures and the liturgy that is celebrated today forms an especially poignant dialogue. If, in our Eucharist, we rejoice in *anamnesis*, a memorial of God's saving work in Christ, then the readings prepare us for this gifted remembrance since they disclose that God remembers us: Elijah is fed, Jesus rescues the disciples from despair and death on the sea, and Paul is strengthened in his conscience by the Holy Spirit. To this end, the **Collect** prays that the God in whom we live and move and have our being remembers the children of the promise: those he has adopted as his own who now stand before Word and sacrament, longing to be fed, like Elijah. The faithful are given food to sustain the journey. The liturgy places special emphasis on the congregation's self-recognition as children of the promise, an awareness Paul himself contemplates: "Almighty ever-living God, whom, taught by the Holy Spirit, we dare to call our Father, bring, we pray, to perfection in our hearts the spirit of adoption as your sons and daughters, that we may merit to enter into the inheritance which you have promised."

The **Collect** and the Scriptures will find an echo in the beginning of the Communion Rite in which we again acknowledge that we are about to be fed, "formed by divine teaching," and "dare to say Our Father." The Spirit has made us children by adoption crying out to God: "Father." For those disciples awash at sea, have no fear, for the Jesus who comes to us is no ghost, but real food and drink. We live then with our brothers and sisters of Israel, since "theirs the adoption, the glory, the covenant . . . and from them, according to the flesh, is the Christ who is over all, God blessed forever."

Strategy for Preaching

If the homily of last week proclaimed the ever-present Lord, this week's readings suggest a more elusive God, yet one who keeps his promises. We will want to proclaim the God who continues to work wonders for his people with whom he has formed a covenant, but also name the grace, often hidden in the "whispering wind" and yes, even in the terror of the night when we seek the Lord for safety.

We know that when Jesus seized upon his messianic mission (cf. Luke 4:16-30) that he was claiming a preaching that would "speak a word to the weary." Christ references Elijah and Elisha as prophets whose mission reached out to foreigners. With this in mind, our Lord kept the many people of God before him in full view and became the Word "fulfilled in their hearing." Jesus and Paul find suitable parallels as sacrificial offerings: Jesus for the whole world and Paul as an evangelizer for both Jew and Gentile. One way of unfolding the Word for the hearer this Sunday is to deploy a monologue homily, using a subjective narration from the point of view of three of the prominent characters in the readings: Elijah, Paul, and Peter. The imaginative preacher will sketch a sympathetic portrait of each, giving a small history of their encounter with this hidden God who has adopted them, but also in occasional eclipse. This particular tactic explores the saving Word from a psychological point of view, looking at the text from the inside out, as it were. The preacher would choose just *one* of these voices for the homily. Here are some composite outlines for each monologue:

I. Elijah

    A. My journey has been hard and difficult, pursued by king and queen alike.

    B. Yet when I seem to hit rock bottom, I always seem to find an angel who feeds me. Did you ever notice that they show up around you when you are most in need?

    C. I don't have to look far. I just listen deeply to find the Lord in the quietness of the wind, the words of the covenant, and the secret God whispers to me as a promise that never fails.

II. Paul

    A. I often feel like an orphan. I was devoted to the law, and they are my people. But I am driven by the Spirit of Christ who moves me forward. Do I have a family?

    B. But no; I will always be poured out for them for the sake of the covenant God gives us all.

   C. Christ makes us all in the same covenant, Jew or Gentile. You folks are my brothers and sisters.

III. Peter

   A. I felt lost on the water, though I spent my life as a fisherman. Did you ever feel like you were sinking and there was nobody there? Then I saw him.

   B. Fear gripped me, but I felt compelled to go to him. I never loved another more than Jesus, even though I doubted. Fear held me until he did.

   C. Why didn't I remember all he did for us? I still wake up at night to ask God to give me the faith I lack. I know he remembers me.

Twentieth Sunday in Ordinary Time

Readings from the Ambo

Isa 56:1, 6-7; Ps 67:2-3, 5, 6, 8;
Rom 11:13-15; 29-32; Matt 15:21-28

From the perspective of Isaiah, the postexilic community of Israel to whom the prophet addresses God's divine words of comfort
is being reformed in God's covenant. This communal invitation
to refashion a people will come about not by ethnic origin, but by
obedience to God's commands and ordinances. It would appear that
Israel's refashioning might occur to the exclusion of the stranger;
but no. Now ancient Israel has always had a complex and usually
turbulent relationship with foreigners. Indeed, broadly speaking, the
chosen people dislodged themselves from foreign practices like polytheism and symbolically traced the origins of this separation to the
call of the patriarch Abraham whose mandate from God was quite
clear: leave the land of your fathers and come to another land. "Come
away and be you separate" rings as something of a refrain throughout
the Hebrew Scriptures. Ethnic intermarriages were forbidden even
as Israel moved into distant and strange lands.

Yet we know that these ethnocentric practices were undoubtedly
practiced to guarantee a formational community, made so by a strict
following of the law of Moses. It would be the commandments of
God that forged a relationship with the Lord God, together with
the sociopolitical practices within community life. This covenantal
testimony would be severely tested during the exile into Babylon,
when God's invitation is renewed for all people by virtue of his
commands. God asks *all people* to come to celebrate in a sanctuary
designed for all nations "for my house shall be called / a house of
prayer for all peoples." Foreigners render themselves the "chosen

people" not by virtue of their connection with Abraham, but by their interior disposition. As God says, "all those who keep the sabbath free from profanation / and hold to my covenant, / them I will bring to my holy mountain / and make joyful in my house of prayer."

God's broadening of ethnic boundaries makes the gospel encounter with Jesus and the Canaanite woman easier to absorb and understand. The disciples reveal what Paul describes in Romans as an encounter with the Gentiles enough to make his (Jewish) race jealous. Our modern, pluralistic attitudes can only be stunned at what amounts to be Jesus' resistance to the foreign woman's pleas. When the woman asks for healing for her daughter, the Lord says that he came only to "the lost sheep of the house of Israel." Even after further petition, the woman receives a rebuke: "it is not right to take the food of the children / and throw it to the dogs." We might wonder where divine compassion has gone. Yet, we ought not to confuse this scene with Jesus' similar encounter with the Samaritan woman in John 4:4-42. The Matthean Jesus rarely interrupts his mission to Israel (his meeting with the Gentile centurion in Matt 8:5-13 is an exception), and we blunt the force of the text if we make this gospel passage conform to our preconceived notion of Jesus. Jesus would hardly be a Jewish man of his time if he responded any differently to a Canaanite in first-century Palestine. At the same time, Christ's own humanity forces the divinity of faith to come to the surface, a call for the woman to unpack her faith not in idols but in God's covenant and promise; this will eventually lead her to the holy mountain of God's healing power. "Please, Lord, for even the dogs eat the scraps / that fall from the table of their masters." She won him over by her faith. Christ then becomes the minister of all people in the exile of sin and death; he is the source of holy power to those who might come to God's sanctuary: made, not born by faith in him.

Connecting the Bible and the Liturgy

A thoughtful option for the preacher/presider to consider for this Sunday is using the presidential prayers **For the Evangelization of Peoples**, which may even be deployed on Sundays in Ordinary Time whenever there is a special celebration for the work of the missions. In a larger sense, we are always celebrating the work of the missions. With the church's call to welcome the immigrant (a topic I intend to explore more fully as a preaching strategy below), this Sunday is a time to remind the congregation that everyone is called to mission in the church. Even if the presider should not choose to use these presidential prayers, these liturgical texts are a marvelous series of threads with which to weave a homiletic thread.

That universal mission activity is clear from the **Collect** for the optional **For the Evangelization of Peoples** because of God's invitation for everyone to draw near to the holy mountain by participating in his saving covenant. "O God, whose will it is that all should be saved and come to the knowledge of the truth, look upon your abundant harvest and be pleased to send workers to gather it." With this initial prayer, some in the congregation might be reminded of the end of the liturgy, of the call to be sent forth at the end of the Eucharist to "Go and announce the Gospel of the Lord." Indeed, in all the recommended dismissal prayers, the command to evangelize without regard to persons or place is an imperative: "*Ite.*" This is the ancient rejoinder to the baptized to live the Gospel and make disciples so that, by Paul's inspiration in his work among the Gentiles, "the Gospel may be preached to all creation so that your peoples, gathered by the word of life and sustained by the power of the Sacraments, may advance in the path of salvation and love."

These prayers carry the additional freight of being able to play the gospel in an extraordinary pastoral register for the purpose of hearing the Word as an invitation to include the broad spectrum of humanity. Jesus faces the Canaanite woman, having withdrawn to the region of Tyre and Sidon to carry the Good News—that is, himself—to a world outside the Jewish nation. Despite the seeming resistance of the Lord and his disciples, the church's prayers encourage us to see the work of the Spirit, Christ's gift, "to sow seeds of truth constantly in people's hearts and to awaken in them obedience to the faith" (**Collect**, second option for Evangelization of Peoples). Indeed, Jesus awaits a response from the Canaanite woman, to "awaken" in her a faith-filled acclamation. The gospel's allusion to the "scraps that fall from the table of their masters" might be read from one perspective as a deep yearning for the food that never fails: Jesus, the embodiment of the covenant of faith. The woman must bypass her own national identity and search her own hunger in order to respond, so that she might be "nourished by these redeeming gifts" (**Prayer after Communion**).

Strategy for Preaching

This Sunday presents a wonderful opportunity to preach "through the readings" about the call to all Christians to evangelize or to be missionaries of hospitality, especially to those who are immigrants. The purposeful use of a gospel where Jesus briefly resists the importunity of the Canaanite woman on behalf of her daughter accentuates the life of faith and the call to awaken the presence of the living God in all people of goodwill.

The U.S. Conference of Catholic Bishops (USCCB) have repeatedly renewed their call to American Catholics to be mindful of the immigrants; this is a mandate that comes not only because of the urgency of attending to the pastoral needs of the twelve million plus Hispanic immigrants but because of the scriptural warrant to welcome the stranger among us. The USCCB calls the Hispanic presence in this country a "blessing," something that, sadly, not everyone (including the gathered assembly) is quick to acknowledge. Yet the parallels suggesting the disciples' resistance to the Canaanite woman ("send her away!") and the open hostility with which some Catholics receive pilgrims from other countries can hardly be ignored. To this end, how can the preacher organize a homily that positions the congregation as something like a new Israel, being reformed with a prospect of the vibrant immigrant population?

One place to start—and this could be a homiletic core idea—is demythologizing national boundaries (real or imagined) and reminding the listener that we share a common fate with all immigrants: we are all of us exiles in the landscape of sin, being brought into the sanctuary of God's merciful grace in Christ. As such, it is God who does the inviting, the receiving, and the reforming; we are simply cooperating with our divine host. The reimagining of boundaries is no small task, because the congregation must contemplate dissolving their own prejudicial boundaries, which everyone possesses, whether they admit to this fact or not.

If the preacher chooses to use the Presidential Prayers: For the Evangelization of Peoples, these texts add further support to a homiletic strategy designed to challenge the baptized assembly into contemporary mission. The homily would do well to develop a theology of missiology that is first of all gleaned from the First Reading and the gospel for this Sunday. Are we all about our nation and securing our borders, or are we headed to God's Holy Mountain to dwell with all people of faith? Resources to consider are numerous, but among the most important are: *Lumen Gentium: The Dogmatic Constitution of the Church; Ad Gentes: The Decree on the Missionary Activity of the Church* (Second Vatican Council, 1962–65); *Prophetic Voices* (USCC, 1986); *Strangers and Aliens No Longer: The Hispanic Presence in the Church in the United States* (USCC, 1993); *Encuentro and Mission: A Renewed Pastoral Framework for Hispanic Ministry* (USCCB, 2002). The preacher should recognize that the issue of immigration is a sensitive one, but the Old and New Testament texts for this week allow for a repositioning of the baptized assembly as a reformed nation. What better moment to preach about the call to mission when our Hispanic brothers and sisters require the church's welcome? An image of God as a head of a family might serve to replace false notions of patriotism, and a suggestion that a gathering in which many members travel far and wide to return to the sacred home is certainly in order; it would enable the congregants to visualize what it means for all people to come to God's "holy mountain and make joyful" in that house of prayer. We are not celebrating a private liturgy with a select group or sect, but the church's Eucharist, the centerpiece of our expression of worship to the Father, where none of us is worthy to gather the scraps from the master's table but made so by faith in Christ's redeeming power.

Twenty-First Sunday in Ordinary Time

Readings from the Ambo

Isa 22:19-23; Ps 138:1-3, 6, 8; Rom 11:33-36; Matt 16:13-20

The passage taken from Isaiah may first strike us as unusually historically specific for a First Reading on a Sunday liturgy. Shebna appears to be a steward or "master of the palace" who has erred through presumption and arrogance. His is described as having "carved his tomb" earlier in the chapter (22:16). Although Shebna's offense to Hezekiah goes unmentioned in its particulars, his vices have been named lucidly enough. We do know that sometime before 700 BC, Eliakim replaced Shebna and the latter was reduced to being secretary, roughly the equivalent of "how the mighty have fallen." The image of the "Key of the house of David" on Eliakim's shoulder represents, obviously enough, the trust invested in the new official. Shebna has carved out for himself a "habitation," but God overturned this place, took the household key, and fixed Eliakim "like a peg in a sure spot, / to be a place of honor for his family."

The keys of new authority also fall into Peter's possession; this transference occurs not because he is replacing another official but because of his faith in Jesus and the disclosing of the Lord's true identity. That confession has come about by a revelation, an *apokalupsis* of the Father in heaven. The result of this affirmation is a name change, which, in a certain sense, seals a new covenantal relationship between the master and the disciple. Peter becomes the rock (*petros*) of the church, or the gathering of other faithful witnesses who acknowledge Jesus' identity as "Christ, the Son of the living God." Like Eliakim, Peter is given power to shut where "no one shall open," or whatever is "loose on earth shall be loosed in heaven." This scene ends with the third section of Matthew's gospel (11:2–16:20) and prepares us for the next section where "Jesus began to show his disciples that he must go to Jerusalem and suffer greatly."

We might ask how and why Peter made his acknowledgement of Jesus' identity; the answer comes from Paul: who has known the mind of the Lord, or who has been his counselor? It is the inscrutable judgment of God that revealed to Peter the mystery of Christ's identity, a mystery made more wonderful when we consider the trinitarian aspects of the Father revealing Christ in the Spirit to Peter. The keys are Peter's, which is to say that the authority abides in the church because of the indwelling of the Triune God who has spoken to the Rock or Foundation of the church. At the same time, however, it is sobering to note the same Rock now confessing Jesus as the Christ, only a few verses later (16:22) urges the Lord to deny his divine mission. The point here seems plain enough: that the Father has revealed the Son's identity when and where he chooses. The keys of authority come not from personal perfection but from responding to God's initiative and revelation.

Connecting the Bible and the Liturgy

The gospel suggests that Peter's confession will become the bedrock of a community of believers—united in disclosing Jesus' identity and made possible by the Father's gift of the Spirit. An expression that enhances the somewhat charismatic role of Peter and the Spirit is a phrase taken from the **Preface: The Twofold Mission of Peter and Paul in the Church for the Feast of Peter and Paul** (June 29). Peter, the preface says, *"hic reliquiis Israel instituens Ecclesiam primitivam"*—"who established the early Church from the remnant of Israel." The **Preface** lays claim less on Peter's *authority* than on *"instituens"* or broadly speaking, *building* the primitive church from the "remnant of Israel." Therefore, *instituens* plays on the name Peter or rock. Furthermore, the Latin word *reliquiis*, translated by *The Roman Missal* as "remnant" is related to the word "relic," which is also the literal foundation for churches and altars. I don't think that "remnant" quite captures what the original text is after, since the Latin suggests a more sacred character to this group that was once part of Israel and became the church. The **Collect** for the Twenty-First Sunday reminds the church of its identity as the sacred inheritors of this *"reliquiis Israel,"* that the Spirit continues to reveal to believers the identity of Jesus: "O God, who cause the minds of the faithful to unite in a single purpose, grant your people to love what you command and to desire what you promise." This is the church asking for a single-minded trajectory aimed at the revelation of Christ—not yesterday, but today. We are the remnant of Israel, the people of God standing before the altar. In a sense, this strengthens our relationship with the people of the covenant now celebrating a new Passover in this Eucharist, which becomes the unfolding of Christ's identity, deepening the belief of the baptized.

The affirmation of Christ's identity among the faithful will be readily apparent in the Nicene-Constantinopolitan Creed. "I believe in one Lord, Jesus Christ, the only begotten Son of God, born of the Father before all ages." The shift in the English translation in *The Roman Missal* moves from the first person plural to the first person singular: "I believe." We are one with Peter, the gatherer of the "remnant," the one who becomes the builder of the community of the early church. The personification of the belief in Christ parallels Jesus' challenge to all his disciples in the gospel. But who do you say that I am? At the time of our recitation of the Creed, we affirm our witness to Christ and his divinity through the Father, by sending down the Spirit, which animates the collective confession of the whole church at prayer.

Strategy for Preaching

Although the First Reading tends to focus on an unusually particular historical moment in the life of a steward in ancient Israel that may seem incidental to us today, I think that this episode in the Hebrew Scriptures should not be dismissed out of hand. Needless to say, the preacher may have to wrestle with the historical specificity of the text in order to glean some pastoral application for the congregation. But if the passage is mined in prayer and taken together with the other readings for the day, together with the liturgical texts, we might find something old but very relevant to any generation: power. The texts ask us at least three questions about power. First, who owns power and authority? The steward is dismantled from his position and replaced with another. How long will the course run before Eliakim is himself replaced? In the gospel, it is Peter who is given power by Jesus, first through a new name and then through a symbolic and figurative gesture of keys. Secondly, where does authority come from? Paul speaks about "the depth and the riches and wisdom and knowledge of God" and wants us to understand that we cannot understand. Thirdly, what is the purpose of power? The Hebrew Scriptures play havoc with anyone who dares to usurp God's power or pretend to access authority beyond their scope, and Shebna is no exception. Power is utterly in the hands of God and its purpose known to the divine will. Jesus tells Peter that the authority he gives the apostle is for the building of the church. Jesus' power is utterly linked to mission and salvation.

In my view, the three questions I propose crystallize a core homiletic idea and form an outline for the homily:

I. Introduction: Power: its universal uses and abuses (many examples, but one contrasting illustration is sufficient)

II. Who owns power?
   A. We are helpless when the (electric) power goes out; we cannot survive, so it seems with other forms of power.
   B. Story of Adam and Eve tries to make sense of power
   C. Illustrations of other narratives (Frankenstein as an "overreacher" tale); political control in history, etc.

III. Where does true power and authority come from?
   A. Isaiah says that power belongs to God alone.
   B. Israel's fate with Assyrians
   C. Shebna's story is a slice of life but suggests that our pretended ownership of power is fleeting.

IV. What is power's purpose?
   A. Jesus hands on authority to Peter in order to build the church. He is renamed.
   B. We are named in baptism as we become part of the "building" of the church, the people of God; we are all foundations.
   C. The church is acknowledged as living and comes from members, the "living stones" animated by the Spirit of the "inscrutable" God.
   D. **Collect** quotations

Twenty-Second Sunday in Ordinary Time

Readings from the Ambo

Jer 20:7-9; Ps 63:2-6, 8-9; Rom 12:1-2; Matt 16:21-27

The First Reading registers Jeremiah's famous red-hot outburst to God, having been sent as a reluctant prophet to announce the captivity of Judah, only to receive shackles in a stockade at the hands of the official Pashhur, who is renamed "Terror All Around." This translation uses the word "duped" for the Hebrew word *patah*. But the Hebrew means something closer to a sexual conquest, to put it mildly. In fact, the rest of the verses disclose just how seductive, even irresistibly so, God has been to Jeremiah. Try as he will, the prophet cannot hide from the Word of God. "I say to myself, I will not mention him, / I will speak in his name no more. / But then it becomes like fire burning in my heart, / imprisoned in my bones."

This is pretty strong language for Christian ears. We tend to think of the word of God as comforting, and, indeed, the Word does console us. But we domesticate almighty God (or think we do) if we believe that consolation is the only relationship we have with the Lord. Devouring the word of God fully and without compromise will ask us to be renewed in our mind, as Paul will tell the Romans. That action will have consequences, as all conversion surely does. Jeremiah's experiences as a prophet tell us that he has endured great suffering and darkness; he has paid the price for consuming the Word. The letter to the Hebrews will later reference our fated relationship with the Holy: it is a terrible thing "to fall into the hands of the living God" (10:31).

In light of Jeremiah's situation, Jesus' conversation with the disciples gives a powerful meaning to the destiny of those who choose to follow the Word Incarnate. The passage in the gospel for this Sunday begins the last section in Matthew; it will set Jesus toward Jerusalem and the cross but also reveal the resurrection. In summarizing his own future, Christ faces a good deal of resistance from Peter, whose response provides our Lord with an occasion for teaching about the cost of discipleship. Of primary importance in this passage appears to be a rock-hard question: what can one give in exchange for his life? Saving life will lose it; losing life will find it. Lose and love are entwined; substitute a "v" for the "s" in "lose" and there is "love," or again, put an "s" where the "v" used to be in "love" and there is "lose." Losing begets loving; that is the paradox of the Christian journey. In a sense, Matthew's handling of these apparent contradictions and questions provide the essential lens with which to view the rest of the gospel, all the way through the passion, death, and resurrection of the Lord. The hearer is asked to understand the fate of Jesus as another Jeremiah, aflame with God's word, but with the faith and trust of the Son of God, who loses everything for the sake of humankind's redemption.

Paul provides universal application for Christ's journey to Jerusalem for the church in Rome when he tells that community to offer their bodies as a "living sacrifice," a *thusia zosan*. Paul's emphasis on the "*zosan*," or living portion of the sacrifice, makes it clear that this gift is ongoing. The background here is a moral exhortation to be transformed (the Greek emphasizes the urgency of this change in "*metamorphousthe*") by renewing the mind and not trusting in the shallow guarantees and pleasures of this present age.

Connecting the Bible and the Liturgy

All the readings remind us that our God is "a consuming fire" (Heb 12:29), but it is we who must become the ancient holocaust for the sake of the kingdom of heaven. It is this same fire that is burning in Jeremiah's bones and urging Jesus to press on to Jerusalem, despite its costs, and to which Paul advises Christians to surrender into as a "living sacrifice." Gathered for worship, the community of believers offer themselves in the Eucharist with Christ, who has surrendered himself for the reconciliation of all humanity. For at the Eucharistic Liturgy we process again to Jerusalem to witness the living sacrifice of the one who made himself "holy and pleasing to God," as Paul tells the Romans. **Eucharistic Prayer III** refers to this offering as *"hoc sacrificium vivum et sanctum"* (this holy and living sacrifice), with *sacrificium vivum* a clear echo of Paul's Greek *thusia zosan*. The eucharistic community is, then, placed in a parallel situation with the community Paul addresses in Rome: both are living sacrifices. In the Eucharist, of course, we become this offering through *grace*: "May this sacred offering, O Lord, confer on us always the blessing of salvation, that what it celebrates in mystery it may accomplish in power" (**Prayer over the Offerings**). Indeed **EP III** further emphasizes the role of Christ in sanctifying the congregation as a living sacrifice pleasing to God, renewed and transformed, a metamorphosis in body, mind, and spirit by virtue of Christ's saving power, when it asks the Father to recognize "the sacrificial Victim by whose death you willed to reconcile us to yourself."

The gathered assembly of the baptized has become, then, an "oblation" (*oblationem Ecclesiae tuae*), a collective Body formed by this very offering, this living sacrifice. Those who have gathered around the table of the Lord for the sharing of Christ's gift of peace and reconciliation, partaking in the One Bread and One Chalice of salvation, make us "one spirit in Christ." The ending here of the "second epiclesis" is an invocation to the Spirit to draw all the baptized into Christ's sacrifice of the cross, so as to share the unity of that offering and the hope of the resurrection.

Strategy for Preaching

Those who think that preaching is about delivering a cheery little Christian nugget of goodwill each week, or some kind of therapeutic mantra to help the congregation negotiate another day, should look again at Jeremiah, Paul, and Jesus himself. Serving God by devouring the Word is always going to mean taking up the mystery of the cross, and occasionally—maybe more than occasionally for some chosen ones—that experience will seem practically overwhelming at times ("You have duped me, O Lord!"). These experiences will compel the faithful to put on the mind of Christ and think as God does and not as human beings do.

So how do we think as God does? Can we imagine putting ourselves at the mercy of God in order to allow us to become more like the crucified Christ? That question might form the homiletic core idea for which Paul's text this Sunday serves as a major centerpiece.

"Offer your bodies as a living sacrifice," is a very powerful plea to surrender our wills and be formed in the image of God. A little caution is in order when dealing with this Pauline text. The preacher should shun a knee-jerk reaction to this text in an attempt to make the homiletic response to Romans 12:1-2 simply about spiritual athleticism and sexual abstinence. There is a powerful alternative to this interpretation and, indeed, much more to be gleaned from this passage. The offering Paul is asking us to make is our very selves, a living sacrifice, which is underlined both in the Scriptures and in the liturgy. The challenge will be to make such preaching practical and realistic, as well as authentically Christian in its intention.

I am suggesting below a structure that would involve the listeners in a self-examination both individually and corporately. All parishes are going to approach the challenge of preaching from varying socio-economic and spiritual horizons.

I. How have I allowed God to shape me this past week? This year?

 A. Points of harmony and growth

 B. Points of resistance

 C. Story for illustration

II. As a church member, how am I an "oblation" offering myself in service "holy and pleasing to God" in spiritual worship?

 A. What is my level of participation at the liturgy?

 B. Image of a couple either communicating well with each other or failing to do so

III. What will be the implications of these challenges for points of conversion?

 A. Paul: Do not conform to this age, but "be transformed by renewal of your mind."

 B. What does this renewed mind look like?

 C. How am I different after the Eucharist has offered me as a perfect offering to God?

Twenty-Third Sunday in Ordinary Time

Readings from the Ambo

Ezek 33:7-9; Ps 1-2, 6-7, 8-9; Rom 13:8-10; Matt 18:15-20

The text from the book of the prophet Ezekiel forms a small part in a larger section (33:1–39:29) that prepares for the devastating fall of Jerusalem. As such, the major thrust of this short selection concerns warnings—both how to give them and how to receive them. Ezekiel has spent his time prophesying against Israel's soon-to-be-crumbling institutions of kingship and temple. The heart of the prophetic work stands precisely at the margins, remaining apart from these institutional practices and behaviors so that these oracles might call to accountability what has become acceptable status quo living. Indeed, the early portions of the book of Ezekiel are filled with the dramatic vocations God has in mind for this new prophet: he becomes the "watchman," or as some translations put it, the "sentinel." These are appropriate images for the prophet who warns the people with the sound of the trumpet (vv. 4-6). It is the duty of the watchman to speak on behalf of the Lord, while those who hear must heed the call to repent from wickedness or just plain apathy. In a sense, the Responsorial Psalm anticipates the communal reaction God longs for to Ezekiel's pleas: "If today you hear his voice, harden not your hearts."

The watchman stands at the ready for the impending destruction, but he is also the herald of restoration as well in the book of Ezekiel (40:1–48:35), where the house of Israel will be raised up again, like so many dry bones. The promise of renewal has its legacy in God's covenant, a font that will never run dry. Jesus imagines that all of the disciples are, in a way, watchman for one another in this new age he

242

is initiating, even as the Christian community holds itself accountable. Indeed, Christ has come to bring peace and reconciliation, so
he can expect nothing less from his own disciples. The warnings or
the correction of sins are persistently in view for the sake of peace
and charity. But Jesus is quite aware of the hardness of heart that
grips everyone; Ezekiel faced the same resistance in his own ministry.
Paul tells the Romans that there really is no other covenant but the
binding principle of love. "Owe nothing to anyone, except to love one
another; / for the one who loves another has fulfilled the law." We
are bound to each other by the ties of steadfast love, the breaking of
which can only be repaired by the faith community's intercession:
because the very gathering of the church in the name of Christ brings
peace and concord, destroying division. The call to worship as one
and to reckon accountability from one another for the sake of Christ
and the righteousness of God fulfills the commandments. "[L]ove is
the fulfillment of the law." In a certain sense, Ezekiel provides Paul
and Jesus with a fitting image: the watchman. From the earliest days
of monasticism, the hermits knew that they had to keep a watch, to
maintain vigil on their own thoughts in order to maintain perfect
charity. Clearly, hardness of heart has its origin in the interior re-
cesses of our being, as the expression implies. So reconciliation and
the call to honesty with others must begin with a careful watch over
our thoughts, before they become actions. Finally, the readings call
us to keep a vigil and watch not on what others are doing, but on the
life of Christian charity that begins in the heart itself.

Connecting the Bible and the Liturgy

The readings for this Sunday powerfully gesture toward the endless need for reconciliation amid the turmoil and strife, which afflict
communities everywhere. Paul even hints at legal language when
he speaks of the Christian community's duty to "owe nothing" but
remember only the obligation of "fulfilling the law." The Eucharist
gathers the baptized together precisely to celebrate the unity of the
Body of Christ, healed of all division. **Eucharistic Prayer for Reconciliation II** offers some significant reflection to parallel today's
readings, especially in regard to the role of grace in making the healing of conflicts possible. As I have already suggested, making connections with the present liturgical texts for the congregation during

the celebration of the liturgy itself is ideal, but the performance of these Preface texts is not necessary to gain a deeper insight into the readings for the Sunday and to discover a conduit for preaching. "Even more, by your Spirit, you move human hearts that enemies may speak to each other again, adversaries join hands, and peoples seek to meet together." We might think of these quotations from the various parts of *The Roman Missal* as something the way Scripture itself is used in the homily: we don't confine ourselves to the Lectionary only, but other references throughout the Bible help support the current Sunday or feast day.

Eucharistic Prayer for Reconciliation II is a consoling text, one that focuses on the power of the Spirit to move our hearts, but there is more: the passage helps to take the sharp edge off of Ezekiel's sobering words, meant to catch our ears. But we also recognize that the Christian community is reproved in the light of our redemption in Christ; we do not deny the evil in the world but understand that God gathers those who sin into an embrace larger than our sin, a cosmic reconciliation. "By the working of your power it comes about, O Lord, that hatred is overcome by love, revenge gives way to forgiveness, and discord is changed to mutual respect." The Lord himself makes it clear in the gospel how much we are to yearn to be back in the center of love, winning back our brother and sister who sin against us. After all, Love has redeemed us and we who worship do so endlessly as a church in the community of love until the end of history. Ultimately this is the Body of Christ, gathered in Jesus' name to which we are called out of our existential loneliness, so that we "may receive true freedom and an everlasting inheritance" (**Collect**).

Strategy for Preaching

The readings for this Sunday present the preacher with the reality of sin but also the Good News that releases us from the bondage of our transgressions. I think that we might use either the **Preface for the Eucharistic Prayer for Reconciliation I/II** or **Preface VII of the Sundays in Ordinary Time** in order to speak of God's promise embedded in the readings, which does not excuse us from transgressions but opens a window into God's forgiveness. Above all, it is the recognition of that mercy that causes, indeed triggers to the point of tears, true contrition of heart. It should be obvious that love cannot be induced by guilt or shame but only the awareness of love in the Holy Other. So it is possible to do some real catechesis on reconciliation and the call to accountability here, or to get the congregation to respond with the psalmist: "If today you hear his voice, harden not your hearts." The assembly will hear that voice of love if the preacher makes this proclamation of the Good News manifest to the hearer.

If we look at the centerpiece of the **Preface for the EP for Reconciliation**, it forms a neat outline for the homily. Along these lines, the core homiletic idea is that we are wired to be sinners, but Christ gathers us together for healing and reconciliation.

I. "The human race is divided by dissension and discord"

   A. Numerous illustrations of war, politics, etc.

   B. Humans as programmed for alienation by nature

II. "Yet we know that by testing us you change our hearts"

   A. The human struggle is a test that unfolds our life in Christ

   B. The church's sacraments help us live this out, particularly the Eucharist and the sacrament of reconciliation.

   C. Sunday readings tie into this and deepen awareness of how God calls us to reconciliation.

III. So it is only in God's power that we are able to overcome hatred by love, that "revenge gives way to forgiveness."

   A. God's grace alone helps us to fulfill the commandments to love.

   B. Jesus knows that the community of love, the Body of Christ is the landscape of forgiveness, which is ongoing like the sacrifice the Lord has gained for us.

A final note here: the first part of this organization is a good example of narrative tension, which should be stretched out until section II. That God changes our hearts (demonstrated by sacraments and the Scriptures) forms a moment of revelation in the homiletic plot. The congregation of hearers then responds internally, "Oh, so that is how we are saved from ourselves!"

Twenty-Fourth Sunday in Ordinary Time

Readings from the Ambo

Sir 27:30-28:7;Ps 103:1-4, 9-10, 11-12; Rom 14:7-9; Matt 18:21-35

I mentioned the background of the book of Sirach in a previous Sunday, but it is worth repeating briefly here: Ben Sira, the author of the book of Sirach, was writing around 180 BC in a world that was gradually becoming hellenized; the memory of the old customs and traditions of Israel was quickly shrinking. Read from a modern perspective, we might see this book of Sirach or book of Ecclesiasticus as bon mots for upright living. Nice. The First Reading makes an appropriate pairing with Jesus' counsel on forgiveness and the handling of anger in Matthew 18:21-35. Also very nice. But the texts are more than wise sayings from antiquity that might just as easily be torn from a fortune cookie. These readings are mandates to return to first things—that is, the covenant between God and his people, the heart of the law.

"Think of the commandments, hate not your neighbor; / remember the Most High's covenant, and overlook faults." In some sense Ben Sira sees himself as the custodian of Israel's memory, provoking the Hellenized Jews to radicalize their return to the basic tenants of the covenant God made with Abraham, Isaac, and Jacob and the law he established with Moses. The stipulations against anger rightly recall the commandments at a foundational level, since two-thirds of the Ten Commandments deal with offenses against the neighbor. Ben Sira is also very practical when he suggests that there are at least three ways to overcome anger or hatred against the neighbor. First, it is best not to "cherish" or "hug" wrath tightly. Holding on to a grudge can be comforting and a source of blindness. Second, remember our

246

own faults and that God has forgiven them. Third, think of death and decay as a way to sober up from sinning. All of these point in some way or other to God's largesse and accentuate divine power over and against human pride, arrogance, and pettiness.

Paul has his own practical wisdom to share. He tells the Romans that the only way to really live is not for oneself, but for the Lord. Endless forgiveness is possible then only if we do not live for our own self-interests. The early church was obviously much concerned about precisely how to handle relationships within the community. Jesus' admonition to Peter to forgive "seventy-seven times" comes in the middle of Matthew's so-called fourth discourse, dealing with community harmony. A glimpse of the kingdom of heaven may be snatched if the precious ego is set aside and we no longer "cherish" anger but look to the interest of the other instead. That abandoning of the self must begin with dissolving the boundaries of the ego that prevent love from emerging. Forgiveness is the erasure of those walls that keep us from one another. The parable Jesus tells about the wicked servant who had no pity on his fellow servant is an endorsement of how the community challenges the self-centered, narcissistic ego. The wicked servant did not allow the king's forgiveness and compassion to enter his heart and so was incapable of forgiving anyone else. It is the community of just servants who bring the activity of their fellow malevolent and unforgiving servant to the attention of the king. So this advice about forgiveness is ultimately a foundation for personal conversion as well as a road map for community intervention.

Connecting the Bible and the Liturgy

These readings form a bit of a bridge with the previous Sunday, which also focused our attention on the need to be reconciled and to forgive. With the powerful gift of peace bestowed on us in Christ, we hope to pass this treasure along to others. **The Penitential Act** and the "Exchange of Peace" in the Communion Rite make suitable connections with the readings and may prove a source of inspiration, especially for preaching.

The words "Lord, have mercy" have become so familiar to us that we may forget that these are intercessory prayers addressed to Christ in the presence of the whole Christian assembly begging for forgiveness. From the very inception of the Eucharist, then, we are witnesses not only to God but to our fellow brothers and sisters that we have sinned—and that in Christ we have been forgiven. With another option for the Penitential Rite, the *Confiteor* publically acknowledges sin with "Through my fault, through my fault, through my most grievous fault," admitting to our common humanity and humbling the baptized assembly before the Savior of the world and one another. I think that when we see all the conversation partners here—Christ, interceding in the Spirit to the Father, the gathered assembly, and the individual penitent—we are already on the road to forgiving our brother and sister "seventy-seven times." The masks are already off as we begin the Eucharistic Liturgy in spirit and in truth. We see ourselves as sinners like everyone else. Additionally, the words spoken by the priest remind all those present that forgiveness has been extended: "May almighty God have mercy on us, forgive us our sins and bring us to everlasting life."

The promise of being brought to "everlasting life" at the close of the **Penitential Act** is twofold: not only is there a pardon granted to the congregation for reconciliation (not to be confused with sacramental absolution in auricular confession) in preparation for the Eucharist, the witness to eternal life on earth, there is more: this is eternal life made possible by the restorative power of forgiveness here and now, since charity is endlessly re-creative: it builds up the Body of Christ; that is, a covenantal promise from God, who asks only that "we overlook faults" as we our faults confess. It may be a challenge to be reconciled when someone sins against us, but the liturgy provides a foundation for healing and peace.

Strategy for Preaching

Although last week's readings concentrate on similar themes concerning the need to forgive and the role of Christ and the community in unfolding that reconciliation, the preacher does not need to be redundant in the homily for this Sunday. By drawing the congregation's attention to the role of the liturgy in forgiveness, there is a new and often overlooked place to proclaim the readings as witnessed through the liturgical action of the church.

The crucial place to begin is at the beginning. As we observed last week, there will be a default position with the preaching for this week as well: some will harp on the lack of true contrition in a culture that fails to recognize sin. Fair enough, and point well taken. But as true as the observation may be about the blindness of contemporary culture to original sin and its consequences and the need to reconcile with one another, the real issue for the preacher will be to recall God's invitation to us for forgiveness (as we see in the **Penitential Act**), which will cause us to want to be forgiven and deserve to forgive our neighbor.

We might consider, then, a threefold structure that would accommodate the very process I have just suggested: we call on God for mercy; we listen to forgiveness; we forgive. This triad forms the core of the homiletic idea and ultimately calls the Christian community to the witness of charity based on God's own initiation of love.

I. We recognize our need for mercy in the depth of our heart; it is a gracious offering to move into the healing presence of youth and transformation, to return to innocence.

   A. Book of Sirach and the return to the covenant

   B. Freedom from the shackles of the past comes with a recognition of God's love for us

   C. Illustration or story filling out A and B

II. We listen to the forgiveness being offered to us.

   A. The church's liturgy is a response to God's challenge of peace in Christ.

   B. As a community we release our sins to Christ and admit them to one another.

   C. **Penitential Act** catechesis

   D. Theological image and explanation: Christ offers himself up on the cross as a gift for our redemption.

III. We are invited to forgive endlessly.

   A. Emphasis on endless forgiveness, even as the liturgy is ongoing in its work in Christ.

   B. Gospel "seventy-seven" is biblical language for endless

   C. Recognize that we are all the same in Christ's Body

   D. Paul's "live for the Lord" happens here at the Eucharist because our own selfish ego boundaries have been broken down as we become One Body, One Spirit in Christ.

Twenty-Fifth Sunday in Ordinary Time

Readings from the Ambo

Isa 55:6-9; Ps 145:2-3, 8-9, 17-18;
Phil 1:20c-24, 27a; Matt 20:1-16a

The section for the First Reading taken from the book of the prophet (Second) Isaiah is commonly thought of as part of a hymn of celebration (55:1-13), which will conclude the second section of that seminal prophet's words to Israel before the third and last section (56:1–66:24) of Third Isaiah. These few lines are a kind of summary of the exuberating language contained in Isaiah that we might see unfolding in course.

First, there is God's invitation, a breaking of the silence of exile. The prophet opens the door to seek the Lord, not in some distant land or in the future but in the present circumstances. The immediacy of God's promise remains an essential piece of the covenant between the Lord and his people. The exile was a wasteland, a netherworld of loss and bondage without a future. This oracle tells of the nearness of the divine presence: "Seek the LORD while he may be found." Second, there is a call to repentance. I don't think we should see anything in this but an urgent longing on God's part for our goodness. Indeed, the turning away from wickedness proclaims a future for healing and wholeness. Third, there is a recognition of God's transcendence. If the first part of the oracle announces God's imminence, the last part underlines the Lord as (W)Holy Other. We sense in this divine disclosure of imminence and transcendence an essential paradox of the divine mystery. A God of mercy and compassion who dwells in unapproachable light is characteristic of the burning bush revealed to Moses: it is a heart on fire with empathy for the poor, yet sacred so that that same presence dwells on holy ground.

A sense of division and paradox also runs through the epistle for today's liturgy. The Second Reading takes us with Paul to prison, where he is under military guard, and expresses his state of being "caught" in more ways than one. Paul expresses his own sense of paradox when he says that he is caught between the two (*sunecho-mai de ek ton duo*), either "living in the flesh" or departing this life to "be with Christ." Paul judges that remaining for the sake of the church at Philippi would be "more necessary" for their *prokopen*. The translation in the Lectionary for the Greek word *prokope* is "benefit," but the meaning really has to do more particularly with "progress," in this case, spiritual progress. So Paul remains with the Philippians because he is interested in their advancement or progress in the way of the Gospel. The irony is that the more Paul feels drawn into the circle of divine love and the transcendent experience of Christ in departing this world, the more his own compassion and commitment to charity and spreading the Gospel urges him toward remaining close to the Philippians for their progress toward Christ.

Jesus' baffling parable in Matthew's gospel remains, in some sense, inexplicable precisely because of the divine mystery whose paradoxical identity we can never know. Jesus approaches the world of the Father from the perspective of the economy of grace, which can only confound what we believe to be our sense of fairness: those who work less *should* get less, because "the last will be first, and the first will be last." Yet that is precisely the point. The parable is not an exercise in Reaganomics but an analogy about the kingdom. We should be scandalized because of the landowner; and we should be just as scandalized by our reaction, intuited by the landowner's final characterization of the laborers when he says, "Are you envious because I am generous?" Indeed, under the optic of the Beatitudes, this question is both frightening and comforting. Terrifying because we cannot predict or control its outcome or judge who will get in or out; comforting, yes, if we realize that we are *all* late to the vineyard. If we see ourselves as toiling for the whole day and deserving of a full reward, we have lost sight of the kingdom completely.

Connecting the Bible and the Liturgy

The language of the liturgy, as well as the Scriptures to which they are married, draw us into an essential paradox of the divine mystery: to recognize that God's thoughts are not our thoughts. Yet to be conformed to the image of the Son of God unfurls itself like a

wondrous banner in the work of charity. There is a sense in which
this paradox is also mirrored in the twofold commandment to love
God and neighbor, which the **Collect** for today's liturgy surfaces: "O
God, who founded all the commands of your sacred law upon love of
you and of our neighbor, grant that, by keeping your precepts, we may
merit to attain eternal life." The summons here, of course, is to love
the neighbor one is able to see as well as the God who remains hidden. There cannot be one without the other. Paul has become a prime
example of the way these greatest of the commandments have been
lived out. Although he is torn, the great Apostle to the Gentiles will
remain for the sake of the community, for their benefit or progress.

Paul also recognizes that the incarnate God expressed himself
in Christ, thus revealing a transcendence that was imminent. Later
in the letter to the Philippians, he says, "The Lord is near. Have no
anxiety at all, but in everything, by prayer and petition, with thanksgiving, make your requests known to God. Then the peace of God
that surpasses all understanding will guard your hearts and minds in
Christ Jesus" (4:5-7). And again, he takes hold of another paradox:
"life is Christ, and death is gain," certainly a meditation on being in
prison and its potential outcome as a martyr, but also an acknowledgement that God's very nearness is a cause for praise and rejoicing
and worship. Therefore the Responsorial Psalm cries out with Paul:
"The Lord is near to all who call upon him," which also highlights
Second Isaiah's rarified utterance of the immediacy of divine mercy.
The congregation assembled for liturgical worship might be drawn
into the way in which the Eucharist also expresses the divine paradox
that God is terribly near when the celebrant reveals the Eucharistic
Lord as merciful but before whose presence we approach as unworthy (though invited) guests: "Lord, I am not worthy that you should
enter under my roof, but only say the word, and my soul shall be
healed." Like Moses, we are caught up in God's eternal holiness and
are unworthy to approach with our sandals still tied to our feet; yet it
is Christ who beckons us to share this paschal meal and who dwells
with us mysteriously under bread and wine, hiding Body and Blood.

Strategy for Preaching

The illustrious teacher of homiletics, David Buttrick, always insisted that preachers should not ask what a Scripture passage *means,*

but what the text is *doing* to a congregation. In addition to creating an inextricable link to the hearer of the Word in the congregation, Buttrick's teaching reminds us that language shapes us. That force of the word should be obvious in the Christian community who are formed by the Word himself, abiding with the baptized each and every day of our lives. That experience of the Word made visible is deepened in the process of preaching at the liturgical homily.

Matthew's account of the parable in today's gospel is formative at its very core: our sense of "justice" is outraged by love. There is a paradox for us to think about! The question for the preacher will necessarily be how to proclaim the readings in a way that replicates a similar challenge: the first shall be last, but the last shall be first. Taken together, the readings provide an opportunity for the preacher to explore some of the church's teachings on social justice in which the marginalized have been excluded from society but welcomed into the kingdom. So the homiletic core idea might be: if we think we have a sense of justice, God is always going to surprise us by the paradox of his love. I think it would be important to explore Second Isaiah's revelation of God's thoughts as utterly different from our own, as well as pondering the implications of the parable as an invitation to come near to the God who is mysterious yet merciful.

A modern version of this parable, in my estimation, is Flannery O'Connor's "Revelation," published as a collection of short stories in a little volume called *Everything that Rises Must Converge*. Before preparing the homily, the preacher would benefit from the way in which the main character's sense of justice and righteousness are "burned away."

Twenty-Sixth Sunday in Ordinary Time

Readings from the Ambo

Ezek 18:25-28; Ps 25:4-5, 6-7, 8-9; Phil 2:1-11; Matt 21:28-32

In their various ways, the readings for this Sunday all speak about what it means to have a change of heart. Paul's letter to the Philippians urges that community to be humble. We might recall that Philippi was among the first of the churches Paul established, but chapter 1 in that letter makes it clear that there was some opposition already present from the origins of that community in Macedonia. Paul's advice to be humble comes by way of a practical example to the suffering he and his fellow Christians are experiencing: Jesus becomes the example *par excellence* in the famous Philippians hymn (2:5-12) extolling Christ's own humility. A dominant metaphor throughout chapter 2 in the letter is the importance of adopting the "mind" of Christ. The theological underpinnings of this injunction are celebrated in the hymn itself, a *kenosis* or emptying of God's very self for the sake of the world. Paul wants to join his own self, together with the community, in the very person of Christ himself through a transformation of behavior: "If there is any encouragement in Christ, / any solace in love, / any participation in the Spirit, / any compassion and mercy, / complete my joy by being of the same mind, with the same love, / united in heart, thinking one thing."

Joining in the mind of Christ will require letting go of preconceived notions, especially of the right to power and moral certitude, humbly regarding others as *uperechanotas eauton* or "more important"—or even "hyper-important"—than the self. Ezekiel, writing in the time of the Babylonian exile, lets the community know that even their notion of what is fair and not fair has been renegotiated by God. The temptation for the exilic community was to blame God and the previous generations who resisted the call to repent and got themselves into their current situation. Ezekiel wants to dissolve corporate blaming and focus instead on personal integrity, a much more productive and advanced state of moral behavior. If someone "does what is right and just, / he shall preserve his life." In a sense, the Israelites had to change an entire mind-set, which was more about communal shame and blame than personal sin and responsibility. Ezekiel is clearly motioning for moral maturity in the return from exile.

Jesus extends to the sinner this same future, one not shackled with generational baggage, but invested in how an individual life can be transformed by a change in behavior. The son who turned his mind around eventually took ownership of his resistance to his father's command to labor in the vineyard, while the other son, probably a pleasant enough fellow, simply paid lip service to the parental request. From the point of view of the overall movement of Matthew's gospel, Jesus is headed with a showdown with sons who have done a lot of talking about God's commands but demonstrated very little behavior change. Indeed, the backdrop in Matthew's gospel is Christ's confrontation with the chief priests and Pharisees after he enters Jerusalem, cleanses the temple, and is questioned about his right to authority (Matt 21:1-28). These events position us to hear a parable about a son who claims a new moral authority by virtue of repentance (the sinners and tax collectors) rather than the pretended allegiance of the religious institution that refuses to change and, instead, stands on the shoulders of their generational legacy and claim to power in and outside the temple precincts.

Connecting the Bible and the Liturgy

Can we change? That is the question that the Scriptures and the liturgy for today propose, not so much as a query about developmental behavior but as a challenge for the baptized for ongoing conversion of life. Some psychologists and sociologists would argue that after about thirty years of age, we are pretty much the person we will always be. That is probably true enough, but the Scriptures and the liturgy propose a change of heart, a moral and intellectual transformation, which is less determined (although influenced) by personality than by adopting humility and the other virtues as constants in our lives.

We must acknowledge, with St. Thomas Aquinas, that "grace builds on nature," and grace is exactly the point here. The humble person has asked for it; so does the humble assembly, baptized and clothed in Christ as a new creation. At the commencement of the Eucharistic Liturgy, the congregation is sacramentally positioned to pray through Christ, thus adopting the "mind of Christ." The assembly, then, asks for the grace of self-emptying to make us more able to witness to the humble Son of God. The **Collect** prays, "O God, who manifest your almighty power above all by pardoning and showing mercy, bestow, we pray, your grace abundantly upon us." Asking for grace in the liturgy at the beginning with the **Collect**, always mindful of God's mercy, is the first step toward putting on what Paul calls "the same attitude that is also in Christ Jesus."

I think that the Rite of Baptism also makes strong connections with the Scriptures for today, a link I have already pointed out. Having been clothed in Christ, it is grace that covers the newly baptized as one who has changed completely. "See in this white garment the outward sign of your Christian dignity" (Rite of Baptism for Children, 60). The change is absolute and irrevocable: we become "children of God" in baptism, and so the mind of Christ has been bestowed on us, not through an act of personal will, but by sacramental grace. And so the **Collect** for today begs God to make "those hastening to attain" God's "promises heirs to the treasures of heaven." The Father's true heir in Jesus' parable is the one who has changed his mind. From our modern perspective, this change is the transformation from original sin into a child of grace. Indeed, the true inheritors in Paul's letter to the Philippians are those who have put on the mind of Christ, even in suffering, by practicing humility. Turning away from the power of sin and abiding in Christ makes us heirs to the kingdom. As the **Prayer after Communion** puts it: "May this heavenly mystery, O Lord, restore us in mind and body, that we may be coheirs in glory with Christ, to whose suffering we are united whenever we proclaim his Death."

Strategy for Preaching

Paul's use of what some believe to be an ancient hymn in his letter to the Philippians is a centerpiece for a theological meditation on the incarnation. The first step in encountering this important passage for the preacher is the need to discover in prayer, reflection, and pastoral encounters the *kenosis* of Christ in a very specific context. How have I experienced the humility of Christ today? I am suggesting here that the parish has indeed set the context for what it means to suffer with Christ, and that Body has put on the mind of Christ the Savior already in baptism; they are poised at the Eucharist to hear the Word preached, having asked God to free them from selfishness and sin and help them to conform to the mind of Christ in the opening **Collect**. Although I did not mention this text in the earlier section, for both prayerful prehomily meditation and preaching itself, **Common Preface I** (said on weekdays) contains some central theological reflections appropriate for the readings, helping the congregation to recognize that we all share in Christ's fullness: "though he was in the form of God, he emptied himself and by the blood of his Cross brought peace to all creation." Like Paul, then, the preacher can point to the humility of Christ and find the source of redemption in this divine self-giving. This preaching is nothing short of the call to self-examination leading to gratitude, humility, and thanksgiving at the Eucharist and forms the core homiletic idea.

A hard look at American culture is a sure and certain starting point for the homily, not for condemnation but as a window to insight. Indeed, does anyone have room today for a deep self-examination of the mind to see if we have put on the mind of Christ and lived out our baptismal promise? From here, the congregation might be challenged to renew their baptismal promises and recognize the status of being a "new creation." Living as children of God has its demands, and the greatest of these is Christian *kenosis*, just as Christ himself experienced.

In order to avoid abstractions, it is important that the homily exhibit concrete examples, emerging from these theological reflections, and I suggest that the parish is both a real and affirming example. How does the parish community of Saint Anselm or Our Lady of Guadalupe empty itself for the sake of the Gospel? What about personal ego and its selfish ambition? There are very positive examples to allude to here in every parish community, and the preacher acts as an encouraging witness to this corporate striving to adopt the mind of Christ. But there are also probably specific ways in which division might be healed in the community: this difficulty faced Paul in Philippi, and it is a crack in every community. How can these obstacles be overcome? Find ways throughout the day to give power away, to give self-interest to someone else, to live for the sake of changing one's mind, like a son revisiting a parent's request.

The Good News is always restorative, if challenging. Christ's very suffering leads to our redemptive participation in his Spirit as we rise with him. Paul's recommendation that the Philippians see Christ as an example of humility is not only a model but a sacramental reality. We enflesh this baptismal occurrence in the workplace at the liturgy and in all we do.

Twenty-Seventh Sunday in Ordinary Time

Readings from the Ambo

Isa 5:1-7; Ps 80:9, 12, 13-14, 15-16, 19-20;
Phil 4:6-9; Matt 21:33-43

Even a cursory glance at the First Reading and the gospel for this Sunday indicates an intimate connection between the two. Isaiah was not alone in speaking about a vineyard as a symbol for Israel, and Jesus would find himself part of a long tradition evoking the vineyard as an allegorical reference to Israel. The other major prophets also used a vineyard in order to represent the fate of the chosen people, albeit somewhat less developed than Isaiah's parabolic reference. Jeremiah (2:21) mentions a choice vine turned wild; Ezekiel constructs an allegory using a vine to refer to Judah transplanted into exile. Even a minor prophet like Hosea and the psalmists find a strong connection between Israel and the vine.

Jesus positions himself squarely in the midst of this prophetic tradition, and Isaiah's "Song of the Vineyard," excerpted for today's Lectionary, forms the backdrop for the Lord's own allegory about trust, betrayal, and murder. In a sense, both Isaiah and Jesus are gesturing strongly in the same direction: God has established a covenant with his chosen ones that was broken, not by anything the Lord did but by Israel itself. Isaiah explains his allegory like this: "The vineyard of the LORD of hosts is the house of Israel, / and the people of Judah are his cherished plant; / he looked for judgment, but see, bloodshed! / for justice, but hark, the outcry!" Along these lines, Jesus allows the parable of the Wicked Tenants to speak for itself, or rather, the chief priests and the people have to answer at the end of the narrative the Lord's question: "What will the owner of the vineyard do to those tenants when he comes?" / They answered him, / "He will put those wretched men to a wretched death / and lease his vineyard to other tenants / who will give him the produce at the proper times." The trap has been sprung as those who answer incriminate themselves: "Therefore, I say to you, / the kingdom of God will be taken away from you / and given to a people that will produce its fruit."

Jesus chooses to picture himself as a kind of new Isaiah for those in the religious institution of first-century Israel and grafts these chief priests and leaders onto the vine that has produced wild grapes. So if the chief priests and Pharisees claim a tradition, Jesus is connecting them to a corrupt vineyard that will be taken away from them. From a strictly literary point of view, Jesus creates a narrative in which the landowner is more and more sympathetic and the tenants more and more vicious. From a modern Christian perspective, it would be hard to miss the parable as something of a retrospective in which the son has become the last of the servants sent to obtain produce but murdered instead.

The bottom line for both Isaiah and Jesus is summed up in Paul's letter to the Philippians: think about truth, honor, justice, purity, loveliness, and graciousness, excellence, and praise; these are the mind-sets that should occupy the destiny of Christians in order to harvest good grapes. God's continued fidelity is available to us if only we would see it, and once we glimpse the Lord's steadfastness, the insistence on the righteousness of the covenant becomes even more lucid. Paul reminds the Philippians that they are to be harvesting the choice fruits of virtue above all.

Connecting the Bible and the Liturgy

Since we have two readings this Sunday that focus on an allegory of the Lord's vineyard and its consequent parallels to Israel, the Eucharist makes a substantial, indeed vital, parallel to the call to a new vineyard that God himself tends, transforms, and hands over.

The **Presentation and Preparation of the Gifts** gives the gathered assembly an opportunity to revisit Israel's covenant with the Lord in a new, sacramental context. Isaiah's bitter invective against Judah is that when his beloved looked for grapes at the harvest, they were inedible, wild fruit. The church, on the other hand, recognizes that it does not have the power to produce a harvest without the Beloved and the intercession of the Spirit. Consequently, the people of God are able only to present the fruits of the harvest, blessing God for his goodness and asking for a transformation as our *potus spiritalis*. "Blessed are you, Lord God of all creation, for through your goodness we have received the wine we offer you, fruit of the vine and work of human hands, it will become our *spiritual drink*." Like Israel, this is a prayer of *berakah*, an oration of blessing to God for the harvest that is offered back in thanksgiving so that "through the sacred mysteries, which we celebrate with dutiful service, graciously complete the sanctifying work by which you are pleased to redeem us" (**Prayer over the Offerings**).

The vine of blessing will become the cup of righteousness, peace, and justice, made so not by our own virtues by the Beloved himself. As the **Words of Institution** say, "Take this all of you, and drink from it, for this is the chalice of my Blood, the Blood of the new and eternal covenant, which will be poured out for you and for many for the forgiveness of sins. Do this in memory of me." In other words, this new and eternal covenant establishes a vineyard that will never run wild with a rancid harvest because the Savior himself has brought this wine to harvest. The Christian community faces the challenge of listening (as always) to the son of the landowner, the servant sent to yield produce. Although the land has been given over to others by the work of Christ, those who recall the memory of this saving action must be attentive. We can either reject him or remember the covenant he gave us as an everlasting memorial. To fail to heed this *anamnesis* risks our losing the vineyard to other tenants. The virtues that Paul asks us to cultivate will help us all to become good tenants.

Strategy for Preaching

I think that the alliance with Isaiah's "Song of the Vineyard" and Jesus' parable of the Wicked Tenants, together with some of the liturgical parallels I have suggested, help identify a strategic road map for the preacher. A good place to start might be with *berakah*. The preacher might develop the language and purpose of "Blessed are you, Lord God of all creation," as the first section in a homily that prepares the congregation to focus on exactly what we are bringing to the altar and how and by whom we are asking it to be sanctified. The homily might further contrast our modern urban/suburban fast-food culture with the experience of agricultural communities in antiquity. All of us are called to offer the fruits of our lives at the altar, to beg the Lord of the harvest to make our vineyard holy. Isaiah and Jesus clearly allegorize the vineyard as a way of discussing a failure to offer God much else except treachery and rebellion. The congregation has the opportunity to do otherwise by bringing what they have, with the help of the virtues Paul has named for us.

But the real transformation of the fruits we bring—literally at the altar with bread and wine, and figuratively with our lives—comes from the Beloved who through the Holy Spirit transforms sin and makes of us an eternal, perfect harvest of righteousness to the Father, the just landowner from whom all blessings come. I think that a story about transformation would be useful here, perhaps a recent memoir, or a narrative that focuses on the power of God outside of ourselves to make things new.

In the last section, an image for mission may be most appropriate, since now the church gathered must ask how it intends to witness to the harvest of the new wine of the kingdom. How do we plan—as individuals and as a church—to pass the cup of salvation on to others and spread the Good News? We do so when the Body and Blood are distributed to the faithful during communion, but can we take that same cup of the new covenant and pass the wine of righteousness and justice to all we meet in the marketplace?

Twenty-Eighth Sunday in
Ordinary Time

Readings from the Ambo

Isa 25:6-10a; Ps 23:1-3a, 3b-4, 5, 6;
Phil 4:12-14, 19-20; Matt 22:1-14

In the Second Reading, we can see that Paul, writing to the church at Philippi, evinces a remarkable sense of detachment, even while in prison. When the Desert Fathers such as Evagrius speak about advancement in the spiritual life, they use the term *apatheia* to describe a state derived from stoic philosophy whereby the individual soul maintains a sense of equilibrium from the passions. St. Ignatius of Loyola would later refer to this spiritual sense as something like holy "indifference," not even preferring good health to bad health. Indeed, learning how to live "in humble circumstances" as well as "with abundance" becomes for Paul a template not for spiritual athleticism but openness to God's Providence, a condition we might call holy indifference. For Paul, and later, the emerging Christian monasticism, the detachment from the passions enables the will to be in accord with God's plan and to be united in contemplative joy. Paul closes his letter to the Philippians with a firm hope that God will fully supply whatever they need "in accord with his glorious riches in Christ Jesus."

Paul is clearly reminding us that we live inside God's Providence. The image of supplying the needs of all shows itself luminously in one of the most stunning promises of hope in the Hebrew Scriptures: "On this mountain the LORD of hosts / will provide for all peoples / a feast of rich food and choice wines, / juicy, rich food and pure, choice wines." The passage from Isaiah used for the First Reading for this Sunday occurs in the middle of what the prophet sees as a final apocalypse (chaps. 24–27), where all shall be made waste and dried up. Chapter 25:6 initiates another (third) eschatological discourse quite different from the previous two, which focuses on God's judgment. That said, our text pours out a table of plenty and hope for death itself to be vanquished. Rich food will be provided for an eternal banquet because "On this mountain he will destroy / the veil that veils all peoples, / the web that is woven over all the nations."

Jesus' parable describes another kind of apocalypse: the kingdom of heaven, which he likens to a wedding feast. But unlike Isaiah's eschatological feast, those invited to the wedding that the king holds for his son miss the invitation completely. Even one who comes as a replacement for the first group of invitees is not well prepared for the feast and fails to wear a wedding garment. The kingdom is an event, then, for which we must wait, long for, and be prepared to embrace in fullness. Jesus' language is bold and his invitation to come to the wedding urgent. The kingdom of heaven is not for the faint of heart and will be inaccessible to those who fail to respond or who do not prepare to receive it with the garment of salvation.

Connecting the Bible and the Liturgy

Interestingly enough, the **Prayer after Communion** for this Sunday's liturgy picks up the language of Jesus' parable, providing the congregation a reference point for the liturgy as a wedding banquet: "We entreat your majesty most humbly, O Lord, that as you feed us with the nourishment which comes from the most holy Body and Blood of your son, so you may make us sharers of his divine nature." Consider the use of the word "majesty," not unusually deployed in the new *Roman Missal*. The word suggests that we submit to a higher order of authority. Here the expression is especially appropriate because of its obvious connection with kingship in the parable in Matthew 22:1-14.

The Eucharist, we know, is like the kingdom of heaven and the site of the heavenly banquet; it is an eschatological feast at the table of plenty, the mountain God has made holy, where the Bridegroom awaits his Bride, the church, feeding her with his Body and Blood. Additionally, it should not go unnoticed that Isaiah provides us with a striking image of a mountainous utopia, where all people come together in peace to share God's bounty and where tears will be wiped away forever.

We do not want to miss the sign of the kingdom of heaven but remain, as Paul was, completely free and available to receive everything that comes to us in God's house. God is breaking into our small world and astonishing us with divine mercy and restoration. These are the promises of the covenant God made with his new creation at baptism. Yet it would also seem that God has invited whomever he pleases to this Table of Plenty, including outsiders. Plainly enough, Jesus sees the kingdom not as a place where we get to decide who is in and who is out: the King brings into his presence the most marginalize of people, and so those of us who stand in the center should make doubly sure that we are prepared.

When **Eucharistic Prayer III** is used, there an expression that gestures toward the holy mountain God has prepared for all peoples. We ask through the power of intercession that the departed find "kind admittance to your Kingdom. There we hope to enjoy forever the fullness of your glory." This is the language of the kingdom in which we ask for God's hospitality to admit our beloved to the wedding feast of the Lamb at the end of the ages. Clothed with the garment of salvation, the departed will surely find a place at the wedding feast.

Strategy for Preaching

The readings for this Sunday are extraordinary in their power to move us by the sheer force of their images, the power of their feeling, and the strength of their narrative: Isaiah's eschatological feast; Paul's highly personal witness of his own preparation for whatever comes; Jesus' parable of the Kingdom of Heaven as a Wedding Banquet. In one way or another, these readings begin to look forward to the end of time and ask us to be prepared for that event by imagining what it might look like. In Matthew's gospel we also sense an urgency, a final trajectory moving us forward. The narrative structure of Matthew heats up as Jesus focuses on the kingdom and the language of apocalypse.

I think we could target the core preaching idea rather simply as something like this: Are we prepared to imagine God's future? Notice that this question is only about imagining. This envisioning is certainly not a doomsday warning that should go flying across the Internet and all of cyberspace to prepare for the end of the world; it is more threatening than that! We have to *change* if we really hear the parable's demands. Jesus has been giving us metaphor after metaphor in Matthew as to what the kingdom of heaven might be compared. In a certain sense, the parable of the Wedding Banquet functions simply as a raw narrative inducing shock in the hearer. So does Isaiah's image of the holy mountain and its banquet for all peoples. These are analogies meant to break into our little world with its own versions of the kingdom of heaven self-inscribed, and into which we have given ourselves membership. Jesus moves us out of our comfort zone, the place in which we control our own destiny. But God's future will not be harnessed, and Jesus as the Sower of the Word will harvest a crop the destiny of which the Father alone knows, since he alone draws up the invitation for the wedding of his Son.

I might suggest an appropriate, albeit disarmingly simple way into this preaching event. In the 1970s it was popular to have a "Come as you are" party. If I remember correctly, the tactic was this: you are supposed to wear to the party whatever you were clad with when you opened the invitation. Not pretty for some. Some unusual outfits caught people very unawares. Maybe that is what the kingdom will look like . . . catching us unawares . . . are we ready?

You probably get the point: how does the in-breaking of the kingdom occur? Preachers will find their own way of discovering surprises. The kingdom of heaven is beyond our imagining, and so we have to let God prepare the table and provide the food. Ours is just to receive its bounty as gift and be grateful. The Eucharist is an endless table giving food for all, which anticipates the kingdom of heaven and its riches. The readings, together with the liturgical texts, allow us to think again, to image anew, and be ambushed by divine love.

Twenty-Ninth Sunday in Ordinary Time

Readings from the Ambo
Isa 45:1, 4-6; Ps 96:1, 3, 4-5, 7-8, 9-10;
1 Thess 1:1-5b; Matt 22:15-21

It would be hard to exaggerate the bewildering sense of shock that would have come upon the ancient hearer of Isaiah 45. The text finds itself in the middle of some of the most compassionate language in the Hebrew Scriptures, voiced by Second Isaiah, a prophet who has become synonymous with the idiom of rebuilding, reconstruction, and return. And who will be the Lord's instrument in the restoration of Israel's fate from exile? Who will lead the chosen nation into healing? Another King David? No; a non-Israelite will be the messianic promise: King Cyrus of Persia. Astonishing.

We know that the "anointed" has long been associated with Israelite kingship, beginning with Israel's request for a king to rule them in 1 Samuel 8 and then, of course, King David. The Davidic monarchy set the gold standard for what would follow; a messianic king would necessarily follow from his line. But for King Cyrus to be anointed and even referred to as "shepherd" (44:28) transgresses the established link with King David as both king and shepherd of Israel. Most alarming for the chosen people, even though Cyrus apparently knew not the Lord, he was called by name and given a title.

The Lord's use of Cyrus to carry out restoration pushes political boundaries into God's universal plan of salvation. God alone holds the true destiny of Israel in his hands, creating an alliance even with those who do not know him. Paul's letter to the Thessalonians fits well in the context of the First Reading because the letter is addressed to the Gentiles. Paul offers the community at the beginning of his address his encouragement and implores them, despite difficulties, to remember that "knowing, brothers and sisters loved by God, / how you were chosen," that is, *ekloge*, or elected by God. The term becomes an extremely important theological reference, since it allows Paul to convey to the Gentiles that out of God's own free will they have participated in *ekloge*. Paul hints at the bond that exists among believers not just in language or tradition but in the Spirit. "[O]ur gospel did not come to you in word alone, / but also in power and in the Holy Spirit, and with much conviction."

The gospel for today, like the two preceding readings, wants to blur divisions. The Pharisees and Herodians (a secular group who supported royalty) seek to trap Jesus and drive a wedge between God and the emperor. The irony is that Jesus, who ultimately stands squarely in the Jewish tradition of Isaiah and the prophets, does not allow himself to be drawn into a discussion about ideological separation in his "repay to Caesar" response. At the same time, *everything* belongs to God, including the Gentile emperor. As we have seen in our encounter with Second Isaiah, even secular rulers come into the province of God's majesty, as King Cyrus functions as an instrument for God's renewal and an image of the messianic age that is to come upon us.

Connecting the Bible and the Liturgy

As with last week's presidential prayers in *The Roman Missal*, we uncover, once again, monarchical language ("majesty"; a direct translation from the Latin singular dative form *maiestati* from *maistatas*), referring to God's kingship or rule, which may strike some as a bit arcane or antiquated, even baroque in its affected ornamentation. St. Teresa of Jesus, for instance, often refers to "His Majesty" when naming God in her works. The previous translation *Sacramentary* leaves out "majesty" altogether. In the present context, however, it seems that the Scriptures for today give us plenty of warrant for understanding God's majesty over (but not necessarily against) Caesar's secular hegemony. The biblical text reckons God as the Holy One to whom secular rulers, even Gentiles like Cyrus who do not know the God of Abraham, Isaac, and Jacob, may become messianic swords in divine hands. We pray, then, at the **Collect**, "Almighty ever-living God, grant that we may always conform our will to yours and serve your majesty in sincerity of heart."

In a certain sense, the liturgy allows us the space to make a transition from the realm of politics to spirituality. I do not see these entities as mutually exclusive, but mutually informative conversation partners. Indeed, if we allow for the lessons of salvation history in recognizing God as the one who subordinates early authority of every kind, how could we withhold our own wills? This is what the **Collect** is getting at, I believe. The portion of the self—the core of who we are—must not reign over God's own authority. So we ask that "we may always conform our will" to God's. The Eucharistic Liturgy sanctifies the wills of the baptized, even as the homily deepens the faith of that listening congregation, so that "through the purifying action" of God's grace at the Eucharist we may be "cleansed by the very mysteries we serve" (**Prayer over the Offerings**).

Finally, there is an interesting resource available in the opening prayer For The Nation or State that might prove to be a useful touchstone for today. While the **Collect** for this option clearly urges cooperation with the civil order and supports the nation-state in its carrying out of justice and peace, there is no doubt who has given Caesar the authority to rule—and might just as easily take this authority away. "O God, who arrange all things according to a wonderful design, graciously receive the prayers we pour out to you for our country (state), that, through the wisdom of its leaders and the integrity of its citizens, harmony and justice may be assured and lasting prosperity come with peace." This is a sobering prayer to the Divine Architect of "wonderful design," reminding the congregation that no political order may establish utopia or lasting peace. The "lasting prosperity" and its link are not economic satisfaction, but the promise of God's future that will only be fulfilled in the coming of the kingdom, God's rule.

Strategy for Preaching

Preaching this Sunday may provide an opportunity to help the congregation to understand and clarify the role of the nation and its governance, vis-à-vis religion. As I am writing this, the subject of "religious freedom" has become an increasingly important topic on which the American Catholic Bishops are focusing more and more attention. The separation of church and state and giving the nation its due is there to protect religious liberty, after all. At the same time, the Scriptures remind us that all civic authority must be subordinated to God, if not by law of the land, then by divine plan and the order of the universe. Civil authorities have their day in court, it is true, but as Jesus told Pilate in their famous exchange in John's gospel, the governor would not have power over him unless it had been given to him from above. Nothing happens outside of God's egis, and this is an important refrain for the Christian community to keep in mind so that we don't compartmentalize church and state: God's law sometimes requires civil disobedience (think of the civil rights issue in the 1960s overturning the Jim Crow laws) or ongoing protest (Roe v. Wade, 1973).

The core homiletic idea for this Sunday could be based on the Isaiah text: God is able to accomplish all things by any means necessary—secular or religious—and will rely on our cooperation. I think the primary focus in this preaching is really about integration. How much of our personal real estate, so to speak, do we allocate for God to own? This is a good image, in my estimation, to challenge the assembly, without moving too abstractly into the idea of surrendering our wills or making the homily a political pep rally about this or that issue. The fact is that we give God a little here and there. But God wants everything, to serve his "majesty in sincerity of heart." Isaiah recollects, echoing the first commandment: "I am the Lord and there is no other, there is no God besides me." Our modern relativistic subjectivity and our American individualism are challenged by God's sovereignty.

That surrender happens by personal sanctification. There are some whose personal purification will occur in the realm of living countercultural values—as the church at Thessalonica did in the time of Paul. These folks dwell in between God and Caesar, at the edge of the coin, but know where the true authority lies. Developing a homily that encourages the congregation to see themselves as being sanctified in the midst of long-suffering—perhaps even a sense of exile—for the sake of the Gospel is both realistic and true enough in a profoundly secular society. This endurance will be gained by those who render what belongs to God alone.

Thirtieth Sunday in Ordinary Time

Readings from the Ambo

Exod 22:20-26; Ps 18:2-4, 47, 51; 1 Thess 1:5c-10; Matt 22:34-40

Spiritual traditions of every kind have always drawn to themselves a portion of the population who are black-and-white thinkers; for some, religion somehow seems to guarantee a degree of certitude. An unfortunate result of this attitude can be dividing up the world between "them" and "us." To these folks, I would direct a steady and thoughtful gaze at Exodus 22:21–26, which stretches not only geographic boundaries but religious ones as well. The selection for the First Reading is taken from what we now call the "Covenant Code" and presupposes an Israelite society that has been settled in Canaan and deals with negotiating sojourners, widows and orphans, the poor and destitute. Far from structuring a religious society based on insiders and outsiders, the covenantal society of ancient Israel welcomed into their midst the vulnerable and defenseless as part of God's commands. The teaching of the Covenant Code would become the foundation of Judeo-Christian law and the bedrock of Catholic social teaching to the present day.

These stipulations did not arrive in Israel overnight or *ex nihil*; rather, they were derived from this early culture's own experience of liberation at God's hand from alienation and social marginalization. "[Y]ou were once aliens yourselves in the land of Egypt," God tells them. The subtext here, of course, is the commandment of the law, which Jesus himself tells the Pharisee is the greatest: loving the Lord God with all our heart, mind, and soul acknowledges that the same Lord has been the fountain of freedom. The second commandment, love of neighbor as one's self, is like it because we pass on to others the gift of liberation we ourselves have been granted.

271

In the end, these social precepts derive from a theological instinct rooted in Judeo-Christian anthropology—we are *imago Dei*, made in the image of God. If God has had compassion on me and others like me, I ought to be an imitator of this same Lord. If the poor cry out, the Lord says, "I will hear him; for I am compassionate." Therefore, Paul tells the Thessalonians that being "imitators" (Greek: *mimetai*) of him or other disciples and the Lord make those in Thessalonica "a model for all the believers / in Macedonia and in Achaia." The word *mimetes* is related to the word "mimic" in English, but that expression harbors a theatrical and shallow state of imitation. Paul is after something like *imago*: you became images of me and of the Lord, reflecting back (mimesis) what you have seen. Having imitated Paul and the Lord, they themselves become a "model" (or some might say "example"). The true and eternal blueprint, as it were, is Christ Jesus, the image of the invisible God. Christ is the perfect *imago Dei*, compassion itself, the "rock of refuge," as the psalmist has it.

Connecting the Bible and the Liturgy

If the Scripture readings for today focus on God's compassion for the poor and the marginalized—and encourage us to do the same in imitation of the Lord—then the liturgy today draws us into the cultivation of the Christian baptized into *imago Dei*. Indeed, we meet in God's Word Incarnate the bottom line of what it means to be a human being made in God's own image, that model for living is only augmented through grace built on the virtues. As the baptized gather to celebrate the Eucharist this Sunday, the **Collect** prays, "Almighty ever-living God, increase our faith, hope and charity and make us love what you command, so that we may merit what you promise."

"To love what you command" really suggests the degree to which we have become imitators of the Lord, something that Paul reminds the churches again and again. There is sound philosophy behind Paul's teaching, since both Aristotle and St. Thomas Aquinas will insist on the practice of virtues in order to become virtuous; the habit eventually becomes inhabited. Commandments cease to become externalized laws or grudging annoyances when they are loved for the sake of God and our neighbor's good, and, as the **Prayer over the Offerings** puts it in relationship to God, they are "directed above all to your glory."

The liturgy itself is also the locus for imbibing the virtues; we become what we worship as we direct our thoughts and actions through Christ our Lord. Surely the supreme way for the faithful to be imitators of Christ is to be taken up into the prayer of Christ in the liturgy of the Eucharist so that God "might love in us," that which he has loved in his Son, as we hear in **Preface VII of the Sundays in Ordinary Time**. The Eucharist is the source and summit of Christian worship precisely because we pray in and through Christ, when we turn away from our selfish interests and serve the living God, and, in the words of Paul, "await his Son from heaven, whom he raised from the dead, Jesus, who delivers us from the coming wrath." In the Eucharist we are not "instructed" in faith, hope, and love, but *become* embodiments of faith, hope, and love, transformed by Christ into Christ, the redeeming offering of himself to the Father on our behalf. Therefore, the **Prayer after Communion** is a petition to God for a grace-filled continuance of what has begun in our participation in the Eucharist: "May your Sacraments, O Lord, we pray, perfect in us what lies within them, that what we now celebrate in signs we may one day possess in truth."

Strategy for Preaching

I am sure that everyone has had the experience of spacing out or drifting off when we have heard a Scripture passage so many times that the words become like so many duplicates sent through an assembly line. With the gospel for this Sunday, the text has even passed into common parlance as a thumbnail sketch of the New Testament. The role of preaching at all times will be to make God's word new and living for the hearer, but this task becomes more challenging if the text is "written off" as one more religious duty. In a sense, the most unfortunate choice for the preacher is to tell the congregation that they have to do what Jesus says because it is the most important thing to do. The liturgy is most instructive here for the preacher when the **Collect** asks God to "make us love what you command." That statement implies that the preacher's goal is to take the assembly through the process of moral conversion, to long to be imitators of Christ, even as Paul begged the Thessalonians to do the same.

How to do this? The core homiletic idea could be that baptism calls us into the responsibility of being blueprints of Christ so that we might build a city of "faith, hope, and love." As I have insisted in other areas and should be obvious by now, this preaching should be concrete. It is not necessary that the homily start with a blueprint and pick up that image with a city (as I have just recommended a possible image), but there is a poetic and narrational logic that fuels the homiletic process with this metaphor.

With the **Prayer after Communion** as inspiration, there is certainly an opportunity to do some mystagogical preaching on the sacrament of baptism, emphasizing that this sacrament makes us an "imitation" of Christ and transforms our fundamental identity. With the participation of the assembly at the Eucharist, the preacher might call upon a christological explanation of the eucharistic mystery, supported by Paul's council to the church at Thessalonica to be imitators of the Lord. The two great commandments are engaged in our sacramental participation: as we worship God, we become imitators of Christ to love one another.

So our worship at the Sunday Eucharist in Christ is really a dialogical frame for an ongoing love of both God and neighbor as we move on to mission. We cultivate the theological virtues of faith, hope, and love and are sanctified to this end in the liturgy we celebrate. It is our continued full and active participation in the sacraments that helps us to fulfill the two greatest commandments, then, and strengthens us to do the same as we preach the Gospel by our lives.

Thirty-First Sunday in Ordinary Time

Readings from the Ambo

Mal 1:14b-2:2b, 8-10; Ps 131:1, 2, 3;
1 Thess 2:7b-9, 13; Matt 23:1-12

The prophet Malachi is known mostly in the Christian tradition for his famous text (3:1-4) announcing to the Lord's "messenger / to prepare the way" before him during Advent (December 23) as well as the First Reading for the feast of the Purification proclaiming: "And suddenly there will come to the temple / the LORD whom you seek." Although the prophet fits well into the liturgical calendar and our familiarity with him is hopefully optimistic, the overall rhetorical design of the book of Malachi suggests a somewhat different style than any of the other prophets.

The intensity of Malachi's language functions by means of a series of rapid-fire questions and their imagined answers; these reflect a kind of Socratic style, which is not to claim influence. But these queries are not investigations so much as accusations hurled at the priest controlling the worship in the temple. Of utmost concern to Malachi is right worship, apparently grown profane by offering blind animals and polluted food at the altar. For Malachi and the prophetic tradition, which insists on orthodoxy or right worship, that which is pleasing to God is keeping the covenant, a charge with which the Levitical priesthood has been especially invested and, evidently, has grown fairly corrupt at the time of Malachi's writing (sometime after the temple was rededicated in 516 BC).

The Responsorial Psalm "In you, Lord, I have found my peace," may sound especially jarring, perhaps even inappropriate after hearing Malachi's punitive invectives. But the psalm provides a mystical passage into Paul's first letter to the Thessalonians and the gospel

in which Jesus denounces the religious institution of his own day as
witheringly hypocritical. These two texts emphasize a heart of right
worship as well and the peace that comes from such praise. Paul tells
the Thessalonians that they received not human words but "as it truly
is, the word of God, / which is now at work in you who believe." Similarly, Jesus advises the crowds and the disciples not to be persuaded by
human language and example of those who "have taken their seat on
the chair of Moses." Like Malachi, Jesus accuses these religious leaders of falsifying the law and looking for "seats of honor in synagogues,
/ greetings in market places, and the salutation 'Rabbi.'" For Christ,
these practices are the height of hypocrisy, falsifying right worship.
The true test of any religious leader will be the degree to which those
who hold power are willing to serve—really serve, unto death. "The
greatest among you must be your servant. / Whoever exalts himself
will be humbled; / but whoever humbles himself will be exalted."

Connecting the Bible and the Liturgy

Since the readings deal in their various ways with the proper condition of the heart for praising God, the liturgy will have a natural
partner with these texts. Malachi's injunction to offer the Lord fitting praise from the heart is, appropriately enough, echoed in the
Collect for this Sunday: "Almighty and merciful God, by whose gift
your faithful offer you right and praiseworthy service, grant, we pray,
that we may hasten without stumbling to receive the things you have
promised." The phrase "right and praiseworthy service" should leap
out at us and be absorbed on a most fundamental level: right praise
that is *therefore* praiseworthy. I hasten to add the obvious in this
context: we are not praiseworthy because we offer God anything by
way of service; that false attribute Jesus ascribes to the Pharisees and
scribes who desire to be called "praiseworthy."

The words "pure oblation" emerge now and again in the **Prayer
over the Gifts** throughout *The Roman Missal*. That pure offering,
however, is made possible only by the Spirit's intercession, an invocation used during the epiclesis: "Be pleased, O God, we pray, to
bless, acknowledge and approve this offering in every respect, make
it spiritual and acceptable, so that it may become for us the Body
and Blood of your most beloved Son, Our Lord Jesus Christ" (**Eucharistic Prayer I**). The One to whom we offer our gifts is also the One

who blesses them and makes them holy. We only become a "pure oblation" by God's saving action.

As with the entire celebration of the Eucharist, this moment in the **Eucharistic Prayer** of calling down the Holy Spirit is necessarily an act of humility, begging, asking, imploring God Almighty to "accept this oblation of our service, that of our whole family," through the intercession of the Holy Spirit to perfect our imperfect offerings, ourselves. Indeed, it is by the power of Christ in the person of the ordained minister that these offerings are made; any personality on the part of the presider is accidental to the essential work of Christ in him. Therefore, the very act of the presider and the assembly offering up the gifts of bread and wine is truly a presentation of the self, stripped of human affectation and earthly power, in a word, sanctified. The Roman Canon further emphasizes this act of service and "pure oblation" when the ritual calls for the celebrant to bow and say: "In humble prayer we ask you, almighty God: command that these gifts be borne by the hands of your holy Angel to your altar on high in the sight of your divine majesty, so that all of us who through this participation at the altar receive the most holy Body and Blood of your Son may be filled with every grace and heavenly blessing." The Eucharistic Liturgy becomes a "pure oblation," brought into God's presence not by rank or privilege, but by God's Angel—Christ Jesus. "And for this reason we too give thanks to God unceasingly, that, in receiving the word of God . . . [we] received not a human word but, as it truly is, the word of God, which is now at work in you who believe."

Strategy for Preaching

Because of their institutional challenge, these readings may always be tough for any church, but not one that is honest and humbly fit for service. Jesus knew that the language of mutual obedience and conforming ourselves to the will of God would be the only kind worship pleasing to the Father. Whether those words come as a liturgical expression or as part of our daily living, the Scriptures for today are not an invitation to dismantle hierarchical church structures (history has shown what strife this has caused), but to purify our attitudes about right worship and live by our Lord's precious precept, "Whoever exalts himself will be humbled, but whoever humbles himself will be exalted." For very good reason, the Rite of Ordination tells the candidate for the Roman Catholic priesthood to model himself on the life of Christ Jesus, "who came to serve not to be served." How about John 13?

When it comes to the homily, the congregation will be quick to perceive true service. Nothing is more irksome to people than false humility, and this attribute is even worse when it is wrapped in religious garb or titles. The preacher, as I have advised earlier, would do well to examine his attitude toward his preaching "persona." It would not be that unusual for someone to feel called to ordained ministry because they *need* to be called by a title. Or perhaps they are just narcissistic enough to like to stand in front of a lot of people week after week and command their attention. Very few professions offer such platforms of more or less instant credibility. So it is vital—crucial, imperative, urgent—that the preacher develop some accountability system along the lines Jesus suggests: it is after all, a clerical culture that both Malachi and Christ address themselves. Self-examination at all times might begin with a simple question, "Am I up here on this ambo to serve or to be served?" These are sober words, but their honest confrontation will mean effective preaching.

That said, these texts for this Sunday must be preached (as always) to the betterment of the Christian assembly as well as for the virtuous improvement of the preacher. The homily might initiate a question for the congregation along the lines of something like this: "Why have we come to Sunday Mass?" (Note the importance of including the preacher himself in this question.) The provocative query will be parsed generationally, to be sure, and these responses might be named in the homily as potential answers to the question. I suggest that the next section develop a personal story (schools of thought differ on whether to include much self-disclosure in the homily, but here it is a clear tactic) involving faith witness: why do I come to celebrate the liturgy and preach the word of God? This brief personal account could then move to a theological reflection on the role of the church's minister as servant of the liturgy for the sake of the people of God. A christological reflection on the ways in which Christ is discovered in the liturgy, using the presidential prayers for this Sunday would fill out this section nicely. The Scriptures for today also offer a challenge to all of us to stay authentic to the liturgy as servants of the Most High God. Christ's own humility draws us into prayer, saving us and blessing us for service.

Thirty-Second Sunday in Ordinary Time

Readings from the Ambo

Wis 6:12-16; Ps 63:2, 3-4, 5-6, 7-8; 1 Thess 4:13-18; Matt 25:1-13

The portion of the book of Wisdom from which the First Reading is extracted introduces a short section (chaps. 6–9) on wisdom as a virtue. The author (the tradition reckons him as Solomon) personifies wisdom as a woman to be desired above all things. The Wisdom of Solomon was written in Greek and, though obviously addressed to a patriarchal Jewish culture, has absorbed some Hellenistic characteristics woven into the diaspora. Described as the breath of God, there is something of the "goddess" about wisdom whom Solomon desires to take as his "bride" (8:2) and who, like Athena, has astonishing powers, "seeking those worthy of her, / and graciously appears to them in the ways, / and meets them with all solicitude."

The author makes wisdom so alluring and attractive, who would not desire her? That is precisely the point. The present text is almost like a love poem, a homage that the king of Israel pays to the importance of acquiring "the perfection of prudence." That Israel has ascribed one of its monarchs as the author of the present text suggests the crucial alliance power has with wisdom, and as the rest of the book demonstrates, the desire and longing for wisdom as a consort becomes the hallmark of the true leader. It is interesting to note that the passages here are really about waiting for wisdom rather than showing us the result of its attainment. "For taking thought of wisdom is the perfection of prudence, / and whoever for her sake keeps vigil / shall quickly be free from care." As alluring as wisdom may be, she does not appear to take up residence for very long but "makes her own rounds."

Waiting at the gate for yet another marriage are the ten virgins who will either choose to be wise or foolish in their vigil for the bridegroom.

The five who were wise brought oil, which is to say, they burned with desire for the bridegroom and were prepared to keep vigil. Their entire attention was directed toward a single purpose: waiting for the return of the bridegroom and getting ready to go out to meet him. This vigil for the bridegroom who is making a sudden, but incalculable return, admits to no diffusion, even when it comes to helping the foolish who were less than prudent in forgetting oil for the lamps.

In a way, Paul's words to the Thessalonians urge them to keep their own lamps burning as well. Evidently confused and perhaps discouraged, the church at Thessalonica was baffled at the delay of Christ the Bridegroom. What does it mean to die before his return? That is a legitimate question for the early church. Paul's letter is an affirmation of Christ's return for those who have not yet fallen asleep and who will be caught up with the dead together "to meet the Lord in the air. / Thus we shall always be with the Lord." The vision of the apocalypse is comforting but also a summons to be prepared and ready for a time we do not expect. Therefore Paul's vision, consoling as it is, is also a preparation for Christ's final return to his Bride, the church, who will join him in heaven.

Connecting the Bible and the Liturgy

From a purely literary perspective, all three readings and even the Responsorial Psalm contain a lot of movement. Wisdom "hastens to make herself known" in anticipation of desire; the psalmist is "thirsty for God," and is "lifting up" his hands calling on God's name. Paul says that the Lord himself, "with the voice of an archangel and with the trumpet of God, / will come down from heaven, / and the dead in Christ will rise first"; and Jesus reminds us that the "kingdom of heaven will be like ten virgins / who took their lamps and went out to meet the bridegroom."

The active movement of the Scriptures this Sunday helps to support the language of the liturgy. In a certain sense, the liturgy today positions the worshiping assembly to be in a kinetic space from the start: this is the Thirty-Second Sunday in Ordinary Time, and we are hastening toward the end of the church year. Even more to the point, though, we are all hastening toward death, a final encounter with the Bridegroom. The **Collect** prays that we run quickly to pursue the things that are the Lord's, including, we can intuit, an abiding wisdom: "Almighty and merciful God, graciously keep from us all adversity, so that, unhindered in mind and body alike, we may pursue in freedom of heart the things that are yours."

I'd like to read the plea to keep us from all adversity as part of Jesus' allegory about the ten virgins. Adversity threatens to steal away the oil we have brought that may come, as it did for some of the Thessalonians, in the form of discouragement and desolation concerning the Lord's return. Resisting adversity comes from remaining constantly watchful, and this attentiveness will keep us in good stead as we prepare for the end—our last days as well as the earth's as we know it. Wisely, Paul fills the minds of the church at Thessalonica with thoughts of God's triumph at the end of time; these images banish despair and replace dark thoughts with hope. To confront such a terminus, as other believers have done before us, and face our mortality and the ephemeral nature of all created things, suggests that wisdom has not only been strongly desired but has been taken as a companion for the journey. Once again alluding to the acquisition of the things that are God in purity of heart, the **Prayer after Communion** begs the Lord that "by the pouring fourth of your Spirit, the grace of integrity may endure in those your heavenly power has entered." The implication of *per infusionem Spiritus tui* is that it is God who will supply the oil of grace for those who wait at the gate for the Bridegroom. Our lamps will never run out of oil since we know what it takes to burn with desire for the return of the Bridegroom and that God supplies all things to those who ask, including wisdom.

Strategy for Preaching

I have already suggested the vital importance of exegeting the assembly before any preaching event. It strikes me that the readings for this Sunday are usually difficult to preach for a number of reasons, most of which concern the composition of the assembly. Some of these factors have come up in other ways when preaching the Lectionary, but this Sunday gives us an opportunity to see how we might confront the biblical readings and the liturgy in the context of contemporary culture.

Wisdom and its desire come with maturity and age, so how do you preach this virtue to a youth group or even a multigenerational assembly? Solomon's world seems a far cry from contemporary

America, to say nothing of five wise virgins waiting for a bridegroom to return. Paul's letter to the Thessalonians was very specifically targeted as an occasional epistle for those who expected Jesus to return at any moment. For those of us today who have adjusted to Christianity without a burning eschatology, what does this letter have to say? Finally, Jesus' parable of the Ten Virgins waiting for a bridegroom will offend some in the congregation because of its strange allegorical and polygamous references, its patriarchal language, and its antiquated views on women. In short, as rich as these Scripture readings are, how can they be made new and relevant?

Once again, I think we should turn to the liturgical texts as a significant conversation partner for this Sunday's preaching. In fact, we might draw the core homiletic idea directly from the **Collect** itself: God desires that we pursue all things that are his in freedom of heart. There is a lot here to support a fine homily. If we unpack the core statement and create some tactics, we first notice a profound starting point: God desires. God wants our good, and so the pursuit of wisdom (together with prudence and the other virtues) will help us to attain that good. A following tactic that will be crucial in order to avoid abstractions: What does wisdom look like? Solomon imagines this quality as a woman, but I think we can contemporize this virtue easily enough for various age groups. The preacher will have to imagine what is important to his assembly, depending on who they are.

Secondly, God not only desires, he wants us to desire. God wants us to pursue all things that are his. The psalmist longs for God. The Eucharist says that they are blessed who are called to the Supper of the Lamb. The baptized long for the Bridegroom, the Lamb of God. How will we run to the altar of God? Is there a story of someone the preacher might illustrate who has pursued a goal with passion? One who burns with zeal for working with the poor or the aging?

Thirdly, we desire the things of God in freedom of heart. We are all given oil for our lamps, and it is up to us to keep ourselves burning with this zeal for God. We do not run to God under duress, but in perfect freedom in a love that casts out fear. In his Rule for monks, Benedict uses the image of "the heart expanding" with "inexpressible delights" as we run the ways of God's commands. The congregation of listeners should be urged to hasten: to seek virtue; to run toward Christ in one another and in the Eucharist; to hasten toward our heavenly home.

Thirty-Third Sunday in Ordinary Time

Readings from the Ambo

Prov 31:10-13, 19-20, 30-31; Ps 128:1-5;
1 Thess 5:1-6; Matt 25:14-30

Broadly speaking, this Sunday's First Reading forms a kind of connective link with last week's Lectionary readings, particularly with the book of Wisdom. Both envision a quest for a partner in life that will make the journey complete. For Solomon, wisdom comes as a woman, seemingly unattainable, yet desirable as a bride; wisdom comes whispering prudence in the ears of a lover. On the other hand, for the author of the book of Proverbs, as we might expect, the choice is more practical: when one finds a worthy wife, her value is far beyond pearls. It is the concrete expression of an honest-to-goodness marriage partner sitting across from me at the breakfast table that is beyond measure.

From a contemporary Christian perspective the selection from the book of Proverbs underlines the incarnational, mediating presence of the human subject. I am sure that most would agree that there is absolutely no reason why "husband" cannot be substituted for "wife." As the historical-critical method has demonstrated over and over again, we need to take into account the "setting in life" with which the Scriptures were framed. Always historicize but don't stop there. Indeed, the Proverbs, like the Psalms that are also part of the Wisdom literature of the Bible, are wonderful examples that, once historicized, can also offer the modern community a new vision as well. Here we note that there is an underlying value driving the search for a life partner: the wife is cherished because she is a place of trust, brings goodness into the home, helps the poor, and is not caught up in the world of charms, but fears the Lord. From this vantage point, the reading really points us in the trajectory of the good, mediated by

283

the life partner; it suggests an eternal value underneath our transitory existence. The Responsorial Psalm underlines these values by singing that the home itself will flourish when one fears the Lord.

The "fear of the Lord" forms the backdrop for Jesus' teaching on the parable of the Talents as well. The Wisdom literature shows us that we must be actively engaged in the pursuit of God's eternal values, whether or not we are a king (like Solomon) or an average person (like the author of Proverbs). Shrewdly, the Wisdom literature represents such divine seeking as a coupling between man and woman. Just as cleverly, Jesus makes this pursuit an economic one. The man who does nothing with his talents is guilty of wasting his life and failing to be actively engaged in seeking God. I am sure that there are those who will read this parable and find there the so-called Gospel of Prosperity, multiplying capital when we follow the right course. But I disagree with this interpretation. The parable's disarming emphasis remains on the right kind of fear of the Lord: not one that covers and buries the gift of life, but one that, in a sense brings life to the home and pursues values like Solomon and the author of the book of Proverbs; this is the one who becomes truly blessed with riches of the kingdom.

And we should negotiate no delay in our journey for such eternal riches. As Paul tells the Thessalonians, the day of the Lord will come "like a thief at night." This is what the in-breaking of God's kingdom looks like: burying our gifts is antithetical because this attitude lives in darkness and fear. "Therefore let us not sleep as the rest do, / but let us stay alert and sober."

Connecting the Bible and the Liturgy

Two of the presidential prayers for this Sunday ring with an unusually remarkable phrase that echoes the wisdom of Israel: "Grant us, we pray, O Lord our God, the constant *gladness of being devoted to you*" (**Collect**). Similarly, the **Prayer over the Offerings** asks that "what we offer in the sight of your majesty may obtain for us *the grace of being devoted to you*." The blessed one who fears the Lord finds him-or herself in constant, devoted gladness (*semper devotione gaudere*), so we ask for the grace of being devoted to God (*gratiam nobis devotionis obtineat*). In other words, we ask for the gift of heartfelt devotion to God in order to abide in *gaudium*, joy.

We can take this as a classic instance of seeking God as being its own reward because gladness and happiness are a result of a search for God, with what we might refer to as good zeal—something like amassing ten talents after being given just one. The **Communion Antiphon** reminds us of our natural inclination to find fulfillment in God's presence, which will naturally lead us to *gaudium et spes*. "To be near God is my happiness, to place my hope in God the Lord."

The liturgy, then, becomes as it always is, a source of life and encouragement for the people of God. If we think symbolically about the gift of baptism, that sacrament might be construed as a single talent we have been given, waiting to be multiplied in love throughout the duration of our lives. We are bound to be discouraged from time to time and live out of fear, burying the gift we have been given. If so, the **Collect** raises us up again as it continues: "for it is full and lasting happiness to serve with constancy the author of all that is good." There are a great deal of values embedded in this small clause: happiness comes from constancy and in serving; God is the author of our being; seeking God means living for the sake of the Creator of all that is good. In some sense, the **Collect** catches us in the process—like the active pursuit of wisdom—living out our faith not in a static way, but dynamically. We come to the Eucharist to give thanks for the "talent" given to us in baptism, the Christ whom we have put on as a garment and so that we may "obtain the grace of being devoted" to God and receive "the prize of everlasting happiness" (**Prayer over the Gifts**). That beatific vision, we know, is to be near God, which, by the gift of Christ and the power of the Spirit, begins but does not end at the Eucharistic Liturgy, the foretaste of the Heavenly Banquet, the supper of the Lamb, where we shall see God as he is, together will all the blessed who enjoy that vision.

Strategy for Preaching

The Scriptures and the liturgy more than hint at the search for happiness and even eternal bliss. Indeed, the question of happiness is an elusive one, the pursuit of which, together with life and liberty, is inscribed in the American Declaration of Independence. Contemporary culture seems directed toward finding happiness and, once grasped, never releases its iron fist. And yet the longing for happiness might be likened to something Oscar Wilde once said about fox hunting, in which the nineteenth-century author described gentlemen galloping after a fox as "the unspeakable in pursuit of the inedible." Try as we may to capture happiness, we find it somehow unavailable. "To be near God is my happiness," is what the psalmist says constitutes real joy, the result of the pursuit of God and God's goodness in constancy and love.

So the core homiletic idea for today should have a strong cultural component, I think. It might look like this: the moment of our baptism brings us nearer to God than we imagine, and at the end of our days we are either going to be closer to Christ or further away; there is no standing still. Since we are moving rapidly toward the end of the church year, there should be some sense of urgency to this preaching, underlining the search for God as the only true and real journey that will yield happiness.

What does this look like? It may be expedient to allegorize baptism as a kind of investment (literally so, since we are given a white garment) that either grows larger or stays a tiny silk dress. The preacher might then contrast this kind of sacred talent and its wise multiplication with other, more ephemeral pursuits typical in modern society. There are lots of these and they are colorful, including the stock market, the search for the perfect house or neighborhood, the expectation of perfection in ourselves and others. Images can be theme park rides only delivering temporary fun, bridges that are half built, vacation tours where the bus breaks down.

It would be useful to cite instances of mediation where God has been revealed and challenge the congregation to ponder these moments in recollection. Proverbs uses a good wife, but there are numerous examples in which God has revealed eternal goodness and happiness; some may have even come in the midst of suffering and illness and loss. As a community of faith (i.e., the parish) we mediate for one another the constancy that is needed. At this point, we should take advantage of multigenerational and cross-cultural difference: young witnesses to the elderly present in the congregation reveal the life of the Spirit: the springtime of innocent, excited faith and the elderly and wise journey of fidelity. Then again, the various cultures present in the congregation display courage, often in the midst of economic and social hardship. Drawing near to one another in the love of God will allow us to sense what true happiness might be like, even as we invest our talent in the love of Christ.

SOLEMNITIES
OF THE LORD
DURING ORDINARY TIME

The Most Holy Trinity

First Sunday after Pentecost

Readings from the Ambo

Exod 34:4b-6, 8-9; Dan 3:52, 53, 54, 55;
2 Cor 13:11-13; John 3:16-18

The brief selection from the book of Exodus is only a swatch from the vast brocade of that magnificent book, yet the passage is quite revelatory for a number of reasons. It is the fourth and final theophany that began with Moses' encounter with the burning bush on Mount Horeb (3ff.). If we look at the previous two chapters before the present selection in the Lectionary for this Trinity Sunday, we note that the rebellion that faced Moses in the desert (and the breaking of the first tablets of the covenant in chapter 32:19) is being "repaired" in chapter 34: God grants Israel another chance (among endless others). Broadly speaking, this subtext—the God of mercy and redemption—will form the constitutive identity of Israel's God throughout their history, even beyond the first covenant that was established with Abraham. God renews his covenant even when the people do not uphold their side of the bargain. And that steadfast love—more than just a legal agreement—becomes crystal clear with the new covenant (34:10-28).

The passage tells us something about Moses and his relationship with God as well, particularly as a friend of God, one who knows him by name (22:17). Indeed the present and last theophany to Moses occurs because that courageous intercessor for Israel asked God to show him his ways (33:13). So Moses has been zealous for God, eager to seek him out, and this unusually transparent relationship with the Holy shows us the powerful and unique role Moses claims as the one who stands in the breach between God and God's people. The theophany discloses not only a merciful and loving God but Moses himself: ecstatic in wonder at the Lord God. "Thus the LORD passed before him and cried out, / 'The LORD, the LORD, a merciful and gracious God, / slow to anger and rich in kindness and fidelity.'" Moses both illuminates and mediates God's presence for the people.

This heart of God becomes radiantly clear, of course, in Jesus' conversation with Nicodemus, who seeks Jesus out at night. The Lord describes God as the One who "so loved the world that he gave his only Son, / so that everyone who believes in him might not perish / but might have eternal life." Here again, we are in the presence of the power of intercession—the greatest of intercessions. But as Son, Jesus makes it plain that it is the power of belief that participates in this divine mediation, the very life of the Godhead. God dwells deeply in the heart of believers only if he is admitted there by faith, born again in baptism.

It is this very indwelling that Paul wishes for the Christian community in Corinth. Although the close of Paul's letter has a familiar ring to it, the Spirit is included together with the grace of "the Lord Jesus Christ / and the love of God." Paul is certainly no stranger to the work of the Spirit, and his pneumatology will play itself out not so much in 2 Corinthians as it will in other arenas of the Pauline corpus. For now, this Trinity Sunday, we are left with a farewell greeting that underlines the work and presence of the trinitarian God for all the ages.

Connecting the Bible and the Liturgy

Since the Trinity is the central tenant of our Christian faith everywhere we look in the liturgy, the signs of God's threefold person are revealed rather explicitly for the faithful on this solemnity in a special and vivid way. Indeed, although the Eucharistic Liturgy is itself the expression in sacrament of the work of the mystery of the Trinity, this Sunday's readings allow us to penetrate deeper into that most sublime doctrine given to the church. Our response throughout this solemnity can be nothing short of the acclaim of wonder Moses uttered at the last theophany in the book of Exodus: "The Lord, the Lord, a merciful and gracious God, slow to anger and rich in kindness and fidelity."

When taken together, the Lectionary readings focus on a different person of the Trinity, as it were: the theophany to Moses in Exodus shows the God of mercy and compassion amid transcendent radiance; Jesus' disclosure to Nicodemus unveils how that divine love is expressed in the incarnate Son; Paul emphasizes the presence of the Spirit working with the Father and the Son in "fellowship." The word Paul uses for fellowship or communion is *koinonia*, a critical word in the New Testament Greek lexicon used to refer to the sacred bond that exists among the members of the Christian family. The liturgy for today works to draw the congregation together precisely as gifted *koinonia*, taking them away from their separate selves and into the center of the life of the one God, though equal and distinct in Persons three. The Niceno-Constantinopolitan Creed expresses the unity of Three Persons in reflecting, quite concretely, on the unity among these mysterious Persons. The Son is not made, but *"consubstantialem Patri"* from all ages, which is just to say from the "same substance" with the Father: not made but begotten. The Holy Spirit *procedit* from the Father and the Son. We might note here that *procedit* is in the present tense, implying that the work of the Holy Spirit is not just part of an event that happened in time once and for all (as in Acts 2), but *ex Patre Filioque procedit*.

The Preface: The Most Holy Trinity allows the presider to sing of the creedal formula in a poetic way, giving thanks for the tenants of faith expressed in the Creed. The **Preface** begins: "For with your Only Begotten Son and the Holy Spirit you are one God, one Lord: not in the unity of a single person, but in a Trinity of one substance." If there is wonder at the complicated vocabulary of the Creed, particularly surrounding "consubstantial" (there probably should be), the **Preface** may help to illuminate the relationship between the Father and the Son.

I would also like to suggest that the **Collect** holds a particular relationship with the gospel, even as this opening prayer echoes Jesus' conversation with Nicodemus. "God our Father, who by sending into the world the Word of truth and the Spirit of sanctification made known to the human race your wondrous mystery." Consider the amplification of the work of the Spirit that the **Collect** brings to the scriptural text: Jesus does not mention to his erstwhile disciple the reality of the Spirit—though the Person of the Spirit is implied theologically—but the **Collect** makes the relationship between the

Three Persons and the work of the paschal mystery quite lucid as it gathers in the assembly into that same Spirit of *koinonia*.

Strategy for Preaching

There is a certain generation of preachers who were trained to simply go through the readings and act as a kind of gloss on their meaning. This method of preaching was a gallant attempt to help the faithful understand the "richer fair" available in the new Lectionary after the Second Vatican Council. But as we know from *Fulfilled in Your Hearing* and other homiletic commentaries, the object of the preacher is to fashion a text that speaks not on but "through the Scriptures." The temptation this Trinitarian Sunday is all too seductive, since each of the readings appears to express another aspect of One God in distinct persons. Preachers should resist this tendency and, as always, strive for an organic text that will crystallize around one homiletic idea.

I know anecdotally from preachers of all faith traditions that this Sunday is notoriously difficult for sermonizing; it seems counterintuitive, given the primacy of place that the Trinity holds as the life and being of Christians, and the animation of the *koinonia* of Christ. Well, maybe it's not so strange. How to explain the inexplicable? But that may be precisely the point: the Trinity is not something that the preacher explains as much as reveals. This revelation can occur by preaching through the Scriptures as well as by quoting salient passages from doctrine or liturgical texts of major or minor euchology such as the presidential prayers and **Preface**. In this regard, though, the liturgical texts' pairing with the Scriptures will be most helpful and thinking of effective preaching as a mystagogical homily a helpful starting point. A related issue that must be dealt with on some level is the question guiding the homily this Sunday, blunt as it may be: So what? That is a pastoral question, indeed a preaching mandate to make the mystery of this solemnity and the readings that surround it relevant to the lives of men and women. So no wonder this is a difficult homily to discover: it forces the preacher to confront the most important and complex and life-giving mystery of the church and make it part of everyday life for the Christian people. That is a tall order.

I suggest we start with the basics: John 3:16. I saw a woman tattooed with this on her face at a rally once. That there are a number of these signs all over America might tell us that this text from John's gospel speaks to a culture crying out for love and mercy. And so with this observation or something like it as an introduction, the core preaching idea for today could be: We long for God's love; we found it in his Son, and he is with us now in the community of the Holy Spirit.

The Exodus reading reminds us that despite their transgressions, God gave the Israelites a new covenant. In a sense, Nicodemus rehearses the same longing for that renewal when he speaks to Jesus; unknown to him, he is speaking with the one who would make that covenant possible. The **Collect** shows us this very moment of salvation. What if we extended this saving moment for all eternity: that is life in the Spirit, life in *koinonia*, the community of the baptized that draws its breath from the divine life of the Trinity. There may be appropriate and necessary references to *The Catechism of the Catholic Church* at this point, especially in sections 237 and following, which brilliantly and concisely interpret the dynamic of the indwelling of the Trinity.

And then a concluding section must address: So what? Example: That Spirit is at work here in this liturgy that empowers the whole church as it proceeds from the Father and the Son, even as we profess our faith as gathered into one Spirit in Christ. As we cry "Holy, Holy, Holy" in the *Sanctus*, we are taken up into the life of the Trinity, even as we confess that undivided unity with our lives. We are a Christian community that cannot be broken because we are animated by the love of the Trinity. God makes a difference and brings us together as one, redeemed in Christ. Illustrate by specific evidence (national, local, parochial).

The Most Holy Body and Blood of Christ
Sunday after the Most Holy Trinity

Readings from the Ambo

Deut 8:2-3, 14b-16a; Ps 147:12-13, 14-15, 19-20;
1 Cor 10:16-17; John 6:51-58

The book of Deuteronomy is divided into five major sections. The First Reading comes from the second part of these (4:22–11:32) and is a discourse on preparing for a relationship with God through the covenant he established. The import of the passages takes its momentum and authority from Moses' first word: "Remember." So this reading appears as something of an admonition to those who have come through the difficult passage in the desert from the bondage of slavery. "Do not forget the Lord, your God, / who brought you out of Egypt, / that place of slavery, / who guided you through the vast and terrible desert / with its seraph serpents and scorpions, / its parched and waterless ground."

The focal point for Israel's memory of God's saving action is manna (*man hu*, or "what is it?"); it is "a food unknown to you and your fathers," Moses says. So there have been at least two generations who have not experienced the feeding in the desert, but Moses (whose memory and experience embraces the entire journey) urges memory as the tool to recollect God's wonders for those who have missed God's action in person. Manna should be seen, then, as a sign that "not by bread alone does one live, / but by every word that comes forth from the mouth of God." Jesus himself will use this truth when he defeats the tempter in the wilderness.

As the Word who has come forth from the mouth of God, Jesus becomes manna, bread for God's people. He details this very self-giving in a graphic way when he says, "Amen, amen I say to you, / unless you eat the flesh of the Son of man and drink his blood, / you do not have life in you." As has been observed before, the Greek verb for "to eat" that John uses in this particular instance is *trogo*, which quite literally means "I chew" or, more colloquially, "I munch." So Jesus' hearers were probably reacting a little like the people of Israel when they first saw the manna: "what is it?" What is he saying!? John emphasizes the nourishing quality of Jesus as real food, as "bread that came down from heaven." Jesus has in mind a new covenant sealed not with manna in the desert, but with his bread for the life of the world. "Unlike your ancestors who ate and still died, / whoever eats this bread will live forever."

Paul's words to the Corinthians famously remind that community that their own nourishment received from the Lord's table is a "participation" in the Body of Christ. Paul once again uses the word *koinonia* to express the reality of the divine in the community of love. In a sense, Jesus was saying something similar: chewing on my flesh and drinking of my blood cannot but allow you to participate in the Body: you become *koinonia*. And for Paul, this Body is One, a theology he will develop more fully later in 1 Corinthians (12:12ff.).

Connecting the Bible and the Liturgy

The Scriptures for this solemnity are rich with eucharistic theology for obvious reasons. To this end, sacred memory, *koinonia*, and the Bread of Life discourse in John all form a web that guides us through an ancient and holy day in the life of the church.

I. Sacred memory: From the perspective of memory, the **Collect** immediately reminds the assembly that God "left us a memorial." **The Preface: The Fruits of the Most Holy Eucharist** celebrates the memorial itself, actively engaging the memory of the gathered assembly when it says, "For at the Last Supper with his Apostles, establishing for the ages to come the saving memorial of the Cross, he offered himself to you as the unblemished Lamb, the acceptable gift of perfect praise." Additionally, **Preface I/II of the Most Holy Eucharist** uses the term *memoriam*, saying that Christ was "the first to offer himself as the saving Victim, commanding us to make this offering as his memorial" (**I Preface MHE**). The theological and scriptural armature for these prefaces is Moses' mandate in Deuteronomy: "Do not forget the Lord, your God, who brought you out of the land of Egypt." Christ establishes "for the ages the saving memorial of the cross . . . nourishing your faithful by this sacred mystery." And so the Lord commands: *"Hoc facite in meam commemorationem."*

II. *Koinonia*: In Paul's world of mystical fellowship, where the faithful join in "participation" in the Body of Christ, we find a very poetic parallel in the **Sequence**: *Lauda Sion* (one of only two *required* for the liturgical year) translated into English in the Lectionary. "Whoso of this food partakes, Does not rend the Lord nor breaks; Christ is whole to all that taste; Thousands are, as one, receivers, One, as thousands of believers, eats of him who cannot waste." The **Sequence** underscores the unity of the Body, reflected in the Body of Christ about to be consumed. The **Preface** for this solemnity says, "Nourishing your faithful by this sacred mystery, you make them holy, so that the human race, bounded by the one world, may be enlightened by one faith and united by one bond of charity."

III. The Bread of Life discourse in John 6, with its highly intense "I am" statements is unavoidably relational. Jesus is saying that we will be different if we eat this Bread of Life, this flesh. "Whoever eats my flesh and drinks my blood has eternal life, and I will raise him on the last day." The divine proposal here from Jesus is not so much a memoriam as it is simply to eat and drink—that is, *participate* in the very life of Christ: be *koinonia* with the Lord and one another in this living bread. He tells them *"Ego eimi ho artos ho zon"* or "I am life bread," which suggests not only an animated present force but one that is ongoing in the work of charity, the central participative life of the *koinonia*. We become what we eat and drink, Christ Jesus, and continue to do so. We will be raised up to eternal life, even as he was raised. That is the (super)natural consequence of becoming one with the Body. "And so, we approach the table of this wondrous Sacrament, so that, bathed in the sweetness of your grace, we may pass over to the heavenly realities here foreshadowed" (**Preface II MHE**).

Strategy for Preaching

As we know, the scriptural and liturgical texts for the Solemnity of Corpus Christi have their roots deeply embedded in the Catholic tradition. In this regard, the day seems to beg for some catechetical engagement. At the same time, the explication of the mysteries of the Eucharist are complemented by the way in which the day speaks for itself as a mystagogical event: it is a powerful witness to the reality of Christ's passion, death, and resurrection, memorialized in his Body and Blood. It was the custom (and still is in some places) for parishes to invest themselves in *Corpus Christi* processions, suggesting that the testimony offered is public in its declaration. The day wants to unfold in the midst of the marketplace, drawing people of goodwill to itself, while also challenging social norms as a countercultural witness to charity and the God of peace and love who gave himself over to death for the salvation of the whole world. In a sense, it is the very public character of the solemnity that makes the day different from the Sunday liturgy, and preachers might take the opportunity to shape the assembly as public witnesses of the sacrament of love. The core homiletic idea, then, might be: We have welcomed Jesus into our lives and even our hearts with this Eucharist, but the Lord also desires to be living with us in community wherever we go.

Here is a short outline:

I. We tend to think of the Eucharist as our private devotion.

II. But we come to bear public witness to John 3:16 so that we become a participation in the Body of Christ.

III. That testimony, then, never forgets the Lord but remembers and helps the whole world see God's salvation.

The Most Sacred Heart of Jesus

Readings from the Ambo

Deut 7:6-11; Ps 103:1-2, 3-4, 6-7, 8, 10;
1 John 4:7-16; Matt 11:25-30

The passage from the book of Deuteronomy chosen for the First Reading is a defining moment for the chosen people—precisely as a unique nation, holy to the Lord. That Israel was selected from among other nations who are stronger and mightier and more numerous than they suggests that their exclusivity emerges not from anything the chosen people have done, but because of God's mysterious love. "It was because the LORD loved you / and because of his fidelity to the oath he had sworn to your fathers, / that he brought you out with his strong hand / from the place of slavery, / and ransomed you from the hand of Pharaoh, king of Egypt." God's own initiative made this liberation possible because of divine mercy, and the covenant was established with Abraham, Isaac, and Jacob out of a covenant of unconditional fidelity.

Moses' recollection of God's eternal love for the chosen people serves to reinforce a response: obedience to "carefully observe the commandments, / the statutes and the decrees that I enjoin on you today." I think we should interpret Moses' call to follow the commandments as a call to love—not as slavish keepers of laws and precepts, but as heartfelt friends of God. After all, why would God liberate the people from slavery, only to reincarcerate them in a prison of laws? The memory of God's love is enough to bring a response to obey out of love. Moses invites us to consider a vital spiritual principle: of remembering how much God loves and to return to that experience of liberation as a ground of who we are as a people chosen by the Lord.

John emphasizes this same love of God, so clearly expressed in the well-known phrase, "In this is love: / not that we have loved God, but that he loved us / and sent his Son as expiation for our sins." Indeed, liberation from the Egypt of our sins has occurred in the Pasch of Jesus the Lamb. We keep his memory as a new covenant in his blood shed for the life of the world. This is the Spirit he has given us so that "we remain in him and he in us." The Spirit keeps us mindful of God's redemptive work and steadfast love by laboring to make all things one in Christ.

No wonder that Jesus calls us to share his yoke and learn from him. Participating in the love of God has been made possible through Christ's redemptive work, even to the lowliest of beings. "I give praise to you, Father, Lord of heaven and earth, / for although you have hidden these things / from the wise and the learned / you have revealed them to little ones." We no longer have to rely on our memory of God's liberation in the wilderness; Jesus has revealed to us the Father in the humility and meekness of human flesh, so that we might find our true identity in the incarnate Word. His yoke is easy because he has taken our sins upon himself.

Connecting the Bible and the Liturgy

The **Entrance Antiphon**, taken from Psalm 33, brings together the language of this solemnity with the enduring love of God expressed in all the readings for today: "The designs of his Heart are from age to age, to rescue their souls from death, and to keep them alive in famine." There is a nice conjunction in this phrase among several things: God's will, divine love, liberation, and eternal steadfastness. Such was the promise God made through Moses and which the great leader of the chosen people repeats to them as a way to underlining the tenderness of God's heart. Divine love is not earned, indeed it is undeserved and, inexplicably, keeps us alive in famine because of *cogitationes cordis eius* (the designs of his heart).

The Eucharist is the memory that the Christian people keep to the God whose heart never fails in *generatione et generationem*, through the work of Christ. The liturgy's action is not unlike prophetic *anamnesis*, which gathers the people into recollection at the table of divine love. So the **Collect** expresses the need for the gathered assembly precisely to remember the love God has given to us, even as Moses reminded the chosen people of their liberation from Egypt: "Grant, we pray, almighty God, that we, who glory in the Heart of your beloved Son and recall the wonders of his love for us, may be made worthy to receive an overflowing measure of grace from that fount of heavenly gifts." It seems to me that the church asks us to feel deeply in our own hearts the wonders God has done and to respond in kind. Similarly, the Second Reading from 1 John remembers that God has loved us first and not because of anything we have done to earn that love, but simply out of the *infinitos dilectionis thesauros*— "the boundless treasures of your love" (**Collect**, second option).

But there is more, as there was for the chosen people. The commandments and precepts provided the people of Israel a way of expressing their response to God's love in obedience and their own steadfastness. The Christian community drinks from the same twin fountain of the love of God and the love of neighbor. Now that we have tasted from that blood flowing from the Savior's heart, we offer one another to drink from our own cup. Since God has loved us so much, so we ought to love one another, to echo 1 John. The **Prayer after Communion** puts it like this: "May this sacrament of charity, O Lord, make us fervent with the fire of holy love, so that, drawn always to your Son, we may learn to see him in our neighbor."

Strategy for Preaching

It is unfortunate that this solemnity always occurs on a Friday, limiting the amount of people who will come through the church doors. The Solemnity of the Most Sacred Heart of Jesus is like a capstone summarizing the work of God in Christ in what is literally heartrending language. The Scripture speaks of unconditional and undeserved love given to us from God and the response we might ponder for the love of our neighbor. Jesus invites all people to participate in his redemptive work, to take on his yoke of humility, so that we might live fuller lives of thanksgiving and praise. The Eucharist is in fact the very Body of Christ lifting up its heart in gratitude to the Father, remembering the paschal redemption of the Christian people brought out of the desert of sin. So the core homiletic idea to consider for today might be: God has loved us with a heart of everlasting fidelity and asks us to respond in our love for him and our neighbor.

We could begin like this: There are few things as poignant as an old Valentine card. We catch them sometimes rolled up and withered on a refrigerator, the work of some first grader for her father. They are paper hearts, fading pictures of winter roses, empty boxes of candy. The day comes and goes as quickly, sometimes, as love itself. Despite the painful transitory nature of the human heart, we still believe that love should be eternal and unconditional. In Cecil B. DeMille's silent movie blockbuster (honestly) *King of Kings* (1927), the opening shot of Jesus several minutes into the film is a very personal gaze right to the spectator. The Lord has just cured a blind person, and together with him our eyes are opened to the loving eyes of Christ. That heartfelt look from the Beloved to the believer has been repeated in artwork too numerous to mention but probably most popularly rendered in portraits of the Sacred Heart of Jesus, once a ubiquitous feature in most every Catholic home. Permanent love is important to us, despite our own inability to keep our promises. The God we know in Christ is faithful, keeps his covenant, and calls out to us, "Come to me, all you who labor and are burdened, and I will give you rest."

Moses recalled that same love of God for the chosen people in the book of Deuteronomy. They were called the "chosen" for a reason: not because they were special, but because they were special to God. Divine love, not Israel's qualities, made them chosen out of all the nations on the earth (a brief recollection of God's activities in releasing Israel from slavery would be useful here).

That love of God has come to the Christian people in a human face, or better: a human heart, one that we celebrate today. Christ among us renders his heart open for our redemption in the Eucharist. We can make no mistake as we celebrate his memory that, 1 John tells us, it is "not that we have loved God, but that he loved us and sent his Son as expiation for our sins." The **Collect** encourages us to "recall the wonders of his love for us," and we do so as we remember Christ's outpouring of his own blood for our redemption. (The listening assembly may be asking at this point for a concrete image of what this love looks like. So a story of sacrificial love in concrete and expressive terms may serve this purpose.)

And so we pass on that love God has given to us to one another. Moses passed on the commandments to the chosen people. We have tasted from the One Bread and the One Cup and bring that same love to one another. All of us will be asked to love not like a paper heart that crumbles and fades but that endures. That may mean loving someone who does not really deserve it because he or she did everything possible to reject kindness. (Examples.) But we keep loving because the Eucharist has bound the Christian community in Christ's blood, which now runs through our hearts. As the **Prayer after Communion** reminds us, the Eucharist is a sacrament of the heart, a sacrament of love: "May this sacrament of charity, O Lord, make us fervent with the fire of holy love, so that, drawn always to your Son, we may learn to see him in our neighbor."

Our Lord Jesus Christ, King of the Universe

Last Sunday in Ordinary Time

Readings from the Ambo

Ezek 34:11-12, 15-17; Ps 23:1-3, 5-6;
1 Cor 15:20-26, 28; Matt 25:31-46

Although generally addressed to the exilic community living in the diaspora, Ezekiel focuses in a special way in chapter 34 on the monarchy that has betrayed both God and God's people. Like Ezekiel before him, St. Augustine deployed the image of the shepherd to confront the abuse of power by secular (and religious) rulers. The leaders of Israel have fed and gorged themselves, according to Ezekiel's oracle, and so they are unfit to lead. The promise of the Lord comes as particularly appropriate to exiles who are dispersed. "I will rescue them from every place where they were scattered / when it was cloudy and dark. / I myself will pasture my sheep; / I myself will give them rest, says the Lord GOD."

Our somewhat sanitized, even saccharine, image of the shepherd in the Christian era ought not blur the reality of one who guards the sheepfold in Israel; he separates, "between one sheep and another, / between rams and goats." Matthew's gospel picks up Ezekiel's prophecy and hyphenates the leader of sheep into the shepherd-king, the judge. For Matthew's narrative, the great apocalyptic judgment represents the culmination of Jesus' teaching, a majestic crescendo just before the process begins where Jesus moves toward his death (26:1–27:66). As such, the great judgment scene becomes an ending in more than one way: a final denouement in Christ's parable and symbol-making before his passion; it is an "ending" for those who hear the story of the judgment between the sheep and the goats and must decide for themselves whether they are on the left or on the right of the King; and the end of the church year, bringing to a close the cycle of readings and symbolizing the end time of judgment for all humanity when Christ comes to fulfill his rule on the earth.

Paul fills out the picture of the end time, creating a theological descant for the Christian assembly on Matthew's apocalypse. In some sense, Paul is rehearsing or recapitulating the very fruits of the Good News itself—the meaning of living in God's resurrection time. "[J]ust as in Adam all die, / so too in Christ shall all be brought to life." Additionally, we ought not to miss Paul's emphasis on the collapse of the powers at the end "when he has destroyed every sovereignty / and every authority and power," certainly meant as an encouragement to the Christians living in Corinth and other Christians persecuted in the emerging church. Paul also picks up a bit of his theology of recapitulation (echoed again in Romans) where he speaks of creation being set free from bondage and decay. In 1 Corinthians, having destroyed death, "[w]hen everything is subjected to him, / then the Son himself will also be subjected / to the one who subjected everything to him, / so that God may be all in all."

Connecting the Bible and the Liturgy

The Scripture readings and the liturgical texts for this feast fully acknowledge that Jesus is King of the Universe, but they also disclose how his kingship will rule. Each of the Lectionary cycles will have their own take on our Lord's kingship.

The Year A Cycle nicely pairs Ezekiel 34 with Matthew 25; they are parallel accounts of shepherding and then dividing sheep from rams (or goats in Matthew). There is really nothing much of the shepherd in any of the liturgical texts, but these prayers focus on kingdom language, which may at first glance seem far from the world of the shepherd tending his flock. But, as I have indicated, Matthew has transformed Ezekiel's shepherd into a shepherd-king: he must divide, as he subjects all things to his rule at the end of time so as to hand over all things to the Father, as Paul tells the Corinthians. Paul's procession of the Son returning creation back to the Father is alluded to in the **Preface: Christ, King of the Universe**. The text contains the idiom of kingship as well as Pauline apocalyptic utterances: "For you anointed your Only Begotten Son, Our Lord Jesus Christ, with the oil of gladness as eternal Priest and King of all creation, so that, by offering himself on the altar of the Cross as a spotless sacrifice to bring us peace, he might accomplish the mysteries of human redemption and making all created things subject to his rule, he might present to the immensity of your majesty an eternal and universal kingdom."

We might also note the inclusion in Matthew's text of the word "nations." Indeed this scene is often referred to as the judgment of *panta ta ethne*, all the nations, which gives this text and its apocalyptic climax a universal, global spin to it. In a very real sense, the judgment of the king is for both individuals and nations, private and public. Indeed, Ezekiel has politicized the Lord God's judgment against the powers by usurping their (political) right and taking up the shepherd's crook in his own divine hands. But Christ intends to picture the king as a judge before whom the nations are assembled, suggesting that all of us will be accountable for recognizing him as either individuals or nation-states. This two-pronged judgment will implicate those who fail to recognize him in both personal and social sin. The entanglement arises, of course, because neither the sheep nor the goats are aware that they have seen him—or in whom. That means that this judgment is alone reserved to the king who will finally be recognized at the end of time.

Strategy for Preaching

In his encyclical letter, *Quas Primas,* promulgated on December 11, 1925, Pius XI instituted the feast of Christ the King to remind the faithful of their spiritual loyalty to the true King, over and against the ideologies that were then emerging in Europe and Russia. The challenge for the preacher will be to make this day relevant for today and to balance the somewhat frightening tone of the readings with the Good News of peace, love, and mercy. There is also an additional paradox to attend to, which surfaces in the Year A Cycle of readings. The vision of the end-judgment (as imagined by Paul and Matthew) contrasts with the compassionate pastor of God as benevolent shepherd (Ezekiel and the psalmist). Taken together, the readings ask us to be mindful of the final judgment but recognize the corporal works of mercy with which we will be confronted when we face the King.

The **Preface** for the feast contains three rhetorical tropes that organize a homiletic core idea: balancing the world of the now with the eschatological vision of the future.

An introduction should do exactly what such things claim: introduce; it may focus on why we have the feast of Christ the King (historical) or on what place the day has in the life of the church (liturgical) or on how it functions spiritually (pastoral). We may not live in a kingdom in America (in fact, we overthrew one over 200 years ago), but we can imagine what it means to give ourselves over to Christ and for our Lord to claim his rule as one who redeems: he is King and Victor over death and so to him belongs:

   I. The kingdom of truth and life

     A. Ezekiel speaks truth to the powers, bestowing new life

     B. Responsorial Psalm (23)

  II. The kingdom of holiness and grace

     A. Relate a story of conversion

     B. Image of God acting in the world: grace discovered

 III. Kingdom of justice, love, and peace

     A. Matthew 25: Imagine all the world as sheep, selflessly giving to one another

     B. What would this look like in the parish? The world we live in?

     C. How am I implicated in Jesus' parable? Would I recognize Jesus in the least of his brethren? The invitation in the gospel is to keep looking and maybe we will find out.